How to Prevent
Computer Crime

How to Prevent Computer Crime

A GUIDE FOR MANAGERS

August Bequai

JOHN WILEY & SONS
New York · Chichester · Brisbane · Toronto · Singapore

Library of Congress Cataloging in Publication Data:

Bequai, August.
    How to prevent computer crime.

    Bibliography: p.
    Includes index.
    1. Electronic data processing departments—Security
measures.   2. Computers—Access control.   3. Computer
crimes.   I. Title.

HF5548.2.B3834   1983   658.4′78   83-6952
ISBN 0-471-09367-X

Printed in the United States of America

10   9   8   7   6   5   4   3   2   1

FOR MY MOTHER AND FATHER

Preface

A 34-year-old claims representative with the Social Security Administration (SSA) embezzled more than $100,000 from his employer with the help of the SSA computers; he created an army of fictitious beneficiaries. The investigators were shocked to find that the entire SSA computer system—which handles more than $150 billion in payments a year—is vulnerable to low-level employee frauds. A Chicago-area teenager used his home computer to penetrate the data processing system of a local university. He threatened to shut down the system unless the university gave him the program he sought. In New York, a computer systems manager reportedly used his employer's computer to create a handicapping system for horse races. In South Korea, criminals used U.S. Army computers to steal more than $15 million in goods and equipment. In San Francisco, a stockbroker with ties to organized crime used his firm's computer to "launder" the mob's money. In Virginia, a European businessman was charged with attempting to steal a valuable computer program for the Soviet Bloc.

The computer has been called the marvel of the twentieth century; it has become the workhorse of our economy. Computers transfer and record more than $500 billion daily. Hospitals, businesses, government agencies, transportation systems, and others use them to record and keep track of their assets, payrolls, inventories, and other valuables. Without the computer, business and government could come to a standstill.

Yet the computer has also attracted the attention of criminals, organized crime, industrial spies, and other malcontents. Crimes and abuses related to computers are said to cost business and government in excess of $100 million annually; some experts place the figure in excess of $1 billion.

Computers have been used to steal assets and trade secrets, create armies of ghost employees, issue checks for nonexistent services, and even in attempts to murder political figures. Crime and abuses related to computer technology are a serious and growing problem. Although there are no simple solutions to this complex problem, the situation is not without remedies. We need not suffer daily at the hands of the computer criminal.

Computer-related crimes can be prevented; the challenge calls for a coordination of various organizational efforts and resources. This book was written with prevention in mind. In easy-to-understand language, it details how you can prevent computer-related crimes.

AUGUST BEQUAI

Washington, D.C.
June 1983

Acknowledgments

After writing this book, I would now like to thank my many friends and associates for their assistance and support. I would like to express my special appreciation to Marian P. Dettor, for her invaluable typing, editing, comments, and patience. I am especially grateful to the many members of the American Society for Industrial Security (ASIS) who took their time to assist me in this endeavor.

A.B.

Contents

Introduction

Little did the ancient Egyptians and Chinese realize that their primitive calculators were the forerunners of machines that one day would help guide ships and airplanes, and even steer spacecraft through the cosmos. The modern computer is the outgrowth of a painstaking and lengthy evolutionary process, which surfaced in the early twentieth century with Herman Hollerith's census machine.

Other scientists and engineers followed in Hollerith's footsteps. The names of machines like the Mark I, ENIAC, Z-3, and SSEC became part of our daily vocabulary; the invention of the transistor in 1948 made it possible to bring this technology to our very doorsteps. Home computers are now part of our everyday lives. Our children play with and learn from them, while we employ them to conduct our daily financial transactions.

The aftershocks of the computer revolution will be felt for many years; we can only speculate as to where it will all lead. Some of its reverberations have already made themselves felt. Like gunpowder, however, the computer lends itself to both good and evil. It has elevated us to a higher plateau of history, but it has also made it possible for the unethical to steal with impunity and even to hold an industrial society hostage.

Armed with this technology, criminals are stealing more than $100 million annually; some experts place the figure in excess of $1 billion. While jurists, scientists, and others continue to debate the scope and implications of the problem, computer-related frauds, thefts, and abuses are becoming daily occurrences. No business or government agency is immune from criminal attack.

In New York, a well known company was forced to sell one of its divisions when it was learned that the latter had become the centerpiece of a $70 million computer rip-off. It is alleged that the caper was masterminded by three corporate employees, and was staged within the company's finance group. The three employees are said to have falsified the computerized general ledger by inflating sales and profits and downplaying expenses.

In Washington, D.C., more than a dozen men and women, including an employee of the U.S. Department of Justice, are said to have been involved in a computer check-cashing scheme; the victim was a group health provider. The fraud is said to have centered in the victim's claims division, and involved the issuance of more than $100,000 in phony medical payments.

Like the Hydra's heads, the forms of computer crime seem to multiply indefinitely; criminals have demonstrated great ingenuity in their *modi operandi*. Those persons who have been entrusted with the responsibility of managing our private and public institutions would do well to study the undercurrents of computer crime. The public would do well to pressure its decision-makers to address this growing problem.

The computer revolution has made it necessary for us to reassess many of our institutions and underlying policies. This book addresses many of these undercurrents; among them are the following:

Criminology.   The computer did not create white collar crime; rather, it has facilitated it by making it easier for this class of criminals to steal large sums of money with impunity and little risk of discovery. It has "democratized white collar crime"; even a clerk with the needed technical sophistication can steal a king's ransom at the press of a button. The computer has also given rise to new types of "informational crimes." Armed with this technology, even a 12-year-old child can gain access to most of our data banks and alter, delete, or copy records. Information has become a commodity; it has both value and a market. As we increasingly move into the era of the electronic office, computer-assisted informational crimes will become a serious problem.

Criminal Profile.   Much has been written on who the computer criminal is; some authors portray the felon as a ten-foot-tall giant, and others as an electronic wizard. The problem, however, is more complex; any simple profile is misleading. The truth is that the computer thief can be anyone who is devoid of ethics, has access to the needed technology, has the requisite technical know-how, and occupies a position of trust. The proliferation of computers has enlarged the pool of potential criminals; it now includes all strata of our society.

Security.   Increasingly, both the private and public sectors are being called upon to take steps to safeguard their EDP systems. Computer security is no longer a luxury; it plays an important role in preventing computer frauds, thefts, and abuses. However, each security program must be designed to meet the specific needs of the organization. No security program is foolproof; criminals have demonstrated an ability to occasionally circumvent even the best of security measures.

Auditability.   The ability to verify the accuracy and authenticity of much of the data an organization stores in its computers is paramount to its very survival. Audits of the computer center are both important and necessary tools. However, EDP systems can pose special problems for auditors; these must be addressed. In part, the answer lies in providing auditors with some training in EDP systems.

Proprietary Software.   Establishing ownership of computer programs has become a serious problem. Federal and state laws do not, at present, fully address this problem; the courts have yet to deal adequately with these issues.

Computer Litigation/Prosecution.   This area of the law is still in its infancy; many legal questions remain unresolved. The courts and legislators have been slow to address this void; for example, many states have yet to enact computer crime statutes. The present void makes the task of both prosecutors and victims more difficult. However, in the final analysis, the form and direction that computer technology takes will, in part, be dictated by its legal environment.

Law Enforcement.   Our police and prosecutorial machinery continues to concentrate its efforts in the area of traditional crime. Few Federal or state/local police agencies have instituted any training programs in the computer crime area, nor is there a public outcry demanding that the problem be addressed. Increasingly, management will be called upon to assist law enforcement; it would serve it well to understand the needs and workings of the criminal justice system. This will facilitate management's efforts to coordinate with law enforcement agencies in the investigation and prosecution of computer criminals.

Education and Training.   Few of our schools and organizations offer any courses or training in the prevention of computer crime. Thus many in managerial positions are insensitive to the problem; this can have a profound impact on the workings of their organizations. Sensitizing management to the problem is both necessary and a key to preventing computer crime.

Lack of Ethics.   Computer crimes flourish in a corrupt organizational environment. Employees often take their cues from their superiors; it would be foolish to expect them to conduct themselves in an ethical manner if their superiors do not. Codes of ethics can play a role in preventing computer capers, provided compliance is equally enforced.

The computer is simply a machine; some call it a "dumb machine." It is a loyal servant; it obeys our every command. We are its creators and instructors; if it is employed for criminal ends, it is because of our doing. Computer crime is, in the final analysis, a "people problem."

It is not the intent of this book to condemn EDP-connected personnel; the majority of these are honest individuals. If the dishonest reigned, society would soon disintegrate and the law of the jungle would set in. Computer crimes are the work of a small number of unethical men and women, both within and outside the organization. It is the problems caused by this group that the book discusses.

Part 1 of the book defines the scope of the problem: types of crimes that are and can be committed with the assistance of computers, and why this technology lends itself to crime. This part also analyzes who the computer felon is, what motivates his/her illegal conduct, and why victims are reluctant to prosecute.

Part 2 addresses the need for and role of security; it details, in easy-to-understand language, the various tools that are readily available to management to stop computer thieves in their tracks. It details how to manage the audit and how to detect and investigate computer rip-offs. Also outlined is the psychology of law enforcement officials, and how to best coordinate your efforts with them. The procedure for establishing an EDP security program is detailed. Part 2 should serve as a "how-to guide" for safeguarding your computers from criminal attack.

Part 3 of the book addresses such novel problems as the theft of high technology, industrial espionage and sabotage, and takeover attempts. It also details the advent of the paperless/cashless society, and the rise of even more subtle electronic ("paperless/cashless") crimes. It draws on present cases and developments; the message for management is: "beware of things to come."

It is not the objective of this book to frighten or cajole; rather, it is to describe a present and growing problem, brought about by the electronic revolution. The computer is here to stay; computers are employed in every sector of business and government. We need not fall victim to computer crime. We can do something about it, but to do so, we must first acknowledge its existence, and then take steps to detect and prevent it. These are the objectives of this book.

PART 1

Why Computers
Fall Victim
to Crime

CHAPTER 1

Understanding the Problem

An employee of a Federal agency took her employer for more than $1 million with the assistance of its computer. A consultant for a large West Coast–based financial institution bilked his employer for more than $10 million in a sophisticated computer caper. Students at a private New York City school used its computer terminal to penetrate more than 20 Canadian computer systems; while several juveniles stole some technical manuals from a telephone company's computer center. These could have been used to shut down a significant part of the company's telephone operations.

Crime and abuses related to computer technology are a growing and serious problem for both business and government. The Chamber of Commerce of the United States has estimated that the annual losses to the private sector from crimes by computer are more than $100 million. Federal law enforcement sources place the losses as high as $1 billion. These electronic crimes are often committed by dishonest employees and competitors; however, their ranks have been joined by professional criminals, foreign spies, terrorists, political dissidents, members of religious cults, and others. Increasingly, management in both the private and public sectors is being called upon to play a role in the prevention and detection of crimes and abuses by computer.

DIMENSIONS OF THE PROBLEM

Currently, there are more than 120,000 computers in use in the private sector. This number does not include the more than 500,000 personal computers, or the more than 10,000 in use in the Federal government. To these must also be added the thousands of other computers that are used by local and state governments. Financial institutions use the computer to record more than $400 billion daily in financial transactions. Computer technology permeates every fiber of our social, political, and economic life. Our dependency on this technology is total; we could not function as a modern society in its absence. In the coming years, the majority of our population may well bank, work, and conduct their daily chores from their homes with the assistance of the home computer.

This modern electronic wizard, however, is vulnerable to criminal attack and abuse. Its uncanny ability to collect, record, store, and disseminate voluminous financial, personal, medical, and other valuable and confidential data makes it an attractive target for criminals. Investigators for the U.S. Department of Agriculture (USDA), for example, have uncovered more than 5000 breaches of their computer security. The USDA computers store such valuable data as:

Confidential U.S. Census Bureau information
Secret crop forecasts
Confidential military research information
Highly confidential commodity-related data

The USDA investigators also found that at least two of the USDA's computer files had been altered.

The growth of computer-related offenses has been linked by some experts to three current developments:

1. The growing number of individuals who are learning or have been taught to use this technology.
2. The spread of low-cost computers (especially personal computers).
3. The large army of men and women (over 2 million private and public employees) who operate this technology.

However, to the above must also be added the inherent vulnerability of the technology itself, and also the lax environment in which it operates. Computer technology is vulnerable because of the following:

1. *It easily lends itself to abuse.* Disgruntled and dishonest employees have set computers on fire, poured paint on them, shot at them, and used them to embezzle large sums of money. Computers in Europe, Africa, Asia, and Latin America have fared no better. Computer tech-

nology has also attracted the ire of terrorists. For example, members of Italy's Red Brigade have bombed computers at a government nuclear facility and research center near Rome; terrorists in West Germany have sabotaged those of private corporations.

The computer has also come to represent, for the politically alienated in many Third World countries, the domination of Western civilization. It has become an outlet for their frustrations. The kidnapping and assassination of business and political officials is giving way to hatred of the machine; few shed tears when computers are attacked. The economic and political losses, however, can be profound; the attacker understands this well. The computer, by its very mystique, has become a symbol of all the evils we associate with technology.

2. *It is a ready-made vehicle.* The computer lends itself easily to criminal abuse; it is a willing accomplice. Computers have been used to embezzle, pilfer, and manipulate funds, and for other thefts. As an example, the accountant for a manufacturer siphoned off more than $500,000 of his employer's money with the assistance of its computer. He created ghost suppliers, and then programmed the company's computer to issue checks to these through bank accounts he controlled. Once the checks cleared, he simply drew out the funds. The theft went unnoticed for four years.

3. *It intimidates the layperson.* The most outstanding feature of modern humanity is its extreme dependence on the machine. We have been conditioned to accept technology as a truism; we hesitate to question it. When we board an airplane, few of us would question its ability to fly safely, nor would many question the ability of computers to guide satellites safely to other planets. The criminal, in part, relies on our dependence on and awe of computer technology; thus when such a criminal directs the computer to issue checks to ghost suppliers, beneficiaries, customers, or employees, we do not question it, even when logic dictates that we should.

It should come as no surprise that many computer-related offenses have surfaced only by accident; even then, many of the victims are reluctant to question or prosecute. For example, when the chief teller of a New York City bank fell behind on his gambling debts, he stole more than $1 million from his employer's funds to pay his debts. With the assistance of the bank's computer he transferred funds (electronically) from legitimate inactive accounts to phony accounts over which he exerted control. His offense surfaced by pure chance when the police raided his bookmaker's operations and came across his name. The felon had managed to fool both the bank's auditors and its security officials. Even when the scheme surfaced, his employer found it difficult to believe. Experts speculated that his fraud could have continued for several more years without being detected.

4. *It operates in a corrupt environment.* Thefts and frauds by dishonest employees and outsiders cannot be blamed solely on twentieth century computer technology. White collar crimes were known as far back as antiquity; they plagued business and government well before the advent of the computer. The American Management Association (AMA), for example, has estimated that the annual losses to the private sector from white collar crime exceed $44 billion[1]:

    a.   *Employees* pilfer between $5 billion and $10 billion.
    b.   *Embezzlers* steal in excess of $4 billion (embezzlers who use computers, however, are said to steal 20 times as much as their traditional counterparts).
    c.   *Corporate officials* account for kickbacks, payoffs, and bribes in the area of $3 billion to $10 billion.
    d.   *Shoplifters* are said to steal more than $2 billion.
    e.   *Arsonists* cause damages exceeding $2 billion in losses to insurers.
    f.   *Check frauds* account for more than $1 billion.
    g.   *Vandalism* exceeds $2 billion.
    h.   *The cost* of these business crimes adds at least 15 percent, on the average, to the cost of most goods (this averages out to $200 annually for each person in this country).

The above losses, however, do not include the losses from white collar crimes committed against Federal, state, and local government agencies, or the thefts and frauds committed by dishonest bureaucrats. Fraud and theft, for example, in government programs and contracts is said to exceed $20 billion. To cite only a few illustrations:

    a.   The military could cut its meat bill by 6 percent if it were not riddled with fraud.
    b.   At least $2 million was paid by a Federal agency for work that was never done.
    c.   One government contractor spent more than $1 million "entertaining" Federal officials.

A corporate executive, when asked by prosecutors why he had defrauded his company out of more than $500,000, replied that he had spent it on "gifts for my wife, on women in Europe, Asia, and Australia, and for my personal entertainment." Crimes and abuses related to com-

---

[1] The Chamber of Commerce of the United States places these losses in excess of $40 billion, while the U.S. Senate Antitrust Subcommittee has placed them at more than $100 billion. These figures do not include frauds against government, or the cost involved in prosecuting these offenses.

puter technology can only find nourishment in a corrupt business and government environment. Computer programmers and operators who witness thefts by their superiors can only be encouraged to do the same. Computer-related crimes are difficult to prevent in a corrupt environment.

COMPUTERS ARE TARGETS

Crimes and abuses involving computers victimize both the private and public sectors. The culprit may be:

An employee
A consultant
A high executive
A competitor
Any individual who occupies a position of trust

Every industry is vulnerable. In a study of 372 cases involving the misuse of computers in both industry and government, the following observations were made[2]:

Institution	Number of Cases	Percentage
Banking	70	19
Education	66	18
Government	61	16
Manufacturing	46	12
Insurance	28	8
Computer Services	24	6
Transportation	9	2
Retail Stores	8	2
Dating Bureaus	6	2
Trade Schools	5	1
Utilities	5	1
Communications	5	1
Credit Reporting	5	1
Securities	4	1
Petroleum	4	1
Other	26	8
Total	372	100

[2] The study was funded by the U.S. Department of Justice, Bureau of Justice Statistics.

Computers can be employed in the commission of numerous categories of thefts and frauds. For example, a study of 365 cases found that:

Vandalism accounted for 62 such offenses
Property and data thefts accounted for 94
Unauthorized use accounted for 68 cases
Financial thefts exceeded all others with 141 cases

The techniques employed in the computer-related crimes and abuses that have surfaced have taken many forms. For example, computers can be used:

To create phony payrolls, false claims, and fictitious employees.
To pad overtime records.
To create phony credit ratings.
To set up phony loan schemes.
To falsify credit and loan accounts.
To embezzle funds.
To pilfer spare parts, raw materials, and supplies.
To steal computer time.
To make payments to fictitious suppliers.
To steal incoming payments.
To pay suppliers twice.
To make fictitious advances to employees.
To overcharge.
To doctor inventory lists.
To manipulate records.
To transfer funds to phony accounts.
To create fictitious purchase transactions.
To manipulate expense accounts.
To carry employees on the payroll beyond their actual severance date.
To ship merchandise to relatives or others for disposal.

Management, however, need not be an observer. It can play an important role in both preventing and detecting crimes and abuses by computer. It can do this, however, only if it understands why computers are inviting targets. Thus management should be sensitized to:

Why computer technology is vulnerable to criminal attack.

What sort of environment gives rise to these criminal abuses.

The fraud indicators ("red flags") in these cases.

As complex as computer technology has increasingly become, the computer itself continues to remain simple in its operations. It is this very simplicity that makes it vulnerable to criminal attack and abuse. There are five basic stages to every computer operation; the computer is open to misuse at any one of these stages. These points of vulnerability are as follows:

1. *Input.* At this stage, information is translated into a language that the computer understands. Many computer-related crimes and abuses depend on the manipulation of the input data; at this stage of a computer operation dishonest employees can cause serious problems for an organization. This can be accomplished by simply:

a. Introducing fraudulent records
b. Altering current data
c. Removing key input documents or
d. Using a combination of the above

In one such case, for example, an employee for a major manufacturer inserted fraudulent data in the company's computer for the purpose of creating ghost suppliers and customers. Corporate checks, to the tune of $200,000, were then issued to these phony accounts; the dishonest employee then simply pocketed the money. The case was finally detected, but only by accident. To add insult to injury, the victim had honored the felon over the years with commendations for "work well done."

2. *Output.* Crimes and abuses at this stage often take the form of thefts of data, customer lists, personnel lists, trade secrets, marketing plans, projected earnings, and other valuable confidential information. These offenses often involve conspiracies between dishonest employees and outsiders; the latter is often a competitor, labor union, professional criminal, or foreign agent (especially in the areas of high technology).

One such case involved a large Eastern drugstore chain; a union organizer is said to have paid a dishonest company employee over $2000 for the firm's personnel list. The list included the home addresses and telephone numbers of the company's nonunion employees. In a separate case, three employees for a major book publisher were accused of selling their employer's most preferred customer list to one of its competitors; while a dishonest employee for an international air carrier is said to have sold his employer's confidential marketing plans to a competitor.

As we increasingly become an information-dependent society, valuable confidential data will command high prices. A sophisticated network of criminal middlemen ("fences") already trades in such data. Output-related thefts and abuses pose a great threat for an organization. The era of the automated office has also brought with it new security-related problems.

3. *Programming.*   At this stage, the computer is provided with step-by-step instructions for solving the many problems it will later encounter. Computer-related thefts and abuses at the programming stage usually involve a dishonest programmer or consultant. These usually take one of the following forms:

a.   Alteration of a program
b.   Deletion of pertinent instructions
c.   Modification of the program
d.   Theft of programs
e.   Copying of programs
f.   Destruction or sabotage of a program

In one such case, a manager for an international chemical company stole his employer's most valuable programs; he then threatened to destroy them unless his employer paid him a $500,000 ransom. In another case, an EDP manager altered his employer's programs so that a few pennies were added to the cost of numerous company purchases; within a period of several years, the felon was able to pocket more than $800,000 through this subterfuge.

4. *Usage.*   Only a small number of companies have enacted security measures to prevent the unauthorized use of their computers. Abuses and thefts involving the unauthorized use of an employer's computers bear close analogy to those involving the unauthorized use of its telephones, photocopiers, or typewriters. However, because computer time is often costly, the unauthorized use of a computer can constitute a serious problem for its owner.

There have been numerous cases (many of which are not prosecuted) where computer operators and programmers have used their employer's computer to carry on their own private businesses. For example, employees at a Maryland state agency are said to have used its computers to keep tab of their weekly football pools. In another case, a bookmaker is said to have used a university's computer to keep track of his bets.

5. *Transmission.*   At this stage, telephone circuits and/or teleprinter lines are used to transmit data back and forth between computers, or be-

tween computers and remote terminals. Thefts and abuses at this stage usually involve the penetration of time-sharing service bureaus. For example, in one such case a felon gained access to a bureau's computer and proceeded to copy data from its customer files. He was also able to extract its billing records, rate ledgers, and general ledgers.

Computers are also vulnerable to electronic interceptive attacks. These can employ many sophisticated techniques; for example, they can take one or more of the following forms[3]:

Browsing
Wiretapping
Bugging
Electromagnetic pickup
Between-the-lines entry
Piggyback entry

An organization, however, need not allow itself to become a hostage to criminal elements; the problem is not without its solutions. A security program can assist management in preventing and deterring crime by computer. The problem, unfortunately, is oftentimes aggravated by management's lack of training and education in this area. Although most modern managers are well versed in a number of subjects that impact on their organizations, they have little or no training in the area of computer-related crime or abuse. It would be as if we were training modern physicians without exposing them to the study of the body's circulatory system.

CONDITIONS THAT PROMOTE THEFT, FRAUD, AND ABUSE

Ironically, many businesses and government agencies promote theft and abuse by computer. They do so by making it easy for dishonest employees or outsiders to gain unauthorized access to their computers. Most corporations and government agencies have enacted few, if any, security measures to safeguard their computer systems. This is unfortunate because many managers take pride in the measures they take to safeguard confidential corporate files, yet an organization's most important "file cabinet" goes unguarded. I am reminded of a lecture I gave in New York City before a group of corporate executives; I asked them, by a show of hands, to indicate if their companies had a computer security program. Less than 20 percent said they had such a program. The majority indicated their com-

[3] These are discussed in greater detail in Chapter 2.

panies had no security program at all. Most companies relied on their private guard force to deter computer-related crimes and abuses.

Without being cognizant of it, most organizations create the very conditions and environment that promote thefts by computer. In large part, these are due to lax or nonexistent security programs. These defects can be summarized as follows[4]:

1. *Hardware security.* A perennial problem with most organizations, hardware security defects usually take one or more of the following forms:

a. There is poor control of the data preparation equipment.
b. Access to the system is poorly controlled (it is not limited only to those who "need to know").
c. Transactions (or other fraud indicators) that have been rejected by the system are usually ignored.
d. At least two people are not always present when EDP equipment is being operated.
e. The computer operations are open to public viewing.
f. System components are located next to open windows, doors, or outside walls.
g. Overall operations are poorly supervised.
h. Auditors have little or no training in EDP operations.
i. Reports and other sensitive materials are discarded in outside (unsecured) trash bins.
j. Computer personnel are not periodically screened.
k. The system generates negotiable instruments.
l. The system is used to transfer credit, process loans, and/or obtain credit ratings.
m. Employee-management relations are poor.
n. Key responsibilities are not separated.
o. The EDP auditors played no role in developing the application programs.
p. The industry is depressed, but the computer-generated data reflects record sales.

---

[4] Check these against your organization's controls to see if they apply in your case. If they do, then you may find that your organization is a prime candidate for a computer rip-off.

2. *Software security.* Lax controls in this area can facilitate the theft, copying, or misuse of programs. Defective softwear security can take one or more of the following forms:

 a. Responsibilities for writing, authorizing, modifying, and/or running programs are not divided.
 b. Computer operators are given oral (not written) instructions by programmers.
 c. Programs do not contain a statement of ownership.
 d. Threat-monitoring capabilities are not built into the programs.
 e. Dubious deviations from the norm are not recorded.
 f. EDP auditors are not consulted regarding needed tests and checks.
 g. Responsibilities for program maintenance are not separated.
 h. Audit trails of program changes are not maintained.
 i. Program debugging is not separate from production.

3. *Data security.* The theft of mailing lists, trade secrets, and other confidential data is increasing. This is made possible by the following:

 a. There is no accounting of documents that are sent for input processing.
 b. Corrections on source documents are not accounted for.
 c. Corrections on source documents are not made exclusively by the originating department.
 d. Source documents are often discarded and are not kept for a sufficient period of time.
 e. Payroll checks and other negotiable items are not numbered sequentially.
 f. Purchase orders are not numbered sequentially.
 g. Outputs are not logged and stored in a secure location.
 h. Tape and disk libraries are not manned or locked.
 i. Accountability for maintenance of the library is not fixed.

4. *Transmission security.* The proliferation of home computers, terminals, and other electronic interceptive tools has made this area vulnerable. You can determine the vulnerability of your system by checking for the following flaws:

 a. Machine-readable cards or badges that identify terminal users are not used.

14

UNDERSTANDING THE PROBLEM

  b. Identification cards and badges are not collected at the end of the work period.
  c. Passwords and security codes are changed only infrequently (or not at all).
  d. Terminal users are not required to indicate when they will next become active.
  e. Scramblers and cryptographic devices are not used.
  f. Access by valid users to specific files is not controlled.
  g. Unsuccessful entry attempts are not recorded.

FRAUD INDICATORS

There are a number of basic fraud indicators ("red flags") to which management should be sensitized.[5] Recognizing them requires little or no technical know-how or training. However, by being able to identify these red flags, management can play an important role in safeguarding an organization's computer from criminal attack and abuse. Some of the more common red flags to be on guard for are as follows:

Staff members give suspicious explanations for missing supplies, property, or funds.
Records have been rewritten for no valid reason.
Records have been altered, modified, deleted, or destroyed.
Signatures on key documents appear to have been forged.
Records appear to be counterfeit.
Inventory shortages are frequent.
Key system personnel are always working overtime.
Records are not kept up to date.
Key system personnel are hesitant (or refuse) to yield control over records.
EDP employees appear to be abnormally sensitive to routine questions.
Complaints by customers, sellers, buyers, and other accounts are chronic.
Complaints by fellow employees are excessive (and based on facts).
Complaints of criminal activity are ignored.
Irregularities and inefficiencies are merely covered up.

---

[5] These are discussed in greater detail in other chapters of the book.

Key system employees refuse promotions and vacations.

Employees loiter outside their own departments.

Confidential financial data is frequently used by employees for personal financial benefit.

Insider data is leaked by insiders to their friends and relatives for purposes of investment.

Trade secrets are illegally sold to competitors.

Decision-making procedures are revealed to outsiders.

Programs are illegally copied and sold to outsiders.

Customer lists are copied and sold by employees.

Other irregularities occur.

The prevention and detection of computer-related thefts and abuses should be a concern of every organization. It is imperative that management understand the conditions and environment that give rise to such offenses. Today's manager must be trained and educated to both identify and assist in remedying such problems. Managers need not become experts in this area any more than they need to become experts in many other areas that have profound impacts on their organizations. Unfortunately, however, too many organizations take the view that, if they close their eyes, the problem will go away; instead, they only facilitate theft and abuse by computer.

2

Crimes by Computer Can Be Easy

An employee for a state agency used his employer's computer to embezzle more than $30,000. A consultant for a Los Angeles bank nearly bilked his employer out of more than $10 million by simply manipulating its computers. A clerk for one of the nation's largest money market funds is alleged to have taken her employer for more than $1 million in a simple computer/wire fraud scheme.

Crimes by computer are a fast growing industry; experts place the annual losses anywhere from $100 million to $1 billion. The average take in a computer caper is said to exceed $400,000 (see Table 1); the likelihood that a computer felon will ever see the inside of a prison is one out of 20,000. The average take in a bank robbery is only $6000; the likelihood that a bank robber will land in prison is one out of three.

As our dependence on computers continues to increase in both business and government, management finds itself at the crossroads: it can make an effort to understand and address the problem or, as in the past, it can sweep the problem under the rug and hope it will go away. In doing the latter, management may be inviting even more audacious attacks by criminal elements both within and outside its organization. Management is limited; it would do well to study, understand, and play a role in addressing the problem.

TABLE 1 SAMPLE COMPUTER CRIME CASES[a]

Victim	Losses[b]
Bank	$10 million
Computer manufacturer	$1.5 million
Financial institution	$20 million
Telephone company	$1 million
Federal agency	$1 million
Money market fund	$1 million
State agency	$20,000
Insurance company	$1 billion
Book publisher	$2 million
Manufacturer	$200,000
Hospital	$40,000
U.S. Army	$20,000

[a] The computer criminal preys both on business and government. No industry or Federal, state, or local agency is secure from thefts, frauds, and abuses by computer.
[b] These losses are in excess of . . . .

CATEGORIES OF CRIMES

We live in the dawn of a new era; the electronic revolution has propelled us into a cashless society. Use of automated teller machines (ATMs), point-of-sale systems (POSs), telephone bill paying systems (TBPs), automated clearinghouses (ACHs), and other forms of electronic funds transfer systems (EFTSs), has become part of our daily routines.[1] The workhorse of EFTSs is the computer. As computer technology has proliferated and come to dominate a large part of our daily lives, thefts, frauds, and abuses by computer have also increased. The likelihood that your organization can become the target of computer criminals (if it already has not been ripped off) is increasing.

Computer rip-offs, however, like other forms of criminal behavior, generally fall into fixed patterns. Although these electronic crimes can take

[1] EFTSs handle daily financial transactions that exceed $100 billion.

many forms, they share a basic commonality; they usually fall into one or more of the following categories:

Financial thefts, frauds, and abuses
Thefts of property
Abuses of data
Unauthorized use of services
Vandalism
Sabotage
Espionage (both political and industrial)

In many of these crimes, the computer plays a key role. It can be both the target and the vehicle of the criminal.

Financial Thefts, Frauds, and Abuses

These can take one of several forms; for example, in an embezzlement, larceny, or EFTS-related fraud, often the criminal merely makes use of the computer to facilitate the commission of a white collar crime. These types of offenses are usually found in financial environments where the computer is used for recording, processing, storing, and maintaining financial data files; they victimize both the private and public sectors. One businessman best summarized the vulnerability of computerized systems to financial rip-offs as follows:

> Once you've built a window into the system, it's there permanently, and large amounts or small amounts of money can pass through that window over a period of time without any change in risk. . . . Business has probably never been so vulnerable to theft.

In one such case, a dishonest manager took his employer for more than $500,000 by simply adding ghost employees to its computerized payroll. He then pocketed their wages. In a separate case, an officer at a West Coast–based bank played a key role in a computer caper that cost his employer over $15 million in losses.

In large part, these financial electronic capers are made possible (both in the private and public sectors) by lax, or lack of adequate, computer security. Management is not security minded, nor has it been trained to be so. One former U.S. Senator has summarized the problem of computer security as follows:

. . . [we have] neglected to take adequate steps to secure [our] computer systems . . . security problems are especially prevalent in [organizations] whose computer systems are involved in the disbursement of . . . funds, economically valuable data and privacy information.

Unless management takes security seriously, electronic financial capers (and the take per caper) will continue to increase.

Thefts of Property

In cases of this type, the criminal makes use of the computer to steal personal property belonging to another; the computer becomes a vehicle for the illegal act. The computer may be used to pilfer or divert valuable merchandise or other goods; oftentimes, these are then sold to legitimate sources. For example, in a California case involving a telephone company, a group of felons took it for more than $500,000 in valuable electronic equipment; they then sold it to legitimate businesses. The criminals had found the secret access code of the company's computer in a trash bin; armed with this, they simply telephoned their orders and instructed the computer where to ship the equipment. The case only surfaced when one of the felons, dissatisfied with his share of the booty, "blew the whistle." The police suspected, but were never able to prove, that the group may have had the assistance of a dishonest company employee.

Abuses of Data

These take the form of unlawful access to confidential (and usually financially valuable) data belonging to another. These offenses often involve a dishonest employee who either directly steals the data, or else assists an outsider in the offense. Crimes of this nature victimize both business and government; they are common in those environments where the programs and files are loosely controlled or where system services and physical facilities are:

Not controlled
Readily available to employees during nonworking hours
Open to the public

The ease with which these offenses can be perpetrated was amply illustrated by several employees of a mail-order company; they are said to have copied their company's most valued customer list and sold it to a competitor.

Unauthorized Use of Services

This usually involves the theft of services; both business and government computers are often used by their employees to play games or conduct their own private businesses. In many jurisdictions, these offenses are misdemeanors; they are punishable by fines of up to $1000 and/or imprisonment of up to one year. However, because computer time is a valuable commodity, the unauthorized use of an organization's computer can prove very costly for the victim; the victim does not even know that it has been taken. Since the penal sanctions are, at best, weak, there is little to deter the criminal.

In one such case, Federal auditors were surprised to learn that a computer belonging to a Federally funded nuclear weapons research firm had been used by many of its employees to store a total of 456 unauthorized files; the computer was being used to play games and to keep track of employees' investments. What disturbed the auditors even more was the fact that a "bomb book" on the system was accessible to all users; this file contained a checklist for setting up and maintaining nuclear tests. In a case involving the New York City Board of Election, a computer systems manager is said to have used the Board's computer to store his handicapping system and horse breeding data.

Vandalism

This usually takes the form of a physical attack directed at the computer system or at any of its components. The objective of these attacks is to make the system (in part or entirely) inoperable. In these offenses, the felon is often a present or former employee, disgruntled or mentally disturbed, who vents his/her anger and frustrations at the computer.

Disgruntled employees have been known to set fire to computer facilities, discharge weapons at computers, and even to spray them with paint. One man is said to have removed all of the labels on several thousand reels of tape; it cost his employer many work-hours to reidentify the data.

Sabotage

With the growth of political turmoil both domestically and internationally, terrorists and the politically alienated have increasingly directed their ire at the computer. In France, for example, political fringe groups have taken credit for attacking several government computer facilities; Japan, South Korea, and Great Britain have also witnessed computer sabotage. In this country, politically motivated groups and individuals have likewise attacked computers, usually systems involved in defense-related research. Saboteurs have even attacked the Pentagon's computers.

The saboteur can also be motivated by economic considerations; for example, a company may orchestrate an attack on a competitor's computers. By sabotaging its record-keeping capability, the saboteur may destroy any advantages the competitor enjoys. The sabotage may even totally destroy a competitor's ability to continue functioning as a viable business entity. In one such case, the target of a corporate acquisition found that its computer had been sabotaged; as a result, its business suffered dramatically and its publicly traded stock fell in price as word reached Wall Street insiders that the company was in "financial trouble."

Espionage

This can be motivated by either political or economic considerations. The Soviet Union, for example, currently has more than 1000 agents operating in the United States; to their number must be added several thousands more employed by Eastern Bloc allies. In search of trade secrets, high technology, and other valuable economic and military data, foreign agents may target an organization's computers. For a price, they can retain the services of dishonest employees; there are also a sufficient number of dishonest businesspeople who can be readily called upon for assistance. In one such case, Federal investigators accused a Belgian businessman of spying on behalf of the Soviet Union. The businessman was arrested when he attempted to smuggle a valuable computer program with military application out of the United States.

Corporate competitors (both domestic and foreign) may also target a company's computers. Both Japanese and European corporations are said to have spied on American companies. As the corporate world increasingly stores confidential (and financially valuable) data, marketing plans, client lists, trade secrets, and other data in its computers, it invites the attention of both competitors and foreign agents.

ELECTRONIC PENETRATIONS

Computer systems, increasingly, have become vulnerable to electronic penetration; this can range from a simple wiretap to the use of a sophisticated imposter terminal. With the dramatic increase in the use of home computers and terminals (more than 3 million) even an amateur criminal can penetrate most computer systems. Felons can easily employ home computers and terminals to tap into the data transmission lines of a system, or even get into the central computer files.[2]

1. *Wiretapping.* This is probably the most common and oldest of the present electronic interceptive tools. The requisite equipment to wiretap another's lines is readily available; it can be purchased at a local computer store for less than $1000. All a felon needs in order to construct a wiretap kit is the following:

    a.   Wireless microphone (about $30)
    b.   AM-FM radio (about $20)
    c.   Cassette recorder (about $30)
    d.   Modern modulator-demodulator (about $200)
    e.   Printing computer terminal (about $700)

By simply connecting the tap directly to a system's telephone or teleprinter lines, a felon can intercept and record messages. A large oil company was surprised to learn that its computer communication lines had been tapped, and the felons had recorded valuable confidential data.

2. *Bugging.* This involves the placing of a microphone in a computer facility. The objective is to intercept oral communications between system personnel. The process is simple, and can provide the felon with valuable information regarding the system, its personnel, and its security.

3. *Masquerading.* In this case a felon gains unauthorized access to a system by assuming the identity of an authorized system user. Systems that have no means of authenticating a user's identity (save for symbolic identifiers) and installations that support remote terminals are often vulnerable to such penetration.

One of the easiest ways for a masquerader to gain entry is to obtain the password and other identifiers of an authorized system user. The felon can do this simply:

    a.   By obtaining (usually from a dishonest user or system employee) a report or document that details the requisite password and identifiers.
    b.   Often, in a system with lax controls, by finding such a report or document that may have been carelessly left exposed.
    c.   By wiretaping a user's terminal and intercepting the identifiers when these are transmitted over the telephone lines.

---

[2] Home computers are making it, experts fear, increasingly easier to illegally tap a system; because most systems employ lax controls, even a 13-year-old armed with a home computer can penetrate a system.

4. *Browsing.* In this case, the felon gains unauthorized access to a user's files by exploiting the system's vulnerabilities. Entry is possible by the simple use of a terminal; for example, if the system does not authenticate terminal entry. Once the felon gains access to the files, they can then be read and copied at leisure. This technique can be employed many times; the felon (unless discovered) can easily browse through the system's entire files in search of valuable data.

5. *Scavenging.* In this instance, the failure of the system's personnel to erase the residual data is exploited; the felon scavenges for valuable data left on the storage media. You should remember that both primary and secondary storage media that are employed to process information can continue to retain that data long after they have been released for reallocation to another user.

6. *Electromagnetic pickup.* Not all interceptive devices are directly connected to a system. There are devices that can be used to intercept the radiation generated by the computer's central processor, telephone and telephone printer lines, and microwave communications. These interceptions, however, may prove difficult to detect. Physical security measures directed at cutting back on the system's exposure should prove of assistance; scramblers and cryptographic devices can also prove valuable.

7. *Spoofing.* The felon exploits the failure of the system's remote terminal users to authenticate, at any given time, that they are communicating with the actual system. The felon employs a masquerading system to intercept the communication lines leading to the terminals, and to provide systemlike responses to the authorized users.

8. *Clandestine code change.* In this case, the felon inserts a code into the system that creates trapdoors; these are later activated by users. For example, the scheme can take the form of a user stealing information from a job card (one that has gone through the system), then resubmitting this information on another job card, along with his/her program. A clandestine code change can be introduced by:

a. The initial designer of the system
b. The manufacturer who services the system
c. Anyone who has access to it

9. *Between-the-lines entry.* The felon connects an unauthorized terminal to a valid private line, and then enters the system whenever a legal user (who continues to hold the communications channel) is inactive. Occasionally, the "sign-off signal" of a valid user is intercepted by the felon, and later used to access the system.

10. *Trojan horse.* This involves the introduction of an apparently useful program that contains a hidden trapdoor, for the purpose of collecting, modifying, or destroying data.

11. *Piggyback entry.* Messages between a computer and an authorized user are intercepted; the felon then proceeds to add or delete information, and to release the modified message to the authorized user.

12. *Trapdoor entry.* The system is probed for unprotected or weak points caused by errors or logic oversights. Once these weaknesses are discovered, they can be exploited repeatedly.

13. *Inadequate parameter checking.* The criminal obtains special privileges by taking advantage of the system's incomplete checking of parameters.

14. *Unknown system exploitation.* The felon takes advantage of certain vulnerabilities that result from a system crash. For example, if some user files remain open, a user can gain unauthorized access to these other files.

With the advances in technology, new and more sophisticated electronic interceptive tools are making their entry into the market. Many of these are simple to operate; students at a New York City school demonstrated this when they were able to penetrate several Canadian systems from the comfort of their classroom. The costs of these technologies are also decreasing, thus making them affordable by even the amateur criminal. Management faces an even more serious challenge in the year to come.

POTENTIAL TARGETS

Oftentimes, you do not need an expensive consultant to tell you whether your computers are a potential target of criminals. There is a simple test by which you can make at least an initial determination.

To test how secure your computers are, ask yourself the following:

Are you satisfied with your present controls?	(Y)	(N)
Are your system access points adequately controlled?	(Y)	(N)
Is it your organization's policy to look into suspicious transactions?	(Y)	(N)
Is your computer facility located in an area frequented by outsiders?	(Y)	(N)
Does your organization take a tough stance on prosecuting dishonest employees?	(Y)	(N)
Does your system store valuable data?	(Y)	(N)

Does your organization enforce its rules and regulations? (Y) (N)

Are employees adequately supervised? (Y) (N)

Are there any employee-related problems at the facility? (Y) (N)

Do any system employees have drug-related problems? (Y) (N)

Are confidential reports and documents discarded in public areas? (Y) (N)

Do employees gamble on the premises? (Y) (N)

Are corrections on source input documents allowed only if authorization is given in writing? (Y) (N)

Has the organization been the target of past criminal acts? (Y) (N)

Are key system personnel given instructions in writing? (Y) (N)

Are audits conducted periodically? (Y) (N)

Do you have a corporate security officer? (Y) (N)

Is the organization security conscious? (Y) (N)

Does top management support security mentality? (Y) (N)

If the majority of the responses to the above were negative, you should give serious consideration to reviewing your entire computer security program (if your organization has one). You may be a potential target for a computer rip-off.

CRIMINAL TRENDS

We are increasingly moving into a paperless society; the electronic funds transfer systems (EFTSs), the electronic office (EO), and the electronic message systems (EMSs) are no longer the stuff of science fiction. The computer revolution has made all this possible; without it, the information revolution would continue to be the province of novelists. Experts, however, fear that the paperless society will also provide a fertile environment for thefts, frauds, and abuses by computer.

There are ample discernible trends and indicators to make management take note. If the present trends continue, we can easily foresee an electronic crime wave in the near future—one that will victimize both business and government. The electronic criminal is today's reality. These trends, unless future events alter them, indicate what we might witness in the coming years:

Massive financial frauds and thefts.
Greater involvement by organized crime.

A wave of terrorist attacks.

Serious privacy abuses.

Massive thefts of intellectual properties.

A growing number of computer-related hoaxes.

Thefts of valuable trade secrets.

Growth of both corporate and political electronic espionage.

Increasingly sophisticated electronic interceptions.

Serious losses of life.

Greater involvement of juvenile offenders.

Many other crimes we cannot yet predict.

Society, however, is not without remedy; both the private and public sectors can play an important role in preventing computer-related crimes and abuses. Among other things, an organization should take steps to establish one or more of the following measures[3]:

Physical security.

Personnel security.

Communications safeguards.

Procedural security.

Periodic auditing.

Support for Federal and state computer crime legislation.

Involvement in every facet of the criminal justice system.

Education and training for key personnel in the prevention of computer-related crimes and abuses.

A code of ethics.

A policy of swift and vigorous prosecution of computer felons.

Prompt civil action against felons to retrieve financial losses.

The above measures are only some of the many that can assist in deterring thefts, frauds, and abuses by computer. However, even the best of measures are of limited value if business and government operates in an environment devoid of ethics. When uncovered, felons are always quick to point out that they "were not the only bad apple." A corrupt environment breeds crimes by computer.

---

[3] These are discussed in greater detail in subsequent chapters.

CHAPTER 3

Computers as Tools in White Collar Crimes

A Miami stockbroker who operated a sophisticated national stock fraud is said to have defrauded thousands of investors out of more than $50 million. The felon is said to have used counterfeit computer printouts from reputable brokerage firms to persuade investors that they were making a profit when in fact they were losing money.

Management for an insurance company used the firm's computers to create play insurance policies that were later sold to reinsurers. Of the company's assets, $143.3 million were found to be fictitious. A teller for a New York City bank skimmed more than $1 million from large client accounts by making a simple computerized correction entry.

White collar crime is said to cost business and government in excess of $20 billion annually. The Chamber of Commerce of the United States places the annual losses to the private sector alone in excess of $40 billion (see Tables 1 and 2 for lists of estimates). A study by the U.S. Department of Commerce has concluded that:

So many employees are stealing so much, that employee theft is the most critical crime problem facing business today.

It went on to note that:

> Management has responsibilities not only to recognize crime as an un-
> necessarily high expense, but also to recognize steps it can take to reduce
> this high expense and to take the initiative in implementing cost-cutting
> policies.

However, the advent of the computer has facilitated white collar
crimes; armed with this technology, the white collar criminal can steal
millions of dollars with greater ease than ever before. This has prompted
government sources to observe that:

> It is estimated that the loss resulting from an average computer-assisted
> embezzlement is ten times higher than the average $100,000 lost from
> traditional embezzlement.

The computer has democratized white collar crime.

TABLE 1   U.S. DEPARTMENT OF COMMERCE ESTIMATED ANNUAL LOSSES FROM CRIMES AGAINST BUSINESS[a]

Business Sectors	Losses ($ Billions)
Manufacturing	3.2
Retailing	6.5
Services	4.3
Transportation	2.3
Wholesaling	2.4
Total	$18.7

[a] The above costs do not include losses as a result
of arson or the moneys spent by business to safeguard itself against these crimes; nor do they include the losses to government. When these are
included, these losses exceed $20 billion annu-
ally.

COMPUTERS MAKE ECONOMIC CRIMES EASY

White collar crime is not a phenomenon of our modern electronic society.
There are ample illustrations throughout history. The ancient Egyptians,

Greeks, and Romans were victimized by white collar felons; King Edward I, concerned about financial frauds, convened Parliament to enact tough measures. Our nineteenth century "robber barons" bilked both the public and government with impunity. Even totalitarian regimes are plagued by economic crimes.

White collar crimes are often defined as being illegal acts or series of acts, characterized by guile, deceit, and concealment, that are not dependent upon the direct application of physical force or violence. Unlike street criminals, white collar felons rely on their intellect, education, training, and technical know-how. Their primary objective is to obtain money,

TABLE 2 COST OF WHITE COLLAR CRIME[a]

Category of Crime	Sources ($ Billions)			
	U.S. Small Business Administration	Chamber of Commerce of the U.S.	American Management Associations	Joint Economic Committee
Arson			1.3	
Bankruptcy fraud		0.08		
Bribery, kickbacks, payoffs		3.0	3.5–10.0	3.85
Burglary	0.958		2.5	
Check fraud	0.316	1.0	1.0–2.0	1.12
Computer-related		0.10		0.129
Consumer fraud		21.00		27.0
Credit card fraud		0.1	0.5	0.500
Embezzlement		3.0	4.0	3.86
Insurance fraud		2.0	2.0	2.50
Pilferage/employee theft	0.381	4.0	5.0–10.0	4.84
Robbery	0.077			
Securities theft/fraud		4.0	5.0	0.291
Shoplifting	0.504		2.0	
Vandalism	0.813		2.5	
Receiving stolen property		3.50		
Totals	3.05	41.7	29.3–41.8	44.2

[a] These figures do not include the costs associated with preventing and prosecuting these crimes.

property, or services; occasionally, they may seek to gain a personal or business advantage. These economic crimes come in various forms; the number of consumer-related rip-offs alone exceeds 800. Computer technology, unfortunately, can and has been employed as a vehicle to facilitate the commission of these offenses; it also makes their detection and prosecution more difficult.

For much of this century, white collar crimes were often associated with individuals in positions of trust and responsibility; well into the 1950s, these were offenses committed by society's elite. When the sociologist Edwin H. Sutherland wrote about these crimes in 1949, he referred to them as violations of criminal law committed by professionals in the course of their occupational activities. Sutherland and others like him studied white collar crimes before the advent of the computer in the everyday dealings of government and business.

Computer technology, however, changed all this; it made it possible for a clerk to embezzle large sums of money. It gave the lower strata of the worlds of business and government access to highly confidential data. Because a large army of men and women was now needed to operate this complex electronic record keeping system, people who had previously been denied access to positions of trust and power now found those doors open. Their technical know-how now made it possible for the dishonest among them to subvert the technology to their needs. It can truly be said that, just as the invention of gunpowder marked the end of an era when the knightly class monopolized warfare, so too computer technology has marked an end to an era where only the affluent and professional elements of society could indulge in white collar crimes.

TYPES OF ECONOMIC CRIMES

Unlike in a paper-based system, computer-related white collar crimes leave few, if any, paper trails. What makes this technology ideally suited for economic crimes is that much of what transpires within it never appears on paper. It can be programmed to "erase" its own trails, making detection difficult. The computer can also, because of its rapid speed and ability to collect, record, and disseminate large amounts of information, be used in complex economic crimes. For example, in the now classic Equity Funding Company fraud, corrupt corporate executives were able to create 63,000 fictitious insurance policies with the assistance of the company's computers. These were assigned a "99" designation; this enabled the computer billing programs to skip these bogus policies when bills were sent to the company's real policyholders. The fraud only surfaced when a former company official "blew the whistle." Even then, it took investigators years to unravel the puzzle.

White collar crimes often fall under one or more of several categories; the more common are essentially as follows:

Bankruptcy frauds
Bribery, kickback, and payoff schemes
Insurance-related swindles
Embezzlements
Pilferage of property
Receiving stolen property
Securities-related frauds and thefts
Tax-related frauds
Illegal trade practices

The above crimes rely, largely, on the manipulation and/or fabrication of records; the computer easily lends itself to such criminal abuses.

Bankruptcy Frauds

These are also known as "scams" or "bust-outs," and account for more than $80 million in annual losses to the private sector alone. The basic technique in a scam usually takes the following form:

The felon purchases merchandise or goods on credit from several suppliers.
The felon then proceeds to dispose of the goods for cash.
The proceeds from these sales are then concealed.
When the creditors press for their money, the felon stalls for time.
Finally, the felon may declare voluntary bankruptcy or skip town, leaving the creditors holding the bag (these then will usually petition the court for involuntary bankruptcy).

In one such scam, a group of criminals bilked creditors out of more than $100,000, and skipped town.

In a computerized environment, where millions of dollars can be transferred in a brief span of time (electronically) to another state or country, tracing the funds could prove difficult for the creditors and/or the authorities. In addition, since a computer can be easily programmed to erase the data it stores, investigators may find it difficult to unravel the puzzle. The modification, fabrication, and manipulation of corporate assets and records so necessary in a scam operation is made easier by computer technology.

Bribes, Kickbacks and Payoffs

These are said to account for more than $3 billion of losses annually, and can involve corporate executives, domestic and foreign government officials, and heads of labor unions. In one such scheme, several corporate officials were said to have paid more than $100,000 to a government official; the payments were made through a numbered secret Swiss bank account. In another case, a corporate executive was charged with taking more than $30,000 in bribes, in return for passing trade secrets to his employer's competitor.

The objectives of the above schemes can vary. However, they are often directed at:

Obtaining a new business
Retaining an old business
Covering up inferior products
Covering up poor services
Securing confidential information
Gaining approval for work done
Securing a contract
Promoting legislation
Influencing political decisions (domestic or foreign)
Gaining an economic advantage

Irrespective of what the objective is, computer technology both facilitates these schemes and makes their detection and investigation more difficult. Funds can be transferred electronically to secret Swiss bank accounts in a matter of minutes, and audit trails can easily be erased. Further, few police agencies are either trained or possess the requisite resources to adequately investigate these offenses.

Insurance Frauds

These account for more than $2 billion in annual losses, and usually take on the form of frauds against:

The insurer

The insured

The company (insurer) stockholders

Frauds against the insurer can take the form of a dishonest company employee inserting fraudulent data in the firm's computer for the purpose of creating fictitious life, health, accident, and casualty claims. Corporate checks are issued to these phony claimants, and the felon then pockets the money.

An insurer can also be ripped-off by dishonest insiders through the manipulation of the insurer's computer. For example, premiums paid by the insured can, through the manipulation of the input, be credited to an account controlled by the felon.

An insurer's stockholders can also fall victim to computer rip-offs engineered by dishonest management. For example, through use of the company's computers, management can alter, modify, or fabricate the insurer's assets, earnings, and expenditures. In one such case, management for an insurance firm fabricated the firm's assets and earnings, with the aid of its computer. Of the approximately $3 billion insurance in force carried on the company's books, approximately $2 billion had been fabricated through manipulation of the computer. Management's report to the company's stockholders predicted a bright future:

In summary, we look forward to another year of growth which will derive essentially from internal operations.

Induced by these fabricated financial reports, stockholders paid as much as $80 for the company's common share.

Embezzlements

Thefts by dishonest employees are presently the primary problem for business. These are said to account for more than $3 billion in annual losses. Experts note that almost 50 percent of the present work force steals at least something from their employers; 8 percent of these, however, are said to steal large sums of money and property. These internal thefts or embezzlements usually take the form of unauthorized use or theft of an employer's assets, equipment, products, services, and other resources.

In an embezzlement, the felon converts for his/her own use or benefit, money or property entrusted to the felon by the employer. Embezzlements can range from the simple to the complex; unfortunately, employers are often reluctant to prosecute for fear of adverse publicity and from lack of confidence in our criminal justice system.

In an increasingly automated business environment, embezzlements have become an even more serious threat. While the traditional embezzler stole, on the average, $10,000 by juggling the employer's books, the automated embezzler steals, on the average, between $500,000 and $1 million. As we increasingly become a cashless society, the losses will increase even more.

In addition, the detection of a computer-assisted embezzlement scheme can prove difficult; there are no paper trails, fingerprints, or forgeries to put management on notice. For example, take the case of the chief financial officer of a large shipping company who, within a period of less than six years, embezzled more than $500,000 from his employer with the assistance of its computer. The auditors finally stumbled on his case by accident. In a separate case, a clerk at a New York City bank embezzled more than $30,000 from his employer; he had programmed the bank's computer to issue dividend checks to his friends.

The majority of the computer-assisted embezzlements that have surfaced were detected by the victim's auditors; they usually surfaced by accident. For example, a clerk for the U.S. Department of Transportation embezzled more than $500,000 from his employer over a period of several years. During this period of time, the felon purchased, with the moneys he had embezzled, 15 luxury cars and a "Go-Go Dance Hall" next to the FBI's Washington, D.C., headquarters. The fraud surfaced only when the felon's bank contacted the authorities regarding several suspicious deposits the felon had made.

Pilferage

The theft of merchandise and goods by dishonest employees accounts for more than $4 billion in annual losses by business. Pilferage schemes often take one or more of the following forms:

Inventory lists are doctored.

Cash sales tickets are altered.

Merchandise is shipped to the home of the dishonest employee or that of a friend or relative.

Tools or products are stolen.

Valuable materials are substituted with cheaper ones.

Bills of lading are altered.

Incorrect shipping labels are put on packages.

Records of incoming shipments are doctored.

Records of outgoing merchandise are altered.

Sales commissions and discounts are manipulated.

Wrong customer is billed.

Wrong product is shipped.

Improper credit is granted.

Fictitious suppliers and customers are created.

Fictitious employees are created.

As corporations and government turn to computer technology to handle their payrolls, shipments, interwarehouse transfers, inventories, billing procedures, and others, they increasingly open themselves up to sophisticated computer-related pilferage schemes. A large department store, for example, fell victim to such a scheme when an employee with knowledge of its sales order processing system placed orders for valuable merchandise; by manipulating the store's computer, he billed his account for only a fraction of the real cost of the merchandise. In another case, a disgruntled manager with a manufacturing firm entered numerous phony orders for valuable goods with the firm's computer; the goods were then mailed to a relative's home.

Pilferage in an automated society is often made possible by poor internal controls. The computer now makes it possible to transfer large inventories of merchandise at the press of a button; goods and merchandise are labeled and shipped by computer. However, the computer also gives the dishonest insider easy access to the employer's inventory files; inter- and intracompany transfers become easy. The felon's pilferage often goes unnoticed because the computer has made it difficult for auditors to detect.

Receiving Stolen Property

Professional middlemen ("fences") often play a key role in white collar crimes. Fences buy and sell stolen property; they thus assist the criminal in disposing of the stolen merchandise. They are said to account for more than $3 billion in annual losses to the private sector. The operations of fences often vary in size and level of sophistication. The following categories are the most common:

Neighborhood fence. This felon usually operates out of a garage, pawn shop, local restaurant, or other local small business establishment. He/she provides a small outlet for stolen merchandise, but lacks the resources and expertise to handle large volumes of stolen goods or highly specialized products.

Specialist fence. This sort tends to specialize in certain types of goods and merchandise. For example, there are specialist fences who trade in high technology items, such as stolen computer bits. These, however, usually disguise their operations under the cover of a legitimate business; the majority of their customers are legitimate businesspeople.

Volume fence. This type handles large volumes of stolen merchandise. For example, a cargo of stolen cigarettes will often be sold by the thieves to an outlet fence, who in turn will sell it to (usually) legitimate business sources. The outlet fence usually employs a legitimate business front.

Many of these fences have at least some ties to organized crime. For example, in testimony before a U.S. Senate Committee, a convicted thief testified as follows:

COMMITTEE CHAIRMAN: How important were these organized crime–connected fences to your operation? In other words, if you did not have them to fence the stolen goods for you and take them off your hands and pay you something for them, could your operation have been successful? Would it have been very profitable?

THIEF: No, not without a fence.

COMMITTEE CHAIRMAN: You would have to have a fence?

THIEF: Yes, sir.

COMMITTEE CHAIRMAN: And you found that requirement fulfilled in the ranks of the syndicate or organized crime?

THIEF: Yes, sir.

COMMITTEE CHAIRMAN: Do you feel that was true in each instance?

THIEF: Yes, sir.

Computer technology has facilitated the theft of valuable goods and merchandise; it has also opened up new markets for the fence. Valuable computer programs and other components command a high price; for example, specialist fences have already been implicated in the role of stolen computer chips. They have provided criminals with ready-made markets for their ill-gotten goods; their customers, ironically, are often legitimate businesspeople.

Securities Frauds and Thefts

These are said to account for more than $4 billion in annual losses to the private sector alone. One U.S. Senate Subcommittee has placed the cost of lost, counterfeit, and missing securities somewhere between $5 billion and $50 billion. Organized crime is also said to have made its way into this arena. A ring of criminals, for example, connected to organized crime, was reported several years ago to be stealing in excess of $4 million worth of stock monthly from Wall Street brokerage firms. In a similar case, a mob-connected fence was said to have purchased $21 million in stolen securities, and then sold them to a legitimate source. The latter used them as collateral at several banks.

TABLE 3   USUAL CYCLE FOR THEFT AND CONVERSION OF SECURITIES[a]

Main targets	Brokerage houses, banks, U.S. mails, and individuals.
Profile of thief	Dishonest employee, who may depend on organized crime for conversion of the stolen securities; the mob may have also used strong-arm pressures to force the corporate insider to assist.
Thieves turn securities	To fences, who control their distribution and conversion.
Conversion	The stolen securities are converted to cash by reselling them through brokers, placing them with banks as collateral, placing them in the portfolios of insurance companies, or taking them outside the United States (Canada, Bahamas, Switzerland, Hong Kong, Germany, Liechstein, or South America).
If taken outside U.S.	The securities are resold, placed in banks as collateral, or used to establish trust accounts.

[a] Organized crime often plays a key role in this cycle.

Securities frauds and thefts usually take on various forms. See Table 3 for one common pattern. The thief can be a dishonest employee, or an organized criminal group of outsiders. Some of the cases that have surfaced, for example, have involved the following:

Executives for a manufacturing company who used confidential corporate insider information for personal investment purposes.

A group of con artists who are said to have puffed up a company's balance sheet by $20 million.

Employees of a Wall Street broker dealer who had been selling worthless securities to the public.

Professional criminals who used bogus securities to inject the appearance of growth in an otherwise worthless corporate shell.

A broker who created an artificial demand for a stock through the use of phony accounts.

In addition, white collar criminals employ a number of techniques in this area; they usually take one of the following forms:

Puffing up a firm's balance sheet
Altering records
Use of foreign accounts
Use of phony credit reports
Fictitious inventories
Phony sales
Ghost buyers
Overseas corporate offices

Computers, however, have been found to easily lend themselves to sophisticated securities-related frauds and thefts. A computer can be employed by a felon to:

Create phony financial statements.
Trade on inside information.
Create worthless assets.
Create an artificial demand for a bogus company's stock.
Create dummy brokerage accounts.
Create nonexistent securities.
Tap confidential insider corporate data.
Transfer funds electronically.
Manipulate the price of a company stock.
Create nonexistent shipments, payments, purchases, and transfers of inventories (these are aimed at confusing a company's stockholders, creditors, and auditors).

In a case similar to the above, management for a publicly held Pennsylvania-based insurance company is alleged to have used the firm's computers to understate its losses and inflate its profits. The ultimate objective was to artificially raise the value of the company's stock.

Tax-Related Frauds

The Internal Revenue Service (IRS) estimates that individuals and companies do not report $75 billion to $100 billion in annual income. This is said to result in a revenue loss of approximately $13 billion to $17 billion annually. IRS sources estimate that, if one adds to this the unreported income from drug trafficking and other such connected operations, some $200 billion in income go unreported annually.

Computer technology, IRS sources fear, could aggravate this already growing problem. Admittedly, the computer records even the most miniscule of transactions; however, it can be manipulated and records can be erased at the press of a button. In addition, IRS auditors are no better trained or prepared than their counterparts in the private sector in the area of computer-related audits.[1]

Illegal Trade Practices

These are said to account for annual losses in excess of $10 billion. They are usually characterized by such things as:

Meetings among competitors to discuss marketing plans

Exchanges of price lists

Communications regarding pricing patterns

Combinations to fix prices

Contracts to restrain trade

Divisions of territories

Agreements not to solicit each other's customers

Refusal to sell or buy

Exclusive dealing agreements

Exclusive distributorships

Pooling of resources

Price discriminations

Seller's agreement not to compete

[1] Unlike the Federal Bureau of Investigation and the U.S. Secret Service, the IRS does not have a formal computer crime training program for its investigators.

Tying arrangements
Collusive bidding
Profit sharing by successful bidders

The traditional smoke-filled room, the exchange of correspondence, documents, and other paper records are things of the past. Today's price fixers need only have their computers communicate with one another; the exchange and dissemination of key data can now be effectuated by automation.

Other Categories of White Collar Crime

Computer technology also lends itself to an array of other sophisticated economic frauds and thefts. Among the crimes that the computer can be used to perpetrate are the following:

Welfare swindles.
Food stamp frauds.
Thefts of government money and property.
Medicare and Medicaid swindles.
Government contract and grant frauds.
Crimes involving electronic funds transfer systems (EFTSs) and/or electronic message systems (EMSs).
Commodity swindles.
Environmental crimes.
Theft of drugs.
Manipulation or alteration of medical/scientific tests.
Diversion of nuclear materials.
Theft of high technology.
Consumer-related swindles.
Industrial espionage.

The computer has not only given rise to new categories of crime, but it has also made it easier for white collar criminals to prey on both business and government. Unfortunately, white collar crimes have always proven difficult to detect, investigate, and prosecute; however, computer technology has now made it even more difficult. Our law enforcement agencies have been trained to detect and bring to prosecution street crimes; they now face the criminal of the suites armed not only with his/her intellect, but also assisted by computer technology.

CHAPTER 4

Meet the
Electronic
Criminal

Four men were arrested in the theft of a company's computer manuals; these detailed how the firm's computer operations could be shut down. A police source was quoted as saying that a shutdown of the system could have caused the company a serious disruption of its business. In a separate case, a California-based gang of "computernicks" provided improved ratings to consumers with poor credit histories. The gang charged fees of up to $1500 for its services; they were assisted by a clerk who worked for a national credit bureau. In return for small fees, he made phony credit entries.

At one of the nation's largest financial institutions, a trusted computer manager conspired to rip-off more than $15 million from his employer. These electronic capers prompted the vice-president of a large financial institution to say that: "If company CEOs really understood the risk we now face, they'd lock us up until we found a solution." The director of software engineering for a communications firm summarized the problem best: "With a reasonable amount of time and effort, a 13-year-old could break into a computer system."

Yet who is this criminal that has caused both industry and government great, and justified, concern? If we are to understand and address the problem of electronic crime, we must by necessity understand who the electronic criminal is, what motivates him or her, and what management's role must be in addressing the threat. On these answers may rest our ability to deter crimes and abuses by computer.

PROFILE OF THE FELON

Unlike traditional crimes, computer capers are not usually committed by the lower socioeconomic strata of our society; they are not the result of depravity. Rather, they are the calculated acts of professionals; they are committed by persons who occupy positions of trust and are armed with the modern technology of our society. They are, in most cases, crimes committed by our technocratic classes—men and women who operate, program, and service our computers.

It has been said that while we have spent billions of dollars and an army of experts to study the traditional criminal, little effort has been made to study the white collar felon; even fewer resources have been expended to study the computer criminal. However, from the hundreds of computer-related criminal cases that have surfaced to date, we have been able to develop some sort of profile (see Table 1). Admittedly, this profile is somewhat misleading because:

It is based only on a small fraction of the many computer-related offenses that daily plague our society.

The cases that have been uncovered and prosecuted usually involved low-level employees, prompting some experts to conclude that our police agencies are not sufficiently sophisticated to apprehend the more sophisticated criminals.

Not all the cases that have surfaced have been handled through criminal prosecutions; many have been disposed of through civil/administrative means, making their study difficult.[1]

There is as yet no one widely accepted definition of what computer crime is.[2]

The Federal Bureau of Investigation (FBI) compiles and publishes annual data on an assortment of crimes, but not on computer crimes (these are usually listed as larcenies, embezzlements, etc.).

There is no Federal or national clearinghouse for the collection and dissemination of information on computer crimes.

---

[1] Because of privacy laws and regulations, the agencies that handled these cases refuse to make all their findings public.

[2] This author had an opportunity to head a Federal study of computer crime, and was thus able to discuss the above with both law enforcement and private security officials. It soon became apparent that neither the law enforcement community nor the private sector could agree on any one definition.

TABLE 1   PROFILE OF TYPICAL COMPUTER FELON[a]

Age	15–45 years old
Sex	Many of these crimes were committed by males, but women are increasingly entering the field
Professional experience	Ranges widely from the highly experienced technician to a minimally experienced professional; in a few of these cases, however, the criminal had little or no technical experience
Criminal background	Usually no previous known contact with law enforcement
Targets of criminal	Both government and business
Personal traits	Bright, motivated, and ready to accept the technical challenge; usually a desirable employee, a hard and committed worker; often the last person you would suspect of committing a criminal act
Fears	The felon is concerned with exposure, ridicule, and loss of status within the community and place of work
Role	In the majority of the cases that have surfaced, it has been a one-person show; increasingly, however, conspiracies of two or more criminals are surfacing
Behavior	At least on the surface, the computer felon appears to deviate little from the accepted norms of society
Employment position	Most of these offenses are committed by individuals employed in positions of trust within a company or agency; the felon has easy access to the computer system
Security	Usually lax or nonexistent
Indicators for management	Is usuually on guard; is the first to arrive at the office and the last to leave; also takes few or no vacations
Justification	Seeks to minimize criminal acts by viewing them as just a "game"

[a] The profile, admittedly flawed, is constructed from the several hundred cases that have been studied by the U.S. Bureau of Justice statistics.

The profile, however, that does emerge from the several hundred cases that have been studied presents problems for management. The computer criminal, oftentimes, can be the average employee within an organization.

The acts of the computer felon are usually characterized by guile, deceit, and concealment. The motives that guide the felon's conduct vary. However, they generally fall into one or more of the following categories:

Economic gain. Theft of money, services, or property for personal aggrandizement.

Robin Hood syndrome. The romantic illusion that the felon is ripping off only the affluent and corrupt, that the victim "has it coming."

Poor security. Employers often invite fraud by establishing few, if any, security safeguards. An organization that is lax on computer security is a tempting target for the criminal.

Game playing. Unfortunately, many data processing professionals treat the computer as a toy.

Hatred of the organization. The criminal may be acting out of revenge for a real or perceived wrong.

Labor-related. Poor employer-employee relations can often result in employee attacks directed at the employer's property; these attacks may sometimes be indirectly encouraged by a labor union.

Economic problems. The felon may be in dire financial straits.

Machine syndrome. Hatred of an all-pervasive technology.

Corrupt management. If the organization and top executives are corrupt, they should expect little else from their employees.

Ego. The challenge of beating the computer and evading detection can prove to be an aphrodisiac for some.

Peer pressure. If other employees engage in illegal acts, there may be few inhibitions.

Emotional maladjustment. Mental illness or instability can also be a factor.

Ideology. Political extremists and terrorists may view the computer as a tool of the "ruling class."

Blackmail. Fear of public exposure, especially where organized crime is involved.

Extortion. The felon may fear for his personal safety or that of his family.

Political. Agents of a foreign country may seek to destroy a country's political-economic viability, or a politician may be seeking to undermine his opponents.

Economic competition. A corporate rival may seek to gain an unfair economic advantage over competitors.

Codes of Ethics. An absence of rules and procedures for dealing with conflict of interest situations and other ethical questions can result in unethical conduct.

At present, the computer criminal is not viewed as a threat to society by either the public or our criminal justice system; our concern is with street crime. Management, in part, facilitates computer crime; few criminals are ever referred to the prosecutors. Many of the computer capers are merely swept under the rug; the losses are passed on to the consumer and taxpayer.

RELUCTANCE TO PROSECUTE

It is no secret that management is often reluctant to refer computer crimes to the authorities. Rather, the culprit is dismissed or transferred to another division or branch. Occasionally, a victim may bring, with great reluctance, a civil action to recoup its losses. In a case in which this author was called upon for assistance, a Texas-based company discovered that one of its managers had copied and sold some of its programs to a competitor. The author recommended, among other things, swift prosecution; the victim, however, merely fired the dishonest employee.

A reluctance to prosecute can hardly be said to serve as a deterrent; it usually only serves to tell others to try their hand. The victim, however, should not always be faulted; complex forces often determine this behavior. Understanding these can serve to assist both a potential victim and the authorities. A victim's decision-making may be determined by one or more of the following factors:

Not dangerous. The computer criminal is not viewed in the same light as the street criminal. Losses from computer-related crimes are usually passed on by the victim to its customers. However, victims often forget that this mode of behavior ultimately has an impact on the public's perception of the organization.

Time consuming. The detection and prosecution of these crimes often taxes the limited resources of an organization. The police will rely on the victim for assistance. Further, the victim's operations may be affected; employees, records, and equipment may find their way to court as witnesses and exhibits.

Expensive. Because the prosecution of computer crimes can easily run into the hundreds of thousands of dollars, the prosecutor faced with limited resources and staff may be reluctant to pursue them. Management is often cognizant of this, and may thus be reluctant to bring the authorities into the case.

Slap on the wrist. It is common knowledge that, even if convicted, computer criminals are often placed on probation or given a suspended sentence. Few victims find solace in this. One manager summarized it as follows: "After you spend thousands of dollars and manhours on the case, you see him walk out a free man. It's frustrating."

Prosecutorial problems. Local prosecutors are often more concerned with street crimes. The public does not perceive crimes by computer as a serious direct threat.

Lack of laws. Although the U.S. Congress and the state legislatures have enacted numerous criminal laws, these were passed primarily to deal with traditional crimes. These laws are thus not always easy to apply to computer crimes.

Viewed as civil. Many of these crimes are often, especially in the areas of thefts of data and software, viewed as civil—rather than criminal—violations. Prosecutors often tell the victim to "hire a lawyer and sue."

Public ridicule. The victim, unfortunately, is often viewed by the public as being greedy, foolish, stupid, and careless. It is perceived as "inviting" the crime. The public sheds few tears for a corporation or government agency that falls victim to a computer caper.

Dirty hands. Some victims fear that a lengthy government investigation may uncover management's dirty laundry. A manager put it this way: "When you invite a wolf into your den, you take a chance."

Corporate liability. Management's failure to take adequate measures to secure the computer could give rise to a stockholder lawsuit.

Insurance rates. Victims often fear that the insurer may raise their premiums—or even refuse to renew a policy—if these crimes become a common occurrence.

Alienating creditors. A victim may fear that its financial reputation and credit rating may suffer as a result.

Encouraging others. There is justifiable concern that disclosure of the crime—a public description of how it was committed—can serve to invite added criminal attacks.

Fear of financial disclosure. The victim may refuse to prosecute because its finances, marketing plans, trade secrets, or other confidential data may become public at the trial.

Little to gain.   Many feel that they stand to gain little from a criminal prosecution, since their insurer "picks up the tab."

Previous denials.   A victim who may initially have covered up the crime may fear ridicule, litigation, and even criminal prosecution if it later makes full disclosure.

Organizational politics.   In-house power fights may discourage disclosure. Managers may fear that disclosure could hinder their professional standings within the organization.

To the observer, it seems incongruous that a victim who has lost millions of dollars would sometimes be reluctant to prosecute. However, there is a logical basis for this. But it carries a price tag. Although some can present numerous arguments for not prosecuting, few doubt that a failure to prosecute can often invite new criminal attacks. The victim is viewed as an easy target; to quote a prosecutor, the victim appears "as a pushover."

POTENTIAL SOURCES OF ATTACK

Computer-related attacks can come from various sources. The majority, however, are committed by one or more of the following three groups:

Dishonest insiders.   Employees, usually those who occupy positions of trust.

Outsiders.   Competitors, maintenance supply and repair personnel, and others not directly connected with the victim, but who usually have some professional dealings with it.

Users.   These usually abuse their authority to use the system.

System personnel who can potentially pose a threat to the system are numerous. These, however, can be categorized by their area of responsibility. For example, operational threats can result from:

Transaction operators
Computer operators
Peripheral operators
Data entry and update clerks
Communications operators

Software-related crimes are usually caused by:

  Media librarians
  System programmers
  Applications programmers

Hardware can be targeted by:

  Terminal engineers
  System engineers
  Communication engineers
  Facilities engineers

Management-connected problems can result from:

  Network managers
  Operations managers
  Data base managers
  Programming managers

Additional threats can be posed by:

  Identification control clerks
  Security officers
  EDP auditors

An organization, however, need not be helpless; there are a number of controls it can employ to both prevent and detect computer-related frauds, thefts, and abuses. These can be employed where:

  The transactions originate
  The transactions are recorded
  The data is transmitted
  The processing occurs
  The data is stored
  The data is retrieved
  The output is processed
  The computer center is located
  The applications system is developed

There are, however, two areas of abuse that should prove of special concern to management; these take the form of unauthorized access and misuse of the system. These two categories of abuses threaten the very accuracy and integrity of the data stored within the system. They undermine the very reliability of the system. Unauthorized access can take one or more of the following forms:

Theft of an authorized user's password and file names

Manipulation of the system (in part or in its entirety)

Gaining control of the system

Removal of the secondary storage media

Exploiting access privileges

Misuse of the system (or any of its components), however, appears to be more prevalent than unauthorized access. Misuse of a system can be the result of:

Authorized users. These may engage in penetration activities through the use of a remote terminal. For example, they may remove or modify the components of the system. However, monitoring the activities of all authorized users can prove difficult, if not impossible.

Operations support personnel. These usually abuse only the components of the system. For example, a tape librarian can mix up tapes and substitute blank tapes for the masters.

System programmers. These can abuse the system either in its entirety or any of its components. For example, they can embed within the system special modifications that can circumvent its safeguards.

System operators. These can modify or replace the operating system or copy its sensitive files.

Customer engineers. These are able to circumvent the system's hardware safeguards when conducting preventive or emergency maintenance.

Program system representatives. These can modify the system by planting trapdoors and also by delivering bogus documentation.

Telephone maintenance personnel. These can attack the system's hardware components.

The potential for abuse of the system comes not only from insiders, but also from personnel who are employed to maintain, service, and operate the system (outsiders). Management's ability to identify potential threats to the system can often play an important role in preventing computer-related offenses. Equally important, the organization should both antici-pate and adequately address all potential threats to the system. This may not always prove to be an easy task; however, it is an important and necessary task for management to undertake.

WHAT TO DO IF YOU'RE VICTIMIZED

A manager at a mail-order firm was told by one of the employees that a computer operator had copied the company's most valued customer list, and was planning to sell it to a competitor. Without taking steps to verify the allegations, he burst into the suspect's office, accused him of being a thief, and fired him. Soon after, the operator filed a lawsuit for defamation; the manager himself was later fired when it was learned that the infor-mant, and not the computer operator, had planned to steal the mailing list.

The modern manager has not been trained to address crime-related problems; yet who, if not management, is in a better position to know and understand the workings of the modern organization? Management is sufficiently sophisticated to be taught the "ABCs" of what to do when a computer caper victimizes its organization. Understanding these basic and simple rules can serve to assist the authorities in prosecuting the criminal.

The "ABCs" of handling an investigation are both simple and non-technical. Today's manager need not be a police officer or attorney to apply these basic rules. When faced with a computer rip-off, remember the following:

Before calling the police, determine if an illegal act has in fact occurred.

Determine what has actually occurred (for example, does it involve the modification of the output/input, illegal access to data base files, etc.?).

Attempt to determine the level of technical sophistication that was needed to perpetrate the offense (this can often tell you if it was an "inside job").

Contact the offices of security director and general counsel (briefly, give them a summary of your findings and observations).

Contact the internal auditors.

Identify potential witnesses to the crime.

Attempt to establish potential motives for the offense.

Attempt to zero in on potential suspects (do not interview any of these at this stage).

Do not tamper with the physical evidence (the police may want to analyze it for fingerprints, etc.).

Review the job description of those employed at the system.

Review the personnel files of potential suspects.

Review your security program (if you have one).

Coordinate "when and how" to bring the authorities into the case with your security director and office of general counsel.

There are some added basic rules that management should be familiar with. These specifically deal with how to handle the suspect; remember that until a computer criminal is convicted of a crime in a court of law, he or she is not guilty of anything. Calling a suspect a "thief" may only result in a lawsuit. With the aid of these basic tools, management can play a key role in assisting the police and prosecutors. Whenever you handle a suspect, keep in mind the following:

1. *Determining the extent and nature of the problem.* When first informed that your organization's computers have suffered a criminal attack, determine:

   a. Whether the act was accidental or intentional (for example, could it have been caused by operator, hardware, or software error?).

   b. Alternatively, could it have been caused by a natural phenomenon (for example, eliminate such natural causes as a flooding, fire, earthquake, winds, or lightning)?

2. *Recording the events.* Once it has been determined that the act was intentional, management should consider recording its observations; these could prove of value to the police. When doing so, consider the following:

   a. Record the events in ink (do not use a pencil, since it is not suitable for a permanent record).

   b. Record only pertinent information.

   c. Your entries should be legible (they are of little value if they cannot be read).

   d. Do not use shorthand.

   e. Use a tape recorder if necessary.

   f. Make sure your entries are accurate.

   g. Have your report typed.

3. *Interviewing the suspect(s).* If a decision is made to interview the suspect(s), keep the following in mind:

a. Approach the suspect in a businesslike manner.
b. Be pleasant.
c. Avoid threatening and foul language.
d. Do not physically detain the suspect.
e. Avoid abusive conduct.
f. Do not suggest answers.
g. Avoid use of physical force.
h. Do not talk down.
i. Let the suspect answer the question in full.
j. Allow the suspect to explain his/her conduct.
k. Be alert to slips of the tongue.
l. Word your questions one at a time.
m. Do not confuse the suspect.
n. Be polite and thank the suspect at the end of the interview.
o. Remember, your report may later find its way to court.

4. *Questions to ask.* When interviewing a suspect, you should prepare your questions in advance, stick to your line of questioning, and inform the suspect that he/she has a right to leave at any time during the questioning. Also elicit, if possible, the following information:

a. All names and aliases used by the suspect.
b. Present address.
c. Date of birth.
d. Present marital status.
e. Names of relatives and friends.
f. Names of outside business associates.
g. Sources of income.
h. Expenditures.
i. Net worth.
j. Credit references.
k. Employment record.
l. Whether the suspect uses any post office boxes.
m. List of personal and real property the suspect owns or controls.
n. List of businesses in which the suspect has an interest.

    o.   List of bank accounts in the suspect's name or under his/her control.

    p.   Other information you feel may be pertinent.

5. *Zeroing in on the suspect.* Compile a list of system personnel—by job description—who had the opportunity to commit the offense. This list of potential suspects could prove of value to the police. The list should include the following:

    a.   *Operations.* Computer operator, transactions operator, peripheral operator, job setup clerk, data entry and update clerk, others.

    b.   *Software.* Media librarian, system programmer, applications programmers, others.

    c.   *Hardware.* Terminal engineer, system engineer, facilities engineer, others.

    d.   *Management.* Network manager, operations manager, data base manager, programming manager, others.

    e.   *Other.* Identification control clerk, security officer, EDP auditor, dispatcher, user, supplier, consultant, salesperson, controller, accountant, others.

6. *Legal concerns.* While handling the investigation, be sure to guard against violating or abusing the privacy rights of both witnesses and suspects. Abusing these could result in a successful lawsuit against you and/or your organization. Note that our legal system guarantees the individual the right to be free from[3]:

    a.   Interference by third parties.

    b.   False statements regarding his/her professional and personal conduct.

    c.   Unauthorized electronic surveillance.

    d.   False arrest.

    e.   Unauthorized searches.

    f.   Use of truth detection devices.

    g.   Defamatory statements (written or oral).

    h.   Assault and battery.

    i.   Infliction of mental distress.

    j.   Public disclosure of private facts.

---

[3] These are discussed in greater detail in other chapters of this book.

  k. Insulting and abusive conduct.

  l. Harassment.

  7. *Preparing your report.* When supervising an inquiry, remember that the authorities will prove more cooperative if you can summarize your findings in a written report. The police have more crime on their hands than they know what to do with; they do not need more business. You may have to "spoon-feed" them in order to induce them to investigate the case further. Your report should thus include the following:

  a. A detailed summary of the facts and events of the case (in chronological order).

  b. A summary of the potential testimony each witness can give.

  c. The name and job description of each witness and suspect.

  d. A list of the available evidence.

  e. The approximate losses you have suffered.

  The electronic criminal is not the supercriminal our media has often portrayed. Often, the felon is someone who occupies and abuses a position of trust. The criminal's motives, level of sophistication, and the type of computer crime perpetrated will vary. The modern manager, if properly trained, can play an important role in preventing crimes by computer. Understanding the modus operandi of computer criminals, and the threat they pose is an important beginning.

CHAPTER 5

Infiltration by
Organized Crime

A member of organized crime is said to have engineered the theft of 10,000 model 2732 microcomputer chips. An associate of a New York Mafia family is said to have created fictitious accounts on the computer of a brokerage firm, and then used them to sell phony securities. A book-maker is said to have used the computers of a government contractor to keep his illegal gambling operations running.

Organized crime is big business in America.[1] Experts say it is this country's second largest business; it is said to gross more than $150 billion annually. Some law enforcement officials fear that this criminal cartel, long active in white collar crime, may have also entered the computer crime area. The head of a Midwestern police agency has warned that organized crime is currently using computer technology to prey on the economy. The amateur computer criminal may soon have to make room for the syndicate; the latter plays tough and for keeps.

POTENTIAL THREAT BY THE MOB

Unfortunately, the business community has for too long dismissed the syndicate as the creation of Hollywood. Organized crime, however, is not a myth; it does exist. Federal prosecutors estimate its net worth at more than

---

[1] Organized crime is also often referred to as the syndicate, mob, outfit, or confederation. I often refer to it in this chapter as the syndicate.

$100 billion. One prosecutor put it this way: "It's bigger than IBM." Its annual income exceeds that of the computer industry; it is an economic power to be dealt with, and crime is its business. For example:

> Illegally placed bets provide it with untaxed profits of more than $500,000/hour.
>
> Its take from gambling operations alone exceeds $20 billion annually.
>
> In one single Midwestern city, syndicate members control or have sizable interests in 89 businesses with an annual income of more than $900 million.
>
> Its loansharking operations are said to net it more than $10 billion annually.
>
> Its annual income from narcotics exceeds $70 billion.
>
> Arson, cigarette bootlegging, and prostitution bring in another $8 billion annually.
>
> Its tax-free profits exceed $40 billion annually.

Organized crime also has ties to some labor unions; it is said to have control over more than $100 billion in union pension funds. It also controls powerful local labor leaders and, through these, exerts powerful influence on some businesses.[2]

The syndicate has also demonstrated an uncanny ability to adapt new technologies. For example, it successfully employed the telephone to construct a national gambling empire; it has also employed mass communications to maintain control over its various investments. It has demonstrated an ability to corrupt both business and political figures. Through blackmail, extortion, threats, and physical violence, the syndicate can subvert computer programmers, operators, tape/disk librarians, maintenance personnel, and other EDP personnel.

Unfortunately, the business community has often underestimated the syndicate's ability to penetrate the private sector. Some in the computer industry dismiss the threat the syndicate poses as mere "nonsense," but ample proof exists to confirm the threat organized crime poses. For example:

> An executive with an insurance firm was forced to issue policies to syndicate-controlled businesses.

---

[2] Payoffs to syndicate figures under the guise of consulting fees are common in many industries in exchange for labor peace.

A large metropolitan newspaper was forced to agree not to attack local syndicate figures, in return for a guarantee that syndicate-controlled unions would not strike against it.

A pipeline company was forced to pay the syndicate protection money.

A high corporate executive received a sizable loan from a loanshark in return for his assistance.

The chief executive officer of an electronic firm is said to have been murdered by the syndicate.

A large conglomerate took on a syndicate figure as a labor consultant, in order to avoid labor-related problems.

A former syndicate member has best summarized his dealings with businesspeople as follows:

> Well, I'm gonna make the score this way. When I sit down with the boss [management], I tell him how much it's gonna cost him in welfare, hospitalization, and all that. Say a plant with 200 people will cost him $4,000 a month—just for hospitalization. So, altogether I make a package out of it. [I'll tell him] it's gonna cost $100,000 a year. Let's cut it in half and forget about it. And walk away. I show him first what it's gonna cost—then how much I'm gonna save by walking away.

People and not computers cause crime. The problem of crime by computer is a people problem. The technology performs only those tasks that it is directed to; it is merely a servant of our whims. However, computer technology does operate in a corrupt business environment. The potential for abuse by criminals is both great and real; organized crime poses a threat. It can both prey on computers and use them to improve the efficiency of its operations, making detection by law enforcement difficult.

UNDERSTANDING THE SYNDICATE

Organized crime poses a serious problem; it has an impact on every facet of our economy. It controls banks, hotels, retail operations, real estate, and is said to have an annual income in excess of $150 billion. In one eastern city alone, syndicate-connected figures own businesses with total assets of over $600 million.

The profits of organized crime are reputed to exceed those of any legitimate single sector of the economy. Its annual revenues exceed those for the telecommunications industry, auto industry, and steel industry; it is second only to the oil and gas industries. Today's syndicate boss is a sophisticated businessperson who views crime as a profession; organized crime presently enjoys a strong foothold in the business sector. Much of its illegal activities can now be characterized as being white collar crimes. It has also, according to knowledgeable law enforcement officials, turned its attention to computer technology.

Unfortunately, the very words "organized crime" evoke, for some businesspeople, images of a handful of men meeting in out-of-the-way restaurants, and plotting crimes. Numerous efforts have been made to explain this phenomenon that we call organized crime. The media has portrayed the image of a national conspiracy, dominated by a small group of ethnic elements. Suffice it to say that organized crime constitutes illegal behavior, on the part of well-organized criminal groups from all strata of our society, whose objective is to gain some economic advantage. It is, in short, a sophisticated economic animal, primarily motivated by financial gain.

Organized criminal activity is not new, nor is it endemic to our society. Secret criminal groups have been with us since antiquity. One of the first known organized criminal groups in America was that of Pierre Moreau (the "Moll"), a French-Canadian who ran an illegal distillery in eighteenth-century America. The nineteenth century saw the rise and proliferation of numerous organized criminal groups in both cities and small towns.

The urban setting gave rise to such criminal gangs as the O'Connell Guards and Bowery Boys in New York City, and the Hounds and Sydney Ducks in San Francisco. By the turn of the century, these small and isolated criminal groups began to grow both in strength and sophistication; some even turned to business and politics.

The early twentieth century also witnessed the coming of large immigrant groups to America's cities. This was the heyday of political bosses; large ethnic constituencies began to play a key role in the nation's political equation. These early criminal groups served their political masters well, insuring that the vote was out in force.

However, during this same period of time, organized crime began to change; it took advantage of the new technologies that had taken root during the late nineteenth century. The telephone and railroads made it possible for these local criminal groups to easily communicate with one another and also to coordinate their efforts nationally. Gambling and loan-sharking thus began to take on national dimensions; other financial crimes were also made possible by these new technologies.

The turning point for the modern syndicate came in 1934; until then, organized crime had been highly fragmented and at war with itself. Italian, Jewish, Irish, German, and other ethnic criminal elements battled one another for control. The late 1920s had witnessed the Sicilian Mafia and Neopolitan Camorra battle each other for control of the New York

City rackets; the early 1930s witnessed the "old leadership" battle the "Young Turks" for control of the syndicate. This latter conflict came to be called the Castellammarese War. At the end of this conflict, the old bosses who had dominated organized crime since the turn of the century gave way to new and aggressive leadership.

Soon after, the new bosses established national vehicles to resolve disputes between the various criminal factions.[3] The new bosses even established arbitration and policing mechanisms to insure compliance with their orders. By 1935, organized crime had become national; armed with the machinery of modern technology, it expanded into new ventures.

The new syndicate chieftains made their way into the world of politics, business, and finance; the syndicate "went modern" and took on its present form. The traditionalist gave way to the innovator, but the new syndicate never fully shed the corrupting influence and violence of the old bosses. However, it did bring with it discipline and organization; it is this that makes it extremely dangerous to the world of legitimate business.

COMPUTERS BECOME ITS TOOLS

Computer technology lends itself to two areas of mob activity: first, the areas of traditional syndicate involvement; and second, the area of white collar crime. The former is usually connected with such activities as drugs, gambling, loansharking, thefts of cargo, and others. The latter involves the world of business, finance, and government. Moneys made in the traditional syndicate areas have been utilized with great success to fund syndicate operations in the world of business.

Computers can easily be used to facilitate the business of the traditional areas of syndicate involvement. They also lend themselves to the laundering and transfer of money, as well as being excellent vehicles for the commission of sophisticated white collar capers.

Drugs

The syndicate's role in the narcotics trade goes back to the turn of the century. During the American Civil War, morphine was used to treat hundreds of thousands of wounded soldiers on both sides; a class of morphine addicts soon arose. Medical experts labeled them as suffering from the "soldier's illness." In 1898, to address this problem, German chemists

[3] For a detailed analysis of the rise of organized crime, see August Bequai, *Organized Crime: the Fifth Estate* (Lexington, Mass.: D.C. Heath, 1979).

discovered a "miracle drug" with which to treat the population of morphine addicts. The new wonder drug was heroin; soon, the heroin addict replaced the morphine junkie.

As the problem of drug addiction continued to grow at the turn of the century, reformers called on the U.S. Congress to regulate the use of narcotics. In 1914, Congress passed the Harrison Act; its objective was to regulate the use and dispensing of narcotics. By the early 1920s, America's drug addicts were forced to turn to illicit sources; a syndicate-controlled black market emerged to meet the needs of the thousands of suffering drug addicts.

This market presently realizes over $70 billion annually; it constitutes more than 1 million active users. The drug trade is both well organized and well financed; it has been effectively employed by organized crime to build a vast business and political empire. Drugs are big business for the syndicate, requiring a sophisticated distribution network.

The computer, however, has made it easy for organized crime to run this multibillion dollar empire. Home computers and terminals can easily be used to keep track of the hundreds of thousands of daily drug transactions; if fearing apprehension, the narcotics dealer can, at the press of a button, erase the voluminous records. Computers can also be used to keep track of the inventory and profits. Wire fund transfers make it possible to transmit large sums of money to overseas bank accounts; a network of computers makes it easy to launder the syndicate's ill-gotten gains. Eavesdropping tools and search warrants will prove of little value to the police in a computerized environment.

Gambling

Said to be a $22 billion annual business, gambling constitutes one of the syndicate's more traditional sources of revenue. It encompasses illegal lotteries, off-track race horse betting, card playing, and wagering on a variety of sporting events. It also employs a large army of clerks, messengers, and auditors. In New York City alone, illegal gambling operations are said to employ more than 50,000 people.

Computer technology, however, should prove of great value to the syndicate's bookkeepers, clerks, managers, auditors, and others who administer and operate these ventures. Computers can easily store voluminous data; they can also keep track of bets, and "hide" the data from the police. Terminals can be used to place bets; computers can be used to keep track of the various betting operations.

The computer thus makes it possible for the syndicate to keep track of its multibillion dollar empire, while making it more difficult for the authorities to investigate its operations. Records can be altered, modified, or destroyed, at the press of a button; today's bookmaker can easily destroy the evidence.

Loansharking

Said to be a $10 billion annual business, loansharking constitutes an "underground banking" system. Loansharks—usually syndicate affiliates—lend money at extremely high interest rates. Their customers are often law-abiding citizens who have no other sources of financing, or legitimate businesspeople who have simply fallen on hard times. Loansharking has made it possible for the syndicate to infiltrate some legitimate businesses. If the borrower fails to keep up with the payments, the loanshark may take control of the collateral—few would dare refuse.

Computers are ideally suited for assisting the syndicate in keeping track of its vast underground banking system. They can be used to record the loanshark's loans, the interest owed on those loans, and payments made by the customers. Computers can also be used to keep track of the loanshark's payroll, profits, and investments. Armed with a personal computer or terminal, the loanshark can run such a business from the convenience of home; at the press of a button, the criminal can engage in home banking. Detection by an ill-trained police force will not prove easy.

Thefts of Cargo

These are said to enrich the syndicate's coffers by at least $10 billion annually. Through an efficient network of middlemen ("fences"), the syndicate has little trouble finding buyers for its stolen cargo in the legitimate business sector. For example, at 4:30 P.M., some cargo might be stolen in New York City; it can be disposed of by 5:15 P.M. that same day through a network of fences. Thefts of cargo are an important source of revenue for the syndicate, one that keeps an elaborate and national fencing mechanism in daily operation.

Computers make it possible both to pilfer property from its lawful owner and to divert it into the hands of the syndicate; they can also help keep track of it. In addition, they can be used to record the sales and profits generated. Through a national computerized cargo theft system, the syndicate could easily run a "steal to order" operation, similar in some respects to a catalog business.

Prostitution and Bootlegging of Cigarettes

These are said to bring the mob over $5 billion annually. Through the use of computer systems, prostitutes can be supplied to meet the specifications of the customer; bootlegged cigarettes can be shipped on demand.

Labor Racketeering

The profits for the syndicate here are staggering. With union pension funds amounting to more than $100 billion, labor unions pose an attractive target. Some have fallen under the control of syndicate elements. Pension funds have been used to assist organized crime in gaining control of numerous businesses. As pension funds increasingly use computers to keep track of their assets, by simply manipulating their computers, the syndicate can pilfer or divert billions of dollars into its coffers. Large sums of money can be moved through mob accounts; funds can be wired to mob-controlled businesses and banks. Records of transactions can be "destroyed" or made invisible at the press of a button. Proving what occurred and how it was done will not be easy for the authorities.

Coercive Practices

Through coercion and the threat of it, the syndicate has been able to both deter competition and to move into new businesses. Since computers are extremely vulnerable to sabotage and vandalism, the syndicate could easily deter a competitor, or acquire a business—at a discount—by simply attacking (or threatening to attack) its computers.

Economic Crimes

Computers also lend themselves to use as tools in white collar crimes. They can easily be used—and have been successfully used by criminals—in stock swindles, insurance capers, bankruptcy frauds, and other economic crimes. The Equity Funding swindle amply demonstrates the power of computer technology as a tool in white collar crimes.

The syndicate has for many years been heavily involved in white collar capers. Syndicate controlled banks and brokerage firms have been used as fronts in sophisticated financial swindles. Organized crime has also demonstrated an uncanny ability to employ new technologies in furtherance of its economic capers. The computer is thus ideally suited to its ends; to fail to acknowledge this is to be blind to reality.

The syndicate can employ computers in two areas: first, private economic crimes, and second, rip-offs involving governmental programs, contracts, and political figures. In the private arena, computers can be used successfully to pull off (or facilitate) the following capers:

Inventory swindles
Commodity frauds
Debt consolidation rip-offs
Overvaluation of assets
Misrepresentation of goods
Precious metal frauds
Falsification of records
Phony reports
Manipulation of corporate stock
Promotion of phony corporations
Energy frauds
Franchises swindles
Investment rip-offs
Diversion of funds
Foreign investment schemes
False billings
Manipulation of employee benefit plans
Phantom employee schemes
Payoff and kickback schemes
Bid-rigging
Price-fixing
Real estate frauds
Insurance frauds
Trafficking in stolen property
International transfers of funds

The use of computers to bilk the government can also prove inviting to the syndicate. Oftentimes, the computer can be used to facilitate the following economic capers:

Misuse of government funds
Misuse of housing funds

Medicare and Medicaid frauds
Welfare frauds
Misuse of government programs
Loan frauds
Mortgage loan frauds
Misuse of development funds
Misuse of roadbuilding and transportation funds
Misuse of education funds
Theft of supplies and equipment
Minority business frauds
Overbilling the government
Payoffs and kickbacks to government officials
Computer services rip-offs
Phony statements for repairs to government property
Tax frauds
Election rigging
Misuse of government securities
Payroll frauds
Ticket fixing

The potential for misuse of computer technology by the syndicate is real; the losses to society can be staggering. It is important to recognize that organized criminal groups prey on our society; we need to explore ways to deter and limit their activities.

USE OF FOREIGN BANKS

Secrecy is paramount to the syndicate's survival; stripped of it, it is like a fish out of water. Foreign financial institutions play a key role in the syndicate's laundering of money. Financial institutions in the Bahamas, Hong Kong, Bermuda, Switzerland, Luxembourg, and Liechtenstein provide safe havens for its laundering operations.

Through a series of secret foreign bank accounts, organized crime can hide its ill-gotten gains from the authorities, and also "wash" illegal money clean. The funds are then transferred back home or to some other nation, through various banking channels, making it difficult if not impossible for law enforcement to trace or detect the movement. The syndicate's dirty money is also used by overseas bankers to purchase securities, gold, precious metals, and other property from such controlled accounts.

Offshore mutual funds have also proven safe havens for the syndicate's "dirty" money. Unlike in the United States, these mutual funds operate offshore with little or no governmental regulation; they are not required to meet any rigid criteria as to their investments and liquidity. Further, their balance sheets are often unaudited. They are thus ideal vehicles of the syndicate; through them it not only launders its money, but also bilks unsuspecting investors.

Computer technology has given rise to the Electronic Funds Transfer Systems (EFTSs); these have already made their appearance in international banking. Billions of dollars are daily transferred and recorded by EFTS computers; law enforcement is presently ill-equipped to identify the syndicate's assets in the midst of these transactions. In addition, the array of privacy laws and regulations, both here and overseas, makes it difficult to identify who authorized these financial transactions.

Through EFTSs, the syndicate can easily hide and launder the billions of dollars it gets from its narcotics trade, gambling operations, and its many other endeavors. Electronic banking also makes it easy for it to carry out its massive illicit international operations. Computer technology enables it to keep track of the millions of dollars it wires to secret offshore bank accounts to pay for the narcotics it smuggles into this country. As we increasingly move into an international EFTS, it will prove even more difficult for the authorities to trace the billions of dollars that the syndicate launders annually. The computer has made this possible.

COMBATTING ORGANIZED CRIME

Admittedly, syndicate-backed computer rip-offs can prove difficult to detect and bring to prosecution; because of its expertise and resources organized crime poses a formidable challenge. However, management is not helpless; it can play an important role in deterring and identifying syndicate-related activities.

Management's program to address syndicate-controlled computer rip-offs should encompass four areas:

Identifying potential syndicate activities
Identifying threats and vulnerabilities
Coordinating with law enforcement
Deterring anticipated or further activities

Potential syndicate activities are not always difficult to suspect. Management can be trained to identify certain "red flags"; these should serve to put the organization on notice that it may be—or already is—the target of organized criminal activity. These identifiers are not foolproof, but they are simple to learn. Management needs no special training. The "red flags" usually take on one or more of the following forms:

A service company with obscure beginnings.
Excessive vandalism to your EDP facility.
Threats to your EDP employees.
"Strong-arm" tactics used against EDP employees.
Pickets and other labor-related problems springing up.
Suspect activity at your computer center.
Suspicious payments.
Physical attacks against your staff.
References that do not check out.
Personnel with criminal records in key positions.
Widespread use of drugs on premises.
Frequent gambling on premises.
Frequent complaints by customers and other employees.
Dubious "labor consultants" offering their services.
Local union with ties to the mob.
Blackmail tactics.
Suspicious fires, accidents, walkouts, slowdowns, and sabotage.
Loansharking on or near premises.
Employee paychecks endorsed over to other persons.
Some employees living beyond their means.
Some employees with serious financial problems.
Key staff associating with syndicate figures.
Frequent cargo thefts.
Customers unexpectedly switching to a competitor with syndicate ties.

Management should be instructed to bring any of the above activities to the immediate attention of the organization's security officials. Management should also be trained to identify potential threats to and vulnerabilities of the system and its personnel by agents of organized crime. The syndicate can exploit these as follows:

1. Threats to the system include the following:

   a. Magnetic tape drive—tapes can be copied and erased.

b. Tape/disk library—labels can be erased, stolen, and destroyed.

c. Card reader/punch—cards can be added, deleted, or punched holes covered up.

d. Disk drive—disks can be copied, stolen, or erased.

e. Diskette unit—diskettes can be copied or erased.

f. Printer—reports can be copied and sold.

g. Tape cassette unit—tapes can be copied or erased.

h. Terminal—terminals can offer opportunities for unauthorized access, sabotage, embezzlement, vandalism, and theft of data.

i. Input—data can be inserted, deleted, and modified.

j. Transmission control unit—electromagnetic impulses can be intercepted and wiretaps can be installed.

k. Trash—discarded reports and copies can be found and used.

l. Distribution—reports can be copied.

2. Personnel vulnerabilities include:

a. Operator—can copy or destroy files.

b. User—can sell data, and receive unauthorized information.

c. Clerk/supervisor—can conspire with outsiders to falsify data or embezzle property.

d. Competitor—can sabotage, spy, and steal.

e. Disgruntled employee—can sabotage and vandalize.

f. Programmer—can steal data, copy programs, embezzle, bypass controls, and attempt extortion.

g. Engineer—can sabotage, access data, and install "bugs."

The syndicate's business is crime; once you have identified potential problems and vulnerabilities, you should coordinate your efforts with law enforcement. Some of the sources you can tap are as follows:

U.S. Department of Justice. This department has specialized units within it to deal with organized criminal activity.

Federal Bureau of Investigation. The Bureau has both computer crime and organized crime investigatory capabilities.

U.S. Department of the Treasury. This department has specialized units within it, such as the Customs Service, Internal Revenue Service, and the Secret Service. Agents of the latter have been trained to investigate computer crimes.

Securities and Exchange Commission. The Commission has jurisdiction over all aspects of the securities industry, and can prove of assistance in securities-related computer capers.

U.S. Postal Inspector's Office. Any use of the mails will give them automatic jurisdiction.

U.S. Attorneys. These are the local Federal prosecutors.

State Attorney Generals. They are the statewide prosecutors.

District Attorneys. They are the local (city) prosecutors.

State Crime Commissions. These are specialized statewide investigatory bodies.

State/city/county police. They are the local police agencies.

Merely opening up lines of communication with law enforcement is not sufficient. You should take several additional measures; among these are the following:

Within the organization. Implement internal measures to encourage coordination and cooperation with the authorities.

Industry-wide approach. Coordinate your efforts with other members of your industry.

Press for vigorous prosecution. The best defense of organized crime is its knowledge that many of its victims will not prosecute. This attitude serves only to encourage its predatory practices.

You should also take aggressive steps to deter anticipated or additional activities by organized crime. Because of its expertise and resources, the syndicate poses a more ominous threat than the lone or amateur thief. To combat its efforts to "rape" your computers, you need tight and sophisticated security measures. The objective of these should be to:

Safeguard the data from unauthorized access, deletion, alteration, or release.

Enact sophisticated measures to safeguard the EDP system and its components from unauthorized access.

Insulate personnel (including maintenance and vendor personnel) who have access to the system or the system equipment from syndicate pressures.

Maintain complete records of each release of information (the record should include the date of release, the requesting and receiving persons or terminal identifiers, and a description of the information given).

Maintain tight management controls (these should include the authority to set and enforce priorities; standards for the selection, supervision, and termination of assignment personnel; and policies governing the operation of computers and terminals).

Make a record, automatically, whenever data is modified, deleted, or altered.

Establish an audit program to assure compliance with system security, verify the completeness and accuracy of data, and maintain system discipline.

Train all personnel with access to the system in the proper use and control of the system and the information contained within it.

Designate a security officer.

Organized crime poses both a serious and present danger; it has demonstrated its ability to both employ and exploit technologies. Your EDP system could easily prove a target. To avert the danger, not only should you acknowledge the problem, but you should also take steps to address it. Closing your eyes will not make it disappear; instead, that may only serve to encourage the predatory practices of the syndicate.

CHAPTER **6**

Lack of Ethics
as a Cause
of Crime

A computer programmer attempts to sell valuable software belonging to his employer to one of its competitors. When discovered, the employer is reluctant to prosecute; it is rumored that the programmer threatened to "blow the whistle" on corrupt company practices. An executive embezzles more than $400,000 of his company's assets through the use of its computer. When the auditors uncover his fraud, his employer simply asks for his resignation; it is said that dishonest conduct was a "way of life" at the company. A computer operator uses a hospital's computer to steal more than $20,000; the victim is reluctant to prosecute. It is alleged that an investigation would have led to exposure of thefts of drugs involving hospital personnel.

The above examples serve to illustrate two key points: first, that crime by dishonest employees has reached epidemic proportions (employee-related thefts are said to account for more than $10 billion in annual losses to the private sector); and second, that some victims are reluctant to prosecute because they have their own "skeletons" to hide. Dishonest management is hardly in a position to prosecute dishonest employees; a corrupt organizational environment is conducive to crime by employees.

In part, the computer-connected crime wave that has hit the EDP centers of both government and the private sector only reflects the overall value system of our society. Corrupt management breeds dishonest employees; a society that pays only lip service to ethics should thus not be surprised when its institutions are attacked by those who harbor the same values it reinforces. The computer revolution has made it possible for all classes of our society to steal; a lack of ethics, in part, is a cause of computer-related crime and abuse.

LAW OF THE JUNGLE

Economic crimes, committed by men and women in positions of trust and power, are not a new phenomenon; computers have only served to "democratize" white collar crime. Even a clerk can now steal millions of dollars, all in a matter of minutes. In addition, the computer has made it difficult to detect and prosecute economic crimes; the thefts are "invisible," and the victim may not know it has been ripped off.

Witnesses and "whistleblowers" often play a key role in uncovering these capers, yet many take the attitude of "why get involved?" The computer criminals themselves, oftentimes, do not view their activity as criminal; it is all part of the game of "taking what they want." This deviant conduct is often explained away as simply "beating management at its own game."

A former client who was under investigation for a computer-connected offense once told me, with a straight face, that: "I don't view myself as a thief. I'm just playing the 'system.'" He found ample justification for his conduct in the unethical behavior of his superiors. After having finished my lecture at a workshop on computer crime, a European criminologist came up to me and commented: "In Europe, we view America as a society obsessed with crime." He was, I felt, not far off the mark. "Stealing," he pointed out, "is a way of life for Americans." In part, he was correct. Unfortunately, we glorify the criminal and label the victims as "dupes" and "greedy."

My European friend was right. In the eyes of many, both here and abroad, we have become a nation devoid of ethics; in some respects, we have become the true disciples of Machiavelli. Ethical conduct is castigated; the honest businessperson, government official, or employee is viewed as being "foolish." The "survival of the fittest" mentality has become a quasi-religious dogma. Ethical behavior in many organizations is the exception, rather than the norm. A former student of mine best summarized this after one of my lectures. "What counts," he said, "is survival."

But the computer has begun to change all this; it makes it possible for both "strong" and "weak" to steal. Top management no longer holds a monopoly. In fact, it finds itself unable to deter or prevent crime by even its low-level employees. In a perverse way, the computer has made it possible for even a 12-year-old to steal from the comfort of his or her home; it has made it possible for any of us to steal with impunity and invade the privacy of others at will. Devoid of ethics, it is the "magic genie" unrestrained.

GLORIFYING THE COMPUTER CRIMINAL

Computer criminals find ample nourishment in the present unethical environment; illegal acts can be justified to the conscience, and others can be kept mute by threatening to expose their "skeletons." As the criminals look about themselves, their ranks are swelled daily by fellow employees, managers, owners of businesses, bureaucrats, politicians, juveniles, and others armed with computer technology. The media glorifies criminal exploits, and the apologists tell us that it is "only a game."

The electronic "Robin Hoods" can also find solace in the knowledge that others also steal. For example, consider the following cases:

The manager for a California bank who helped thieves bilk his employer out of more than $10 million.

The fiscal officer for an Illinois college who was charged with stealing more than $500,000 of the school's money.

The New Mexico government official who pocketed more than $30,000 that was earmarked for the poor.

The Chicago tax collector who embezzled more than $40,000 of taxpayer funds.

The corporate executive who masterminded a multimillion dollar kickback scheme.

The Miami stockbroker who took investors for more than $20 million.

The company president who bilked stockholders out of hundreds of thousands of dollars in a solar energy fraud.

The city attorney who embezzled more than $17,000 in Federal funds earmarked to help small businesses.

The tax assessor who received thousands of dollars in bribes for making $80 million worth of fraudulent cuts in property tax assessments.

The clothing manufacturer whose massive price-fixing scheme bilked consumers out of millions of dollars.

The defense contractor who is said to have paid more than $10 million in bribes to both domestic and foreign government officials.

The bank official who laundered millions of dollars for big time narcotics dealers.

The corporation that set up a secret slush fund to reimburse its executives for illegal political contributions.

The businessman who paid members of organized crime to steal trade secrets from a competitor.

The doctor who bilked the government out of more than $1 million in phony claims.

The retired New York City housewife who took the city for more than $80,000 in a welfare fraud.

The medical researcher who fabricated his cancer research data.

The judge in a Midwestern city who was charged with accepting bribes from convicted felons.

Given the above illustrations—they constitute only a "minutia" of what we read daily—there can be little wonder that crime by computer is running out of control. It can hardly be said that the present environment in government and business will serve to deter or discourage the computer criminal. The latter simply joins the ranks of many other white collar criminals, with little to fear from dishonest fellow employees and management.

WE ILL-TREAT "WHISTLEBLOWERS"

Before a computer thief can be prosecuted, someone has to come forth and "blow the whistle" on the caper. It is the witness who provides the authorities with sufficient information to conduct a successful investigation. Computer capers are often invisible crimes; detection is difficult. Thus the role of the witness is an important one; many capers surface only when a witness "blows the whistle" on the criminal. The witness thus stands at the center of the computer crime investigation; without his/her assistance, few computer criminals would ever be prosecuted. The witness often makes the difference as to whether the authorities will prosecute.

Yet witnesses must be encouraged to come forth; both business and government should encourage whistleblowers to bring to their attention the illegal acts of their managers and fellow employees. Witnesses, however, have not always been treated fairly by our criminal justice system; society looks upon them with suspicion. Their fellow employees view them as "turncoats."

To be a witness in a criminal case is a difficult enough task in any country; the witness is asked to give up time and labor to assist the authorities. In most cases the only return is the solace of knowing that the interests of society have been served by bringing a criminal to the attention of the authorities. The manner in which we treat witnesses in America leaves much to be desired.

There are ample cases—in both the private and public sectors—that demonstrate the manner in which we abuse and sometimes even punish our witnesses. We need only read the daily newspapers for evidence:

When a Federal employee blew the whistle on fraud in his agency, he was stripped of his powers and sent to a "do-nothing" job.

When a clerk for a major air carrier informed on several dishonest union employees, his superiors transferred him to another city rather than risk a confrontation with the labor union.

When an executive with a large bank told Federal investigators that some of his associates were involved in a kickback scheme, he was dismissed by his employer.

When a security director with a large retail firm informed his superiors that one of the firm's vice presidents had been embezzling funds, he was told to take no action.

An employee who charged that his manager was paying off local union leaders was threatened with physical violence.

A broker who blew the whistle on associates who had been involved in a multimillion dollar stock fraud was blacklisted by the industry.

A clerk who was to testify about payoffs involving his company and organized crime figures was found dead in his car.

Crimes by computer can sometimes prove difficult both to investigate and to prosecute. The authorities are often frustrated by the complexity and demands of the investigation; some cases take years to solve. The absence of witnesses makes the task even more arduous. Yet the ill-treatment of witnesses only ensures that others will be reluctant to come forth and assist; it only reinforces the old adage that "minding your own business is best." The computer criminal finds only solace in such an environment.

ROLE OF ETHICS

Ethics have been defined as being everything from "a moral code of behavior" to the "conscience of a society." When asked to define ethics, the late Dr. Albert Schweitzer said:

. . . (it is) the name we give to good behavior. We feel an obligation to consider not only our personal well-being, but also that of others and of human society as a whole.

Ivan Hill, a former director of the Ethics Resource Center in Washington, D.C., and a long-time proponent of ethics in both business and government, has defined it as:

. . . behavior (that) recognizes and rests within a shared interest. On a practical level this shared interest effects an ordering of society's economic means by which the individual can pursue his own ends. It is the recognition and personal acceptance of this basic order that we call ethical behavior.

Hill has also proposed a "four-way test," as he calls it, to assist a person in making a determination as to whether his conduct is ethical. The test is as follows:

1.   Check to see if your conduct fits in with the ethical principles embodied in our society.
2.   Check what impact the law will have on your conduct. For example, will your conduct be in violation of any Federal, state, or local statute or regulation.
3.   Check to see how your conscience responds to that conduct.
4.   Ask God (if you do not believe in God, then Hill proposes that you pretend God exists) whether your conduct is ethical.

There is also a large body of writing by the great philosophers of Western civilization that addresses the question of what ethical conduct is. Suffice it to say, however, that ethical conduct must be viewed as that mode of behavior that is in accord with the Judeo-Christian traditions of the West; on a more pragmatic level, we should view it as that conduct that ensures the survival of the most prized values and institutions of our civilization. The late Earl Warren, Chief Justice of the United States, best summarized the need for ethics as follows:

If there were no sense of love in families, if there were no sense of loyalty, if friendship meant nothing, if we all, or any large proportion of us, were motivated only by avarice and greed, society would collapse almost as completely as though it lacked law.

Even the best of laws, computer security, and training for our law enforcement agencies will not deter or result in the apprehension of computer criminals; they find both comfort and support in corrupt organizational environments. The only way to ensure that computer-related crimes and abuses are eradicated is, as a friend of mine once said in jest, to "put a cop under everyone's bed." But in the process we would be losing our freedoms.

Ethical behavior constitutes compliance with a body of rules and regulations that have come to form the very foundation of civilization. It is not merely an idealization of what a human being should be, but rather what he or she must be, to ensure the survival of our species and our way of life. Ethics in any organization must start with top management; it must set the example, and employees must be both encouraged to and rewarded for following its lead. Codes of ethics in the era of the computer are not a luxury; rather, they are a necessity.

NEED FOR ETHICAL MANAGEMENT

Unfortunately, in its drive for efficiency, profits, and performance, management can prove blind to the need for organizational ethics; many within management are not always sensitive to the need to establish a code of ethics for their organization. This is not to say that management is not knowledgeable regarding the role ethics can play. Many managers do confirm that they are:

Cognizant of the need for codes of ethics.

Aware that ethical conduct is largely dependent on peer pressures.

Conscious of the profound influence that management's conduct has on its subordinates.

In agreement that ethics can be taught to employees.

Management's problem is thus not one of not understanding the value of codes of ethics; rather, it is one of applying these to their respective organizations. "It is," as one manager said to me, "always the other guy who needs it." As a result, many private and public organizations have no codes of ethics; the workforce is left to fend for itself. Employees often feel alienated; some even perceive themselves as having been wrangled. The computer industry itself has no code of ethics for the millions of men and women who operate and maintain the technology. This is a "perfect" formula for thefts and abuses by insiders.

A study by the Ethics Resource Center of Washington, D.C., confirmed that, although top management occasionally pays lip service to the need for ethics in the workplace, little is done to carry this out. The study sought to determine how extensive was the use of codes of ethics in the private sector, the role they played, and the value placed on them. The researchers based their study on interviews with:

Chief executives of Fortune 500 companies
Top officials of trade associations
Deans of graduate business schools

As regards the chief executives, the researchers sent out 650 question-naires and received only 248 (38 percent) responses. When reviewing these, the researchers found that:

Many of the executives said their companies had some code of ethics.
Most of those who had such codes observed that they were only several years old.
Many said that their companies updated their codes periodically.
Only a small number of the companies with codes distributed them to their employees.
The majority provided the new employee with only a brief orientation in their codes.
Most of the codes dealt with general rather than specific principles.
Few of the codes contained any enforcement provisions within them.
Many of the companies imposed no sanctions on employees who violated their codes.
Some sanctions took the form of dismissal.
Most of the codes did require that employees report violations.
Some of the codes specified how these violations should be reported.
Most codes specifically prohibited the giving or taking of favors, and conflict of interest situations.
Many of those responding agreed that codes of ethics could play an important role in promoting ethical conduct.
All agreed that, in the absence of ethical conduct by management, codes of ethics would prove of little value.
Many indicated that employees who had committed a crime were usually only dismissed.
Most commented that criminal prosecution was rare.

The researchers also found that organizations with fewer than 2500 employees were more likely to distribute their codes of ethics to their employees than the larger organizations. The latter, however, were more likely to indoctrinate their new employees in their codes. However, many organizations still do not have codes of ethics; those that do often fail to enforce them adequately.

Regarding trade association representatives, the researchers sent out 600 questionnaires; they received only 244 (41 percent) responses. Of these, the researchers found that the responses differed little from those of the Fortune 500 chief executives. In general, they found that:

Some of the trade groups had enacted their codes only in the last several years.

Many updated their codes periodically.

Most codes provided for some kind of enforcement action.

These actions often took the form of a grievance hearing.

In most cases, the sanction was expulsion from the association.

The researchers sent 134 questionnaires to the deans of graduate business schools; of these, they received 57 (43 percent) responses. Since schools of business play an important role in educating and training most of today's top management, their responses are of particular interest. For example, the researchers found that:

Few of these schools offered any separate courses in ethics.

Those that did enrolled fewer than 10 percent of their student bodies.

Many of the deans indicated that their schools lacked trained or qualified instructors to teach these courses.

Some indicated courses in ethics had a low priority at their schools.

Others indicated that there was a need for teaching materials in this area.

The study's findings demonstrated that codes of ethics in the private sector have not as yet won widespread approval; in addition, education, training, and teaching materials in this area are often not adequate. Further, the business schools have neglected the study of ethics. Many of the codes in present use are relatively new. However, there is a growing recognition that such codes do serve a useful function and should be supported.

IMPLEMENTING A CODE

Codes of ethics can serve to establish guidelines and procedures that can play a role in safeguarding an organization against computer-related crimes and abuses. The code requires management to abide by the same rules and regulations as the other employees; it also calls on management to take the lead. The perception that an employee has of an organization is shaped, in large part, by the conduct of his/her superiors. Derelictions by management not only have an impact on employee morale, but they also serve to:

Erode the very moral foundation of the law.
Provide the employee with a rationalization for illegal conduct.
Breed employee cynicism.
Make it easier for outsiders to subvert your organization.
Undermine confidence in your organization.
Undermine confidence in our political institutions.
Debase our economic system.
Encourage employees to regard unethical conduct as the norm.
Undermine the needed trust between management and the employees.
Breed mistrust among the employees themselves.
Reinforce the view that stealing is acceptable because the "big boys" do it.

A code of ethics, however, can play an important part in establishing (and reinforcing) employee confidence in an organization. This, in turn, serves to deter and prevent crime and abuses by computer. It does this because:

It enhances trust and cooperation within the organization.
It keeps management and employees informed of developments that have an impact on their organization.
It keeps management and employees abreast of laws and regulations that can have an impact on their conduct.
It discourages abuses resulting from peer pressures.
It clearly defines unacceptable or illegal conduct.
It promotes the interests of both the organization and those it serves.
It prohibits unauthorized compensation.

It provides a minimum level of competency.

It restores employee confidence in management.

It weeds out potential thieves.

It anticipates potential difficulties.

It serves as a deterrent.

The human animal has demonstrated, throughout recorded history, a propensity to abide by good laws and moral leadership; most people, fundamentally, want to "play ball by the rules." Most deviations from the norm occur when people view the rules and regulations as unfair, biased, or outmoded; rebellion is the exception, rather than the norm. A code of ethics that is perceived as being fair, just, and meaningful can serve to combat computer-related crimes and abuses (as well as other forms of white collar crime) because:

It establishes honest conduct as a paramount fixture within the organization.

It establishes accepted peer conduct.

It defines a level of accepted professionalism.

It discourages criminal behavior.

It provides clearly defined guidelines and procedures.

It sets out specific sanctions.

It encourages ethical conduct.

It provides an incentive for those who conduct themselves ethically.

It establishes training and education programs to identify and deter problems.

It reinforces ethics in the workforce.

It specifically addresses such areas as security, liability, privacy, and access to confidential data.

It clearly spells out the role of the computer in your organization.

A MODEL CODE

Codes of ethics can serve both an organization and an industry well. At present, the computer industry would do well to study and adopt some industry-wide code of ethics. The problem of crime and abuse by computer not only touches numerous organizations, but also affects the industry itself; a failure to establish and promote self-policing mechanisms can only serve to invite government regulation.

To win the support of the various constituencies that make up an organization or industry, a code should—at the minimum—stress:

The highest ideals of the industry or profession
The value of ethics in business
The need for due process
Specific rules and regulations
Adequate enforcement vehicles
The need for a review process
Adequate and fair mechanisms for handling of complaints
The need to safeguard the privacy of the individual

However, for a code to win the support of the various constituencies within a workplace or industry, it must also be viewed as fair, impartial, legitimate, and effective. To be so viewed, it must incorporate within it certain specific safeguards; a failure to do so could lead to abuses of the code. To prevent this, the code should provide for:

A complaint process. It should be specific about to whom the complaints are to be directed, the manner in which they should be addressed (for example, in writing or orally), and how detailed they should be as to violations alleged.

A committee or individual to review complaints. An organization can choose to have a committee, as opposed to simply one of its officials, review and act upon a complaint. Since there are merits to both sides, the organization should tailor this mechanism to meet its specific needs.

Screening. Logic dictates that not all complaints will have merit or can be acted upon. Limited resources and personnel make this task impossible; the code should provide for a screening mechanism to weed out frivolous charges.

Hearing. Once it has been determined that a complaint has basis to be heard, the matter should then be referred to a committee for a hearing. This group should review the evidence before it, interview the complainant and the accused, and accord the latter an opportunity to present rebuttal evidence.

Decision. Whenever possible, the decision should be in writing.

Finality. There should be finality. Have the accused sign a statement accepting the finality of the committee's decision—otherwise you will find yourself in a "Catch 22" situation.

Deterrence. Sanctions should be specific and adequate. These can range from a warning to suspension, dismissal, or prosecution.

The code's provisions should be applied and enforced equitably; its fairness will, in large part, determine its success or failure. If the perception is that it is only for cosmetic purposes, or solely for controlling employee behavior, the code will prove of little or no value.

TESTING YOUR CODE

Some organizations already have a code of ethics in some form.[1] Unfortunately, many present codes were developed in response to public pressure and fear of government regulation. Some of these serve only a cosmetic function. To test the adequacy of your organization's code, you should check to see if it provides for at least some of the following:

An obligation not to abuse one's position of trust or power.

Details of the obligations of management and the employees.

Assignment of full responsibility.

Definition of the organization's obligations to the public.

Consideration of the need to safeguard the privacy and confidentiality of information.

Sanctions for misrepresentations and the withholding of information.

Swift and meaningful sanctions against violators.

Stress on cooperation and the team spirit within the organization.

Emphasis on the need for service.

Stress on honesty and integrity.

Requirements that employees disclose illegal or unethical conduct.

Assignment of specific enforcement functions to individuals within the organization.

Definition of unauthorized conduct.

Requirements that conflict of interest situations be avoided.

Requirements that employees/management present fair, honest, and objective viewpoints.

Prohibitions against using the organization's resources for private reasons or personal gain.

---

[1] Federal law requires such a code for employees of the Executive branch. See Ethics in Government Act of 1978 as amended by Public Laws 96-19 and 96-28; also see Executive Order 11222. Unfortunately, the Federal agencies have paid mostly lip service to these laws and regulations.

Tough sanctions for anyone who exploits or abuses the weaknesses of the computer system.

Requirements that Federal, state, and local laws and regulations be complied with.

Requirements that law enforcement agencies be informed of cases involving illegal conduct.

In addition, your code should be disseminated throughout the organization and be known to its management and employees. Test your code to ensure that:

Your employees are familiar with it.

It is updated periodically.

It is in writing.

There is an orientation program for new employees.

It is distributed throughout the organization.

It is specific.

It provides for specific sanctions.

It treats all layers of the organization equitably.

It provides no preferential treatment.

Specific reference to the EDP center is made.

Top executives are specifically required to conduct themselves ethically.

It has the support of top management.

There is employee support for it.

It may be that some of your staff belong to various trade/professional associations. If this is the case, check to see whether these associations have codes of ethics and, if so, whether:

The codes are updated periodically.

They are not merely for cosmetic effect.

They have meaningful enforcement provisions within them.

They have been discussed with the appropriate government agency.

They are equitably applied.

Since trade/professional associations are social instruments, they can exert an important influence on some of their members. Support for ethics and establishment of such codes by them can prove important in restraining the potential unethical conduct of some members of your organization.

Professionals want to present the best image possible to their peers; it would serve them ill if they were viewed as unethical by fellow professionals. This will reinforce your organization's code.

Since most organizations have some form of in-house training, this too can prove to be an important vehicle for introducing management/employees to a code of ethics, or acclimating them to the need for ethical behavior. Thus your training director should take steps to ensure that:

Your training programs include instructions on ethics.

The instructions are mandatory.

They are updated periodically.

Specific readings are assigned.

Instructors with both a background and interest in ethics are used.

The instructions stress the value and importance of ethics.

Unfortunately, some managers view instructions in ethics as being of little value. One executive approached me after one of my lectures to tell me that his company was in the business of making money and not promoting the Boy Scouts. Several months later I learned that his company had fallen victim to a computer rip-off. He subsequently changed his tune. Codes of ethics are compilations of rules and regulations that stress the more worthy behavior in our society; they merely serve to tell both management and employees that honest conduct is valued. They serve to place both management and employees on notice.

Having had the opportunity in my career as an attorney to see all sides of our criminal justice system, two things have become apparent: first, few persons steal in our society because they go hungry; and second, the majority of those who steal will justify their conduct by telling you that "everyone does it." What has always concerned me is that so many of us believe the same; such an environment serves the computer criminal well.

Codes of ethics will not abolish crimes by and abuses of computers, nor will they always be enforced equitably by every organization. They do, however, serve to put us all on notice by telling us that we cannot survive long as a free society if we "steal ourselves blind." They are indicia that we must cooperate and work within acceptable limitations if we are to survive. Great civilizations have come and gone; the computer now makes it possible to fall faster.

PART 2

How to Safeguard
Your Computer

CHAPTER 7

The Need to
Understand
Computers

The computer is used today to keep track of inventories, design highways, diagnose disease, generate trade names, set printing type automatically, track airplanes, conduct wars, and do an array of other things. In 1950, there were only 15 operational computers in the entire United States; by 1960, the number had grown to more than 40,000. Their use and proliferation grows daily.

The computer revolution has made its way into our very homes; more than 1 million Americans use their personal computers to play, study, and conduct their daily business transactions. Today, we live at the dawn of a new age, largely made possible by computer technology. Yet few of us fully understand the profound impact of this technology on our daily lives; of greater concern is the fact that so many of our decision-makers know so little.

DEFINING THE MACHINE

A computer may be described as a machine that performs complex processes on information, without the need for manual intervention. Computers fall into one of two types: special or general purpose. Special purpose computers are designed for specific tasks; they are wired internally to repeat the same sequence of operations. They are often referred to as limited purpose computers. For example, computers employed by the airlines for making reservations are usually of the special purpose type.

A special purpose computer cannot be made to perform new tasks by simply changing the instructions that guide its operations; to change its function, it is necessary to rewire the entire computer. The special purpose computer is not programmable, unlike the general type.

The general purpose computer, however, can be employed to perform numerous tasks. This is done by simply changing its instructions. There is no need to rewire it; the user simply changes the program. In so doing, one also changes the tasks it will perform; thus, because of its flexibility, the general purpose computer can be employed in a variety of roles.

General purpose computers usually fall into two categories: analog (these are employed in the sciences) and digital (these are employed in business). The difference between these is not so much in the way they process the data, but rather in the volume of data that they handle, and in the number of calculations they perform on that data. For example, in the case of scientific problems, only a small amount of data is used; however, hundreds of thousands of calculations are performed on it to produce the desired results. Small amounts of data and a large number of calculations are typical of the tasks analog computers perform.

In the case of digital computers, just the opposite is the case. A large amount of data is processed; however, only a small number of calculations are performed on it. For example, processing the payroll of a company with 5000 employees requires only a small number of calculations; these are repeated 5000 times.

Digital computers also differ from their analog counterparts in several other respects: they take longer to solve a set of equations; they have greater storage capacity; and programming them is easier. It is their storage capacity and the ease with which they can be programmed that makes them desirable for business-related tasks; they are also easy to operate and maintain.

Digital computers are also characterized as belonging to one of several generations; each generation is distinguished from the other by the electronic components within it. The first generation digitals are distinguished by their extensive use of vacuum tubes and also by their large size. Some of these first generation digitals were so large that several rooms were needed to store them.

The second generation digital is often characterized by its extensive use of transistors. They tend to be small in size, some no larger than an office desk. The third generation digitals are characterized by their use of integrated circuits; they employ millions of tiny microelectronic circuits. These are also characterized by their small size and immense speed.

Often no larger than a file drawer, they operate thousands of times faster than their giant predecessors.

The role of the computer is to assist us; they were developed to carry out calculations in a matter of seconds that would take a human being many years. Modern society has become so complex that the pencil and paper can no longer keep up with our needs; computer technology is essential to any large organization, where there is a need for fast and accurate decisions.

The computer by itself is a "dumb machine"; it is incapable, at least for the present, of acting independently. It relies on human guidance; errors, malfunctions, abuses, and thefts connected with the computer are "people problems." The good or bad that computers cause is a direct result of human intervention. They reflect our ethics, eccentricities, abilities, performance, and inner frailties; they are mirror images of our inner souls.

FORERUNNERS OF OUR MODERN COMPUTERS

The oldest known computer in history is the abacus. It was widely used by such ancient peoples as the Egyptians, Indians, Chinese, and Romans. It continues to enjoy widespread use in many parts of present day Asia. The turning point in the history of computer technology came in 1642; it was at this time that the mathematician Blaise Pascal invented the first known mechanical calculator. Pascal's box-size calculator was simple in its operations. Calculations were carried out by a series of wheels within it; these moved from a nine to zero and then a second wheel advanced one digit.

Thirty years later, the German mathematician Gottfried Leibnitz developed plans for a mechanical device that could perform multiplications; the machine was completed in 1694. However, it fell short of its inventor's expectations. In 1820, the French scientist Thomas of Colmar invented a calculator similar in design to the Leibnitz machine. Thomas sold some of these to the French government, but the Thomas machine, too, fell short of its inventor's expectations. These forerunners of the modern computer were not taken seriously by the business community; businesspeople were not willing to invest in their construction or use them in everyday business. They were viewed as mere mechanical toys.

The inventors, however, continued their pursuit; new and better machines made their appearance. In addition, a new element had now entered the equation; Europe's industrial revolution had brought with it the problems of a complex economy. The business community now needed efficient mechanical calculators to enable its army of bookkeepers and clerks to stay abreast of a changing and increasingly sophisticated economy.

Europe's governments were also growing in sophistication; they were becoming more centralized. They needed mechanical calculators to enable them to keep track of their citizenry for purposes of the census, taxation, and services. The demands of this modern business and political environment sparked inventors like Joseph Marie Jacquard to improve on the efforts of Pascal and Leibnitz.

Jacquard's machine was modeled after an automatic loom, first invented by Jacques de Vaucanson for weaving tapestries and rugs. Jacquard's machine used punched sheets of stiff paper as controls; these proved inexpensive to replace. This machine also fell below its inventor's expectations. Nevertheless, it was to become a forerunner of the modern special purpose computer.

In 1824, Charles Babbage was able to obtain the financial backing of the English government; Babbage wanted to construct a calculator that incorporated a system of punched cards. The machine was to be used to perform algebraic functions and print its results on paper; as it turned out, it was able to handle only simple mathematical problems. It proved of no value in handling complex algebraic calculations. Although a discouraged English government eventually withdrew its financial assistance, Babbage carried on with private backing. After 40 years of trial and error, he constructed a successful analytical engine.

The Babbage invention represented a radical breakthrough; it displayed all of the basic features of the modern digital computers. Its memory had the capacity to hold 50,000 digits, and the control functions were carried out through the use of a system of punched cards. The analytical engine also had the ability to add, subtract, and multiply in less than a minute. The Babbage machine made it possible for Torres Y Quevedo to later construct a typewriter-controlled analytical machine.

The late nineteenth century also witnessed the invention of an American key-driven calculator. During this same period, William S. Burroughs constructed his listing-accountant; the machine incorporated many of the features of Pascal's mechanical calculator. Burrough's adding machine, however, differed in at least one respect from its many predecessors; it was specifically designed for mass production. It served to launch the Burroughs Company into the modern computer market.

Herman Hollerith graduated from Columbia University in 1879 and soon commenced work with the U.S. Census Office. After three years he left the Census Office for a job at the Massachusetts Institute of Technology; it was here that he started work on his census machine. Eight years later, Hollerith constructed a highly successful mechanical calculator; it incorporated some of the principles of Jacquard's automatic loom machine, and also employed an automatic card feeding system.

Hollerith's machine had been completed just in time to help conduct the national census. It soon found widespread application in the accounting area. By the turn of the century, Hollerith's machines had won the confidence of the business community. They were used by the large railroads to keep track of their boxcars, insurance companies used them in their actuarial work, and large retail stores employed them to keep track of their inventory.

In 1896, Hollerith had founded the Tabulating Machine Company (TBC); in 1917, his company merged with two other growing calculator firms and became the International Business Machines Company, Ltd. (IBM). By 1920, Hollerith's computing machines were widely used both in this country and Europe. One of his machines was used in 1927 to compute the positions of the moon; the information was punched into 500,000 cards. The computations proved extremely accurate; the Hollerith machines proved to be of great value to both astronomers and mariners. The age of the modern computer had come; Pascal's dream had been realized.

A NEW DAWN

Punched-card machines gained popularity with several large companies in the early 1930s; the demand for faster and more accurate mechanical calculators increased with the demands of modern business. In 1937, Professor Howard Aiken approached IBM with a new proposal; he wanted to construct a giant computing machine. IBM consented and the Mark I (Automatic Sequence Controlled Calculator) was completed six years later. The Mark I was a modern day marvel; it could multiply two 23-digit numbers in six seconds. It marked a breakthrough in modern computer technology.

The 1940s witnessed a series of other breakthroughs; the Bell Telephone Laboratories constructed their Model I computer. The Model I was a giant computer, capable of adding, subtracting, multiplying, and dividing complex numbers faster and more accurately than any of its predecessors. Bell followed its success with the Model V computer; this was a general purpose computer. It was well-received by both business and government.

The next important breakthrough came in 1946. Two scientists at the University of Pennsylvania, John Mauchly and J. Presper Eckert, constructed the now famous ENIAC computer; like the Bell Model V, it was a general purpose computer. It performed 5000 arithmetic operations a second; it was 1000 times faster than its rivals. The Mauchly computer also proved to be extremely reliable.

Other computers also made their appearance during this time. IBM came out with the SSEC model (Selective Sequence Electronic Calculator) in 1947; it soon became one of the more widely used commercial computers of its day, and a model for later manufacturers. During this period, John von Newmann constructed his EDVAC. Although smaller in size, it had a larger memory capacity; it also used fewer tubes, and soon became a model for the industry.

The Europeans were also busy; in 1944, Konrad Zuse constructed the Z-z in Germany. Five years later, a group of British scientists constructed the first stored program computer.

In 1951, the Remington Rand Company constructed the UNIVAC I (Universal Automatic Computer); it was smaller than ENIAC and could add in two microseconds. UNIVAC also made use of magnetic tapes as input/output mediums; this was another breakthrough. It was used a year later by pollsters to analyze the outcome of the national elections; with great accuracy, it predicted that Eisenhower would win the Presidency.

The 1950s witnessed the rise of fierce competition between the growing number of computer manufacturers; General Electric, Sperry Rand, Honeywell, and Control Data Corporation had by this time joined the field. Honeywell introduced its Datamatic 1000 series, but IBM was able to maintain its lead with the construction in 1953 of its Model 701. It further strengthened its position two years later with the construction of its Model 702.

These first generation computers made extensive use of vacuum tubes. Although first invented in 1948, the transistor would not be used until 1959. The second generation of computers made widespread use of transistors; as a result, they were smaller and more efficient. IBM introduced the 709 TX computer, Philco Corporation its TRANSAC S-2000, and the Burroughs Corporation the 5000 System. Some of these second generation computers were ahead of their time in both design and size.

The third generation computers started making their appearance in 1964; IBM entered the market with its System 360, Control Data with the 6600 System, and Sperry Rand its 1108 System. The IBM 360 was so successful that it assured the company the leadership of the industry. Texas Instruments developed its Advanced Scientific Computer, and Burroughs introduced its 5500 Series. General Electric made its third generation entry with the 600 Series, while Honeywell introduced its 200 System.

This period also witnessed the rise and growth of the mini-computer industry. The mini-computer revolution was made possible, in large part, by the use of micro-programming techniques. Digital Equipment Corporation was one of the leaders in the mini-computer market; it gained a strong foothold in 1968 with the introduction of its PDP-8 System. Two years later, it introduced the PDP-11, more powerful and efficient than its rivals. Data General Corporation also made its entry into the small but growing mini-computer market; it introduced its NOVA and super-NOVA series. Hewlett-Packard and Inter-Data soon followed with their own models.

The mini-computer revolution had taken off; it now meant that small businesses could also purchase and employ the benefits of computer technology. The mini-computer was soon joined by the micro-computer; computer technology now made its way into the home.

Computer technology had advanced beyond the wildest dreams of its early founders. Computers that can speak, read, write, and even think are developing. Computers that presently link elaborate data processing networks, and electronic funds transfer systems have become daily occurrences. Computer technology progresses daily; the revolution, we are told, is still in its infancy. Yet the technology has also given rise to abuses; criminals have also been quick to see its value.

WHAT COMPUTERS DO

The public perception of computers is that they are giant electronic calculators that perform processes previously handled by armies of clerks chained to their desks. The computer, however, serves a wide variety of tasks connected with the processing of information; of special interest are the collection, storage, organization, calculation, communication, presentation, and control of data.

The dramatic advances in computer technology have increased the ability of computers to collect data. Through audio and visual inputs, these data collection functions have increased dramatically; computers now have a limited ability to recognize human speech, read directly from a variety of typewriter forms and hand printed texts, and detect patterns in video images. This has served to augment their collection capability.

Computers can likewise store large amounts of data for long periods of time; they can do it in an electronically readable form that is easily and quickly recoverable. The methods employed vary; for example, holes in cards and magnetic impulses on tape. Computers can also be used to organize data in a format that makes it more suitable for specific tasks; they can be employed to simplify and restructure vast amounts of raw data to assist decision-makers.

Computers are also employed to perform numerous arithmetic calculations at speeds that are millions of times faster than entire armies of clerks.

For example, they can carry out sophisticated statistical calculations on large amounts of data, or perform highly complex scientific analyses. If connected by telecommunication systems, they can transmit large amounts of data across states and countries; they can also communicate and work with other computers. This latter case constitutes a computer network. Computers can also present information in a variety of different forms. The uses to which they can be put are limitless.

BASICS OF THE SYSTEM

The basic elements of any computer system can be divided into two elements: hardware and software. The hardware components consist of the: central processing unit (CPU); input/output devices; and auxilliary storage. The software components consist of a collection of computer programs, which are planned procedures for solving problems. A program is no more than a series of instructions to the computer, to be performed on the data; the instructions are prepared by a programmer and fed to the computer. Without its programming elements, a computer would lack direction; it would become immobile.

The CPU is the computer's brain. It consists of the circuitry that controls the input/output units and the auxilliary attachments. The role of the CPU is to intercept and execute the instructions it receives from the programming elements; it also contains storage devices that hold the program and data. The CPU receives data from the input and file storage units; it then performs a variety of arithmetic and logical operations on the data; it also transmits the results to the output and file units.

The CPU itself consists of three basic units: memory, arithmetic and logic, and control. The memory unit stores the data, while the arithmetic and logic unit carries out the CPU's operations. As for the control unit, it ensures that the computer follows the instructions it receives from the program.

Like the CPU, the input device plays an important role in the operation. It accepts the raw information that the computer uses; the information can be read from such media as paper tapes or punched cards. Typewriter-like input devices are also widely used. The input device converts the information to a language that the computer understands. If the information is punched into cards or paper tape, an electromechanical device known as a reader is used to scan the information and then convert it into electronic impulses. These, in turn, are communicated to the computer. Modified electric typewriters or teletype machines are also frequently employed as input devices; these enable the operator to communicate directly with the computer.

Output devices take information (as instructed by the program) from the CPU and record it on some type of medium. These mediums can take the form of a printer, display unit, paper tape, or punched card. Typewriterlike devices are usually preferred for low volume output; these are often located either at the computer center or at a remote terminal.

Video-display units have also gained acceptance as output devices; with these devices, the information is displayed on a televisionlike tube. However, what makes these units attractive is their ability to handle large volumes of data; they can also generate additional data rapidly. Unlike the printers, the video-display devices do not produce a hard copy. Paper tapes, magnetic tapes, and punched cards are also widely used output devices. Of these, the magnetic tapes operate at the highest speeds, but cost more.

The auxiliary storage is the computer's filing cabinet. Data can be stored in one of several such storage devices; the ones used most often are the magnetic tapes, disks, and drums. These, however, differ in both cost and performance. For example, data stored on magnetic tape files must be maintained in a predetermined sequence; the new input data is also stored in the same sequence. Magnetic disks, however, are considered more efficient than the tapes; data on disks can be corrected, changed, or modified with little difficulty. Disks, however, are more expensive. Magnetic drums have also proven to be excellent storage devices; data on these can be retrieved with greater speed than from tape or disks. Because they are expensive, however, their use as storage devices has been limited.

The computer program serves two main functions: it must provide the computer with instructions that tell it what operations to conduct, and it must also specify the data on which it is to act. Programs fall into one of several categories. The more common of these—used mostly in handling inventory, payrolls, and accounts—is the application program. Another common one is the packaged program; these are mostly used for routine processing. Packaged programs, however, can also be modified by the user to accommodate specific needs. There are two other programs that are also commonly used: the compiler and the assembly. These are often purchased directly from the manufacturer; they are used to translate application programs into computer language.

Programs, however, are not all written in the same languages. The more common types are FORTRAN (Formula Translater) and COBOL (Common Business Oriented Language). FORTRAN is mostly used by the military, while COBOL enjoys widespread use in the private sector. At present, there are no uniform programs (or languages) within the industry; this lack of uniformity has stifled the growth and direction of the industry.

DATA PROCESSING PRINCIPLES

Regardless of the size of an organization, all automated data processing cycles follow certain basic stages.[1] The first stage in any cycle is the input. This refers to the collection of all the required information, in a form that is convenient for processing. Once the information is collected, it is then processed to produce the desired output result (or output). The second stage of an automated data processing cycle is the processing itself. Here all the necessary calculations are performed on the input data, in order to produce the desired output.

The input stage in an automated data processing cycle is defined as that stage at which the collected information is recorded in the system. The data, however, must be recorded in a form the system understands. For example, in a manual system information is recorded on paper by pencil or pen. In an electronic data processing system, however, the data can be processed in one of several forms; for example, on punched cards and tapes, magnetic tapes, or disks. Some source documents, however, can be used directly as inputs into the system; for example, data can be entered directly through the keyboard of a terminal located several hundred miles away from the computer center.

Data at the input stage can also be coded; this serves two purposes. First, the data is reduced in size; second, sorting the coded data is often quicker and easier than sorting alphabetized (letters) data. At the output stage, the information that is required can be prepared in a format that is most useful to the organization. For example, the information can appear in printouts, punched cards, or magnetic tapes.

Regarding the storage of data, this can be carried out in a number of ways. For example, it may be:

Typed on paper
Punched into cards
Written onto magnetic tapes or disks

In part, the medium selected to store the data will depend on two things: the type of data that is to be processed, and the length of time the data is to be stored.

The original information (the source document) is usually stored for a fixed period of time, in case the accuracy and/or authenticity of the out-

---

[1] The data processing cycle is a systematic method by which data is handled and the desired information produced.

put is questioned at a later time. Once the information is recorded, it is also usually stored in the same medium. For example, data that is recorded on magnetic tape will usually be stored on the same; data that is recorded on punched cards will usually be stored on punched cards. The purpose of this is to permit the data to be used in more than one data processing cycle without having to return to the data entry stage. It makes it possible for the output to be stored until it is needed. Regardless of the data that is processed or the medium that is employed, all data processing cycles start with a raw data source and culminate in a meaningful output.

Most data processing requirements fall into one of three categories:

Batch processing. This involves voluminous data that is not processed as soon as it is generated. For example, in the processing of charges made on a credit card, the merchant will hold these until the end of the day or week; these are then all sent at the same time to the credit card company for batch processing.

On-line data processing. In this case, the data is processed as soon as it is generated; this is often done by remote terminal. The user is on the line while the data submitted to the computer as input is being processed. For example, a scientist may be involved in an experiment in which several days are needed to work out the computations. Through a terminal the scientist enters the information and a few instructions to the computer; within a short period of time, the computer completes the computations and prints the results at the terminal.

Real time data processing systems. Here, data is entered in the system immediately for future use. Airline reservation systems are an example of such systems; when the travel agent receives a request for a seat on a particular flight, he or she enters the necessary information in the computer through a terminal. The computer then sends, as output to the terminal, information about the status of the seats.

The time-sharing industry is a direct outgrowth of the modern developments in data processing. A company or individual simply buys a computer system and then rents its processing time to others. The computer is programmed to accept requests for processing from remote locations and to share out the available processing time among the various users. Customers are charged a fee that is determined primarily by the amount of computer time they use. With the expansion in telecommunications, data processing will take on new forms; its basic principles, however, should remain the same.

INPUT/OUTPUT DEVICES

Many of the computer-related frauds, thefts, and abuses that have surfaced have involved the manipulation, alteration, copying, and/or theft
of input/output data. It is thus important that management both understands and is knowledgeable about input/output devices, as these pose a
tempting target for criminals.

Input devices can take one of several forms; a CPU, at any one time,
can have many such devices connected to it. The function of an input device is to convert data into electrical impulses; these are then transferred
to predetermined locations in the storage. The input itself can be one of
two types:

Instructions on how to process the data
Data that must be processed

Some of the more common input devices are the following:

1. *Punched card.* First used in 1887 by Dr. Hermit Hollerith to process data for the U.S. Census Bureau, this input device continues to be
widely used. It has the advantage of being easy to prepare, verify, sort out,
and collate. It can also be interpreted by the human eye. Data from the
punched cards is then transferred to storage by means of a card reader,
which acts as an input device; this makes the punched card a very versatile
input medium. However, there are also some disadvantages to using it;
for example, it can be bent, folded, and mutilated, making it difficult to
process through a machine. Individual cards can also be easily lost when
they are being sorted.

2. *Magnetic tape.* This medium has certain advantages over the
punched card. For example, data can be transferred to and from the tape
at very high speeds; in addition, they can store much more data. A single
magnetic tape, for example, can record the equivalent of over 100,000
punched cards; further, a tape containing data that has to be used only
once a week can be stored out of the system when not in use. When the
data is required, the operator simply replaces the tape on the drive unit.
But the magnetic tape also has several drawbacks:

a. The data on it can only be processed sequentially.
b. Records can only be read in the order in which they are written.
c. It cannot be used for both input and output operations at the
same time.
d. Identifying the tape itself can sometimes prove difficult.

e. The stored data cannot be read by the human eye.

f. Elaborate labeling systems have to be used.

3. *Keyboard terminal.* This is often referred to as a typewriter terminal; it can be linked to the system by means of telephone lines. For example, a branch office hundreds of miles away from the computer center can send input data and receive output data by way of a keyboard terminal; the operator can also use it to communicate with the computer.

4. *Display terminal.* This is similar to the keyboard terminal; the significant difference between them is that data on this is displayed on a screen, and not printed out as is the case with the keyboard terminal. It can be linked by telephone lines to the system. The display terminal provides a quick and easy method of updating data stored in the computer. Operators who know the program for the computer system are able to access individual records within a file and add or delete information.

5. *Magnetic disk pack.* This can also serve as a useful and flexible auxiliary storage device; the pack consists of a series of metal disks. Data is recorded on these in the form of tiny magnetic spots, each character being represented by a unique combination of spots. Since these spots can be placed very close together, the typical disk pack can hold the equivalent of several hundred thousand punched cards. In addition, each record in a file stored on a disk is located at a known spot; this makes it possible to have access to data in a particular record very rapidly, and new data can be added to the record rapidly. Packs make it possible to both read and write records in sequence.

6. *Magnetic drum.* This is a large metal cylinder that rotates at high speeds past fixed rewrite heads; data is stored on the surface of the drum in the form of magnetic spots. It can store more data than magnetic disks or tapes, but it is also more expensive.

7. *Data cell.* This can serve as both an input/output device and an auxiliary storage. It is often used when large amounts of data have to be readily accessible for processing on short notice. The cell combines both magnetic tape and magnetic disk technologies; each cell contains a strip of tape on which data can be recorded. When the data on a particular strip is needed for processing, the cell is simply moved mechanically to a rewrite station.

There are also several devices that can only be used as output mediums. The better known of these are the following:

1. *Line printer.* This comes in many sizes and types, and is one of the more common output devices in use today; it can produce outputs that can be read by the human eye. It can produce up to 15,000 lines of output per minute, and the characters are produced on the paper in much the same way as with a typewriter.

2. *Dot-matrix printer.* As is the case with the line printer, this output device creates characters on paper. Both this and the line printer are known as impact printers.

3. *Nonimpact printer.* These devices create characters by heat, electrostatic energy, or laser beams. There are several types of nonimpact printers. The more common of these are:

    a.   Electrostatic printers.

    b.   Thermal printers (these produce only one copy at a time).

    c.   Laser printers (these use beams to burn characters on paper).

The dot-matrix printer is preferred because of its high speed, but it is also very expensive.

DEVELOPMENTS IN TELECOMMUNICATIONS

The telecommunications revolution has made it possible for a user to communicate with the main computer from a terminal many miles away; the data is sent over telephone lines. When transnational communications are involved, data can be transmitted via satellite communications. Before the advent of developments in telecommunications, the use of an EDP system was limited to the computer facility.

Telecommunications connects users to EDP systems through a number of different terminals. Some of the more common of these are the following:

Intelligent terminal. This type is used to perform some editing and data checking functions, through logic circuits constructed into it; micro-computers can sometimes be employed as intelligent terminals. Simply by being linked to a main computer, a micro-computer can easily be employed as a terminal.

Graphic terminals. This kind of terminal is used for the display of complex charts and diagrams. For example, an architect can enter detailed plans for an office building, and project a front view of the structure on the display screen.

Silent portable data terminal. This is small and can be carried around anywhere; the only requirement for its use is that there be an electrical outlet close to the telephone. This type of terminal has almost unlimited uses; it can easily lend itself to abuse. A freelance programmer, for example, can use it to access a computer from a client's office, or even his own apartment.

Remote-batch terminal. This type is employed to submit large quantities of data to a main computer, and to print the output when the processing is completed. It consists of a printer, card reader, and minicomputer. Remote-batch terminals are used to keep track of inventory.

Audio-response portable terminal. This terminal does not require an electrical outlet. It is an audio-response unit that can fit into a briefcase; the user contacts the computer by simply dialing the appropriate telephone number.

Point-of-sale terminal. This is usually found at retail stores. Some of these record data on magnetic tape for later processing; others are connected directly to a central computer and operate on-line. They are playing an important role in the cashless revolution.

Terminals make it possible for users to communicate with computers in other cities and even other countries. They have extended the reach of computer technology, and brought its benefits to millions of men and women. Terminals, however, can also be employed to steal or manipulate data, sabotage a system, or pilfer assets. In the wrong hands, terminals can lend themselves to serious criminal abuses.

UNDERSTANDING PROGRAMS

A central computer can perform a multitude of tasks at very high speeds; it can do this while it is connected to several dozen terminal devices. But computers have to be told what to do and how to do it. The instructions that guide computers are known as programs. They are prepared by programmers in a language that the computer can understand. The program tells the computer:

The type of input data it will receive
The calculations it will perform
The order of the calculations
The kind of output it will produce

Programs vary in sophistication, application, and cost. However, all programs, by and large, share a commonality: six basic developmental stages. Understanding these can assist you in better analyzing program-related abuses. These six basic stages are:

Analysis of the problem.

Development of flow charts that describe the solution.

Writing of the program in some coded form (understandable to the computer).

Compiling the object program.

Debugging the program.

Documenting the program.

Concerning the program itself, it usually falls into one of the following four general categories:

User prepared programs. These are prepared within the organization, and are designed to perform specific tasks peculiar to the needs of the preparer.

Report generators. These are used to produce reports from a data file or a series of data files. They are simple to use and can be purchased from a computer manufacturer.

Applications programs. These are mainly purchased from a computer manufacturer or a company that specializes in writing programs. They come ready to use.

Utility programs. These are purchased from the manufacturer, and are used to perform routine tasks.

Regardless of your organization's size, or the nature of its work, remember that programs can be copied, manipulated, or stolen. Their loss can have a serious impact on the ability of an organization to compete or carry out its functions. It behooves you to institute some form of program security.

FUTURE CHANGES

From their earliest history, computers have been used to keep records and exchange information. They have increasingly come to replace manual systems in both government and business. In the 1950s, computers were mostly used as calculators and as controllers of large record systems. The data was usually stored on magnetic tapes or punched cards. The 1960s witnessed the rise of the mini-computer and time-sharing systems; the telecommunications revolution made it possible for the latter to evolve. The 1970s witnessed the rise of communication-based computer systems and networks.

The 1980s should witness a continuation of the computer revolution. We should witness:

A growth in the use of personal computers.

An expansion in the number and size of computer networks.

The growth of information services.

The expansion of computer-based information services, such as bibliographic and data-based search, electronic publishing, electronic banking, and the like.

Growing competition among the corporate giants for the data communication services market.

An increasing variety of data communication services.

A higher level integration of data services in such industries as insurance, banking, travel, entertainment, law enforcement, commodities/securities exchanges, medical services, and others.

But the computer revolution may be stifled by subtle economic and technological forces. Among these are the following:

Overall cost of computer hardware.

Cost and difficulty of setting up and maintaining high speed data communication links.

High cost of producing software (the high cost of the software has already partly retarded the growth of computer technology).

Growing software bottleneck (programming is labor intensive, its costs are rising, and the number of programmers is not keeping pace with the demand).

However, regardless of what direction the computer revolution will take, criminals have already identified it as a potent weapon for theft, fraud, and abuse. Professional criminals have now joined the ranks of the amateurs. The challenge to management, hence, comes both from the technology, and from human frailty.

CHAPTER **8**

Auditing
the Computer
Center

Over a period of several years, a clerk at a shipping company embezzled more than $500,000 merely by manipulating the company's auto-
mated expense and inventory accounts. An employee took a Federal
agency for more than $1 million over a one year period in a "ghost em-
ployee" scheme. A programmer took a credit card company for more than
$50,000 simply by making some "extra" program changes. The computer
was programmed to deposit $100 in his own account every week.

Computers have been used by criminals to manipulate sales, payrolls,
accounts receivable, and assets, and even to invade the privacy of customers and taxpayers. The opportunity for fraud by computer continues
to grow. In spite of the above examples, however, an organization can reduce its risks. Adequate audit controls and safeguards can play a role in
preventing and deterring many of the present computer-related crimes
and abuses. Understanding how and when to employ these tools should
aid in this task.

POTENTIAL EXPOSURES

Audit techniques and controls can prove effective in limiting an organization's vulnerability. The risks can take one or more of the following
forms:

104

Theft and fraud. These crimes can be committed either by insiders or outsiders. Employees at every level of the organization, with access to the computer center, can pose a potential problem. These crimes are often difficult to detect and may involve not only the theft of funds, but also the misappropriation of data and software. Audits can have a deterrent effect. Dishonest employees may be reluctant to press their luck.

Error and malfunction. As a result of negligence or a failure to properly service the system, errors and breakdowns can plague the system; audit techniques can serve to identify some of these problems.

Loss of assets. Audits can serve to identify losses of money, assets, or data that an organization has suffered. Often, the organization may not be aware of its losses.

Legal considerations. Federal, state, and local regulators often exert some form of control on EDP systems, especially those that operate in interstate commerce. Audits can often ensure compliance with the legal-regulatory environment.

High costs. Every organization incurs some unnecessary expenses and revenue losses. The audit can serve to identify and eliminate these problems.

Audit controls have served to reduce and eliminate many of the above potential organizational problems. They can also serve to identify methods to improve the efficiency of an organization. The advent of the computer has, if anything, augmented the need for audits. Auditing the computer center will serve both to identify problems and to insure the accuracy and integrity of the data.

ROLE OF THE AUDITOR

The advent of the computer has revolutionized the role of the auditor. He or she must now acquire sufficient knowledge of this new technology to insure that the organization's controls and safeguards are adequate to both protect against and identify thefts, errors, inefficiencies, malfunctions, and other irregularities.

The auditor, however, faces some serious obstacles; these are in part a result of the new technology, and also partly a result of organizational interests at odds over limited resources. Understanding these can assist you in making better and more efficient use of the auditor. Many of the problems that you should be cognizant of take one or more of the following forms:

Inadequate audit capabilities
Small EDP audit staffs
Limited budgets
Large workload
Inadequate documentation
Lax security
Technical difficulties
Friction between staffs
Shortage of available assistance from outside auditors
Lack of management support
High turnover
Hardware and software problems
Poor quality of available audit software
Poorly trained personnel
Internal politics
Overextended staff
Poor supervision
Inadequate planning
Rising costs

The EDP auditor should be knowledgeable in the field, but selecting the "right" auditor is not always simple. There are, however, certain qualifications that you should look at when making your selection. These qualifications should include:

Good working knowledge of EDP systems.
Knowledge of program languages.
Grasp of the role and capabilities of the computer.
Familiarity with EDP audit methods and terminology.
Ability to communicate (both verbally and in writing).
Ability to get along with others.
Knowledge of audit techniques.
College or equivalent degrees (usually in areas of business).

ROLE OF THE AUDIT

The EDP audit is multifaceted. Its roles differ somewhat from those of the internal audit; in large part, this is because of the computer. The role of the EDP audit within an organization is to:

Provide technical support and assistance to the internal audit staff.

Review security.

Uplift the competency level of the EDP audit staff.

Employ the computer as an audit tool.

Provide periodic review of the EDP system.

Ensure the accuracy of the data.

Make it possible to reconstruct data in case of a disaster.

Analyze risks.

Test adequacy of controls and contingency plans.

Determine skill of and limitations of EDP staff.

Review and appraise the EDP function.

Determine compliance with the organization's policies, plans, and procedures.

Appraise the quality of performance.

AUDIT OBJECTIVES

The objective of the EDP audit is to insure the accuracy, authenticity, and reliability of the system's input, stored data, methodology, and output. The EDP audit serves to:

Trace both legitimate and phony transactions through the entire processing sequence.

Insure the authenticity and reliability of the computer programs.

Check out transactions that are not meeting specified standards.

Test the system's security.

Identify existing and potential problems.

Verify the files and records in the system.

The audit also serves additional functions; the more important of these are:

Insuring that necessary financial and operational controls are both designed and used in the system.

Promoting accurate record-keeping, reducing waste, and encouraging computer security.

Enforcing compliance with the organization's rules, regulations, and code of ethics.

Identifying and recommending improvements in personnel, physical, and software security.

Promoting consistency in the security program.

Developing checklists of questions for management to consider.

An audit team, however, should be representative of the organization's needs; it should have on it more than individuals with auditing backgrounds. Insure that the team also includes:

General management
Legal department personnel
System designers
Programmers
Tape librarians
Members of in-house security
Individuals familiar with computer technology

A well balanced audit team will serve to minimize conflicts between the different departments; it also assures that the team will take the "big organizational picture." Diversity insures that all views and interests are represented in the audit.

The audit should not, however, concern itself with nor waste limited resources on insignificant exposures to risk. Further, periodic unannounced audits can serve to keep the computer center personnel on their toes, and dishonest employees will think twice before ripping off their employer.

AUDITING THE COMPUTER SYSTEM

The ability of any organization to survive in an EDP environment rests, in part, on its data banks. In an automated environment, voluminous data flow through the system almost invisibly; it is guided by unseen hands. Frauds, thefts, abuses, ineptness, negligence, and ignorance can cause costly, if not irrecoverable, losses. These, unfortunately, can occur with great speed in an EDP system, often with little or no way to trace or detect what happened. For these reasons, EDP audit controls and safeguards are increasingly important.

The audit does more than simply verify the accuracy, adequacy, reliability, and authenticity of the data stored in the computer system. It also serves to identify actions and changes occurring inside the system. Unfortunately, not all organizations can or do implement adequate audit controls; limited resources often make this difficult to do. In addition, the needed EDP audit expertise is presently in short supply, but the need for audit controls continues. Management is called upon to implement them, if it is to attest to and rely on the accuracy of its EDP system.

Audit controls and safeguards should be tailored to meet the specific needs of your organization and EDP staff. Before implementing your audit tools, first review the existing controls and safeguards, and then determine ways to update and modify these to meet the needs of the EDP system. In so doing, however, consider the following:

Resources available to support your audit program.
Existing safeguards to protect your data and programs.
Controls available for changes in your master files.
Controls in use for the utility program.
Existing plans for system generation.
Controls available for program changes.
Ability to monitor the system's activities.
System access safeguards.
Available training for staff and management.
Effectiveness of existing application controls.
Available contingency plans.
Use of independent auditors.

However, when preparing to audit an EDP system, remember that there are marked differences between it and manual systems. The key differences can be summarized as follows:

Data storage.   In an EDP system, data is not stored in a form an auditor can read. It must first be printed on paper or on a screen before it can be reviewed.

Use of experts.   When auditing an automated operation, you will need the services of experts—unless you have the in-house talent. In addition, be sure that someone in your organization does have some knowledge of EDP controls so that the expert can be supervised.

Audit trails.   These take on a different form in an automated system. There are no paper records or trails to examine. The data is stored on magnetic tapes and disks, in electronic form.

Controls.   In an automated operation, these can be constructed into the hardware and software.

Coordination.   Coordinating audit activities in an EDP system can prove difficult. In large part, this is a result of the diverse skills necessary for the project.

Basic understanding.   You will need a grasp of computer technology to assist you in supervising the audit.

The implementation of periodic reviews and the maintenance of strong internal controls can play an important role in assisting your organization in deterring and identifying computer-related abuses and thefts. EDP controls also serve additional objectives: they can also detect errors, mismanagement, and other irregularities. Strong internal controls will also serve to insure that:

Transactions are executed only in accord with management's instructions.

Financial statements are prepared in accord with generally accepted principles.

Accountability for assets is maintained.

Access to assets is only in accord with organizational policies and directives.

In order for audit controls to be meaningful, however, they should cover the following:

Specific procedures for documenting changes.

Review of the organization of the system.

Controls in the software and hardware.

Access to the system.

Access to the data files.

Review of the system's overall operations.

Review of the input, processing, and output stages of the system.

NEED FOR A MASTER PLAN

In order to insure the effectiveness of its EDP controls and safeguards, an organization should take adequate steps to establish administrative procedures. The objectives of these should be to:

Reduce uncertainty on the part of the EDP staff.

Improve the effectiveness of the audit.

Inform the system personnel of the organization's policies and objectives.

Identify and allocate priorities.

Improve the coordination of your organizational resources.

Keep costs low.

Management should also take steps to improvise—or develop where none exists—contingency plans to address any unexpected problems. The objective of the contingency plan should be to assist the organization in responding efficiently, rapidly, and effectively to any problems that may arise. Management should also take the needed steps to insure that key organizational personnel have been briefed and kept informed of all contingency procedures. To be effective, a contingency plan should encompass at least some of the following:

A list of the names, addresses, titles, and telephone numbers (both home and work) of key system personnel.

Specification of the responsibilities of each EDP staff member.

Specification of the various options available in case of an emergency.

Detailed instructions for implementing the needed activities.

Specification of the role of each person responsible for carrying out these actions.

Provisions for changes in the plan.

Details of the training necessary for key system personnel.

Provisions for training and refresher courses for key personnel.

Provisions for the uplifting and improving of the quality of important personnel.

The training of key personnel constitutes a key component of any successful audit program. It can be accomplished by:

Registering personnel at universities and colleges.

Using professional schools.

Sending personnel to seminars and conferences sponsored by professional/trade organizations.

Providing in-house training.

Using on-the-job training.

If audit controls are to prove effective, management should take steps to insure that the duties and responsibilities of key system personnel are specifically defined, and also divided. No one person should be permitted access to more than one of the following:

Systems analysis.
Programming.
Data-based administration.
Computer operations.
Tape, disk, and document libraries.
Input and data conversion.

The role of audit controls is to insure that system personnel have been rotated within their own functional areas, no system employee has had an opportunity to become too familiar with any specific production programs, and all system personnel take their designated vacations. Further, should your organization have serious employee-related problems, you should take steps to insure that troublesome employees are either segregated or terminated.

REVIEWING THE CONTROLS

If you are called upon to either supervise or conduct an audit, it is important that you first review the following four key controls:

Administrative
System
Processing
Operational

Each of the above four controls should be carefully reviewed to insure that they both meet and comply with your organization's needs and policies.

Administrative Controls

If these are already in place (consider implementing them if you do not have them), check to insure that:

You have a master plan.
It meets your organization's needs.
It is specific.

It is reviewed periodically.

You have a backup for the system.

The backup is periodically tested.

Key personnel know about the backup system.

Emergency procedures are known to key personnel.

Emergency drills are conducted periodically.

Operating procedures are current.

The organizational chart is updated periodically.

Key employees are bonded.

Employees are screened periodically.

The training program is reviewed periodically.

You have an orientation program.

You have a code of ethics.

Ethical conduct is encouraged.

Employees are briefed periodically on organization objectives.

Job rotation is practiced.

Duties are segregated.

Single-person access to the system is prohibited.

Procedures used to terminate employees are adequate.

Passwords are employed.

Maintenance personnel are kept out of sensitive areas.

Vendor service personnel are closely supervised.

Monitors are employed.

Control procedures are updated periodically.

All system shutdowns and start-ups are recorded.

Controls over tapes, disks, and cards are adequate.

There are security parameters.

The system is tested periodically.

System Controls

These relate to the computer's operations; they also incorporate the input, application, output, and storage controls. When checking these controls, make sure that:

The processed data is not altered, modified, or destroyed.

All processing is authorized.

All data entry is authorized.

Only authorized personnel have custody of the records.

Sensitive forms dealing with input instruments (such as purchase orders, invoices, checks, or requisitions) are prenumbered.

Sensitive forms are stored outside the computer facility.

Each document is verified by a separate operation.

Control totals are used to insure that the input data has not been changed, lost, or modified (before or during) the processing.

Processing Controls

These can be constructed into an automated system to assist it in the detection of erroneous and fraudulent data inputs. These controls should:

Include checks against predetermined transactions, codes, tables, or other data.

Be used to identify data having value higher or lower than predetermined limits.

Insure that the data entering the system is the same as that coming out.

Insure that the files are in proper sequence.

Employ arithmetic checks to validate the results of the other computations.

Employ internal label checks.

Insure that invalid conditions are investigated.

Insure that programs are thoroughly tested by others as well as by the original programmer.

Catalog the programs in the program library.

Keep programs under tight control.

Assure that only properly authorized changes are made.

Insure that flowcharts associated with programs are readily available.

Operational Controls

These should be reviewed periodically to insure that:

The environment within the facility is operational.

The location of the facility is secure.

The construction material is fireproof.

The air conditioning, dehumidification, and humidification systems are adequate.

The power source is uninterrupted.

The files and other sensitive data are stored in secure vaults.

The backup files, programs, and other vital documents are stored in secure outside locations.

Fire protection devices are adequate.

The steps taken to prevent accidental erasures are adequate.

The storage devices are kept free of pollutants.

The library has controls.

The files and documents kept in the library are recorded.

The files are labeled for identification.

The external labels are coded.

The steps taken to insure the accuracy and completeness of the input data are adequate.

The output data is distributed only by authorized personnel.

The output data corresponds with the input information.

PROBLEMS AUDITORS FACE

In many organizations, unfortunately, management views the EDP auditor as a necessary evil. In large part, this stems from management's poor grasp of the role the audit plays. Often this serves to create a gulf between the audit department and the rest of the organization. This serves to undermine the role of the auditor.

Management should be aware of the causes for some of the problems between it and the EDP audit staff. These, in large part, stem from:

The complexity of EDP systems

Management's insecurity

The audit of the other professionals

Fear that the EDP auditor is an "empire builder"

Controls that may not have been implemented when the system was developed

Poor communications

Uncertainty about whether it is worth the cost

The "two hats" that the EDP auditor wears

The fact that the profession is still in its infancy

Oftentimes, these problems can seriously hinder the auditor's efforts. Understanding them, and also recognizing the value of the audit process, will enable the organization to best utilize the audit tools.

AN AUDIT CHECKLIST

The audit checklist should assist you in detecting both intentional and unintentional omissions, deletions, modifications, alterations, and attacks directed at the EDP system. When conducting an audit, determine the following:

Who authorized the transactions?

What steps were taken to ensure clear lines of responsibility and authority?

Who reviewed the input?

Who approved the internal entries?

Who approved changes in the software?

What procedures were employed for requisitioning and accounting for blank stock?

What procedures were used to identify and correct errors and malfunctions?

What steps were taken to insure the accuracy of data transmitted?

What checks were employed to detect the loss (or nonprocessing) of data?

Who serviced the computer facility?

Who kept an inventory of critical parts?

What steps were taken to restrict access to the facility?

What was the policy toward outside visitors?

Was a machine utilization log kept?

What steps were taken to prevent erasures of tapes?

What controls were imposed on the late hour shifts?

What controls were employed in the library?

Who reconciled the output and input totals?

Was a logbook of completed tasks kept?

Were couriers screened?

What vital forms were controlled?

Was the sensitive output printed in a secure area?

Who maintained the visitors' log?
Were sensitive reports shredded?
Were cards and badges used to limit access?
Were closed circuit television sets employed?
Were entry points guarded?
Were detection devices and alarms employed?
Was there central monitoring?
Were the terminals secure?
What were the hours of the computer facility card?
Were security officers employed?
Were authorized users identified?
Was access to sensitive files limited?
Were employees required to identify themselves?
Were passwords used?
Were passwords changed frequently?
Were locks employed?
Were all suspicious activities recorded?

The auditing of an EDP system need not prove any more difficult than the audit of a manual one, if properly planned and if the needed experts are used. If properly carried out, audit controls and safeguards can go a long way toward detecting and preventing computer-related errors, malfunctions, abuses, thefts, and other irregularities.

CHAPTER 9

Detecting and Investigating Computer Frauds

A police operation ended with the arrest of several members of a chip-stealing ring; the thieves had planned to steal 75,000 integrated circuits, said to be worth more than $500,000. In a separate case, several dishonest employees for a computer manufacturer were charged with grand theft; they allegedly ripped off more than $1 million worth of their employer's micro-computers. Three employees of another firm were accused by their employer of planning to sell valuable confidential marketing plans to a competitor.

Computer-related thefts are on the increase. Their detection and investigation is not always easy, yet management is increasingly called upon to assist in these areas. Its role in the detection and investigation of computer capers often can play a role in the government's decision to prosecute.

CHARACTERISTICS AND ENVIRONMENT

Traditional street crimes are characterized by force and violence; the modus operandi is often noted for its simplicity, and the felon is usually someone from the lower socioeconomic strata of our society. Sreet crimes often fall into a fixed pattern; in addition, they are easy to detect and investigate. Their prosecution, with few exceptions, is a simple matter.

Computer capers, likewise, share certain common features; they can prove difficult to unravel, and their prosecution is often costly and time consuming (save for those cases where the defendant pleads guilty). They share some additional characteristics:

Dishonest insiders are involved (directly or indirectly) in a large number of these rip-offs.

Victims are usually reluctant to publicly acknowledge that they have "been taken."

Many of these crimes are "invisible" and it may take years before the victim knows it has been ripped off.

Deception is central to these crimes.

EDP personnel are often key figures in any investigation.

Investigators are often intimidated by computer technology (although this will change as computers become everyday tools).

Evidence can prove difficult to collect and analyze.

Experts are often necessary to assist in the investigation.

Prosecutors often shy away from these capers.

Convicted computer criminals often receive only mild sentences ("slap on the wrist").

Computer crimes also share an additional characteristic: they thrive in a corrupt organizational environment. The computer criminal is especially attracted to organizations where top management either tolerates or directly encourages corrupt practices. An organization that is permeated with white collar crime can be certain that computer crime will follow in its tracks.

There are several red flags that should serve to put management on notice that its organization is ideally suited to computer crime. These corruption indicators could take any of the following forms:

Socializing. If key EDP personnel mingle with outsiders who are alleged to have criminal ties or backgrounds, you may be open to a criminal attack.

Competitors. If one of your EDP managers or employees leaves your organization and joins that of a competitor, this could be an indication that he/she is taking your trade secrets, valuable marketing information, valuable customer-related information, and/or other potentially valuable data along (this is especially true in cases involving industrial espionage).

Complaints. These are common, and could be an indication that your EDP personnel may be engaged in some kind of unlawful activity.

Whistleblowers. If whistleblowers are discouraged from coming forth and testifying or supplying information as regards corrupt practices they have witnessed within your organization, you may be courting criminal attack (whistleblowers often serve as important vehicles for uncovering potential computer-related capers).

Rules and regulations. If these are not enforced, or if disciplinary action is not taken against those who violate them, your staff may read this as a lack of willingness on your part to prosecute unlawful conduct.

Expenses. If the costs of your EDP materials and services are out of line with those on the market, then your EDP personnel may in fact be bilking the organization.

Gratuities. If some of your EDP personnel are receiving gifts in the form of tickets to sports events, travel tickets, or other gratuities from outsiders, the latter may be corrupting them.

Inflated contracts. If contracts for computer-connected services appear to be inflated, then you may be facing a kickback or bribery scheme (it is not unusual, for example, for manufacturers and providers of services to make payments to personnel in return for inflated contracts).

Sham payments. These often take the form of payments for nonexistent services and may be recorded as expenditures for public relations work or advertising (in some sham schemes, the money is funneled through phony advertising or public relations firms).

Falsification of records. These occurrences may indicate that someone is manipulating your sales, assets, dividends, and other moneys coming in and through your organization.

Payroll frauds. It is a simple process for a dishonest employee to add his/her friends, relatives, and others to the organization's payroll.

Phony suppliers. These frauds often involve the payment of money to shell companies and others for nonexistent supplies. These frauds are usually committed by dishonest employees who may either be assisting or are being assisted by dishonest outsiders.

Fictitious transactions. Payments are made for phony transactions, often involving friends or companies in which the dishonest insider has an interest.

Misusing confidential data. This often involves an insider who is leaking valuable information (which has a commercial value) to an outsider.

Phony loans. These take the form of loans extended to friends and relatives who might otherwise not qualify.

Padded overtime records. This problem is especially common in the governmental sector.

Loss of equipment. This involves the manipulation and pilferage of the inventory.

Misuse of services. This means the unauthorized use of services by dishonest insiders for their personal benefit.

Theft of payments. This involves the stealing of incoming payments from legitimate sources (the dishonest employee will usually cash the checks and pocket the money).

Paying twice. This entails issuing two checks to a supplier, and keeping the second check for personal use.

Unclaimed wages. This means pocketing the wages of a deceased, dismissed, or ill employee.

Carrying an employee. This entails carrying on the payroll, beyond their actual severance date, an employee who has either left the organization's service or who is deceased.

Unauthorized shipments. This involves the shipment of goods, equipment, and other material to friends and relatives.

Incoming shipments. This means declaring incoming goods or equipment short.

Not every organizational environment is corrupt, nor is corruption the sole cause of computer crime. However, an environment that condones or reinforces corrupt practices also invites computer crime. In such an environment, computer criminals find it an easy matter to justify their illegal conduct; in addition, those about them will be too taken by their own criminal acts to be concerned with the misdeeds of others. Learn to identify such an environment, and make efforts to remedy it; if one employee steals, peers may attempt to mimic him/her.

TIP-OFFS AND PRELIMINARY CHECKS

Even a more experienced investigator can sometimes be caught off guard by the computer criminal. However, there are some tip-offs that should signal to even the average manager that something may be wrong with the EDP system. These often take the following forms:

Complaints by non-EDP employees as regards the functioning and reliability of the system become common.

When questioned, EDP personnel give evasive and suspect answers.

Records are missing or destroyed.

Some EDP personnel work unusually long hours.

Customers, creditors, beneficiaries, or others never receive their payments.

Checks have forged signatures.

Supplies and equipment are missing.

Records are not kept up to date.

EDP staff sweeps irregularities under the rug.

Complaints by outsiders are chronic.

Some staffers refuse promotions and vacations.

Nonemployees loiter near the computer center.

Cost of operating the EDP system surges dramatically and unexplainably.

Payments are made to companies or individuals with known criminal ties.

Some EDP personnel are known drug users.

Should you decide to act on any of the above tip-offs, be aware that your inquiry may require a commitment in time and resources that you should be well prepared to bear.[1] Often management embarks on a potential computer crime trail, thinking the answers will be simple, and the facts easy to unravel. This may be the case in some situations, but it is not the norm. Thus, while planning your inquiry, consider the following:

Are you prepared to commit a sufficient amount of time, energy, and resources to the inquiry? Since many of these capers can require long periods of time to investigate and prosecute, you should be prepared to expend the requisite resources.

Experts may have to be retained to assist you in your investigation. In such a case, be sure to retain the services of quality individuals.

---

[1] An inquiry consists of informal steps to determine whether a crime has in fact occurred, and its scope. It is not a formal investigation; it should be viewed merely as preinvestigatory steps, taken to determine if further action is necessary. Although more limited in scope, resources, time, and effort than a formal investigation, it can nevertheless be demanding and taxing, especially when confronted with a complex computer caper.

Your inquiry may require you to test the EDP data or files. You may also have to shut down the system for a period of time, and should give ample consideration to this.

Also consider cataloging all of the preliminary evidence you gather.

Your efforts should be planned in such a way so as not to tamper with the evidence.

Review all potential legal problems that may arise in the course of your inquiry with members of your legal staff.

Consider the various Federal/state/local police agencies that you can call on for assistance.

Be sure the inquiry is well managed and coordinated with other organizational units. This will serve both to conserve your resources and to ensure that the inquiry is carried through in an expeditious manner.

Commence your inquiry as soon as you have identified a potential crime. This will ensure that the criminal will not have erased his/her tracks.

Be sure that the inquiry is in compliance with the law. The abuse and misuse of power by management can leave it open to a civil lawsuit.

In addition, as you embark on your inquiry, be prepared to consider several added factors. Among these, do not be surprised if you find:

The criminal (especially if a professional) makes every effort to throw you off the track.

The crime involves a conspiracy between dishonest insiders and their outside associates (increasingly, computer capers are taking on a professional appearance).

The suspect makes every effort to convince you he/she did not know the conduct in question was illegal.

The staff of some of your divisions proves uncooperative (many have their own skeletons to hide).

Witnesses are reluctant to come forth and testify.

Allegations made against the suspect(s) meet with a dead end (jealousy, professional rivalries, and other personality quirks may lead some employees, even the best intended, to make unsubstantiated charges).

The inquiry appears to be sinking in quicksand (often, you will find that allegations only cover the tip of the iceberg).

The scope of your inquiry takes periodic shifts (one crime may lead to another, and criminals are often involved in several illegal acts at the same time).

The police approach the problem half-heartedly (if they take an interest in your case, it will usually occur once the inquiry uncovers hard evidence).

The inquiry leads to personal clashes and friction with other managers or divisions (bureaucrats guard their turfs aggressively).

When zeroing in on potential suspects, the following considerations are some to keep in mind:

Ascertain who authorized the transaction(s).

Check who prepared the input documents.

Determine who approved the purchases.

Assess who prepared the initial records.

Review who recorded the initial (and following) transactions.

Check who prepared the supporting documents.

Computer capers often can be detected by a number of tip-offs; management can be trained to identify those, and to determine their validity. Unlike a formal investigation, the inquiry gives you the out, the back door to take, just in case you reach a dead end.

ASSESSING THE CRIME

Managers are not investigators, nor are they trained to be so. However, they are increasingly being called upon to play some role in the investigation and prosecution of computer crimes. Thus they are required to understand the role and task of the investigatory process.

There are several preliminary investigative considerations that today's management should be versed in as regards the problem of EDP-connected crime. By simply learning how to identify and analyze these criminal acts, management can assist in the investigation and prosecution of the computer criminal. The basic investigatory steps are as follows:

Before doing anything else, always ascertain whether a crime has in fact been committed. This is not always easy to do, and you should consult with your legal department.

Attempt to identify the nature and type of crime involved. For example, ascertain whether the illegal act involves the theft of property, data, or moneys. If it involves a physical damage to the system, determine if it is sabotage, vandalism, or merely an act of God (natural phenomenon).

Determine the degree of technical know-how that may have been needed to pull off the caper. By ascertaining the level of technical know-how, you also limit the size of your pool of suspects. The more sophisticated the crime, the smaller your pool of suspects.

Make an effort to identify all of the potential suspects by name, and examine the role each plays in the system. This will prove of value later on to the authorities.

Establish possible motives for the crime. These can range from the simple to the complex, from the logical to the bizarre. Some examples include revenge by a disgruntled (present or former) employee, industrial espionage or sabotage (by a competitor), game playing (by a prankster), financial need (by someone pressed for funds), and many other potential motives. Examine these closely.

Identify potential witnesses to the crime. Few criminal cases ever reach the prosecutorial stage, unless someone comes forth to assist the authorities. The value of someone's assistance will rest on the witness's credibility, reliability, and knowledge of the facts in question. Compile a list of individuals who may be knowledgeable as regards the crime, and pass this on to the authorities.

Be careful to identify the physical evidence. However, do not tamper with it. Simply identify it for the authorities, and assist them only as requested.

Always record any initial interviews you may have with any potential suspects or witnesses. Pass this information on to the police.

Always safeguard all evidence at the crime scene. Do not misplace, damage, or destroy the evidence.

Review your organization's history, to determine if there have been other similar instances in the past. Criminals have been known to strike more than once.

Review all prior instances of criminal activity in detail. Determine and detail any similarities between these criminal acts.

Compile summaries and job descriptions for each of your suspects and witnesses.

Review the personnel files of all potential suspects. In addition, check with their former employers to determine if they faced similar problems when the suspect was in their employment.

Consider your potential competitors, and prepare a list of these, and also their possible motives.

Determine the impact of the illegal act on your organization's viability, financial health, and share of the marketplace.

Examine the history of your EDP system and the background of its staff.

Determine if the system has had similar difficulties in the past (check with your director of security).

Consider whether the criminal act may in fact be only the tip of the iceberg. It could be part of a larger and more complex fraud.

Assess the resources and personnel you can make available to the government investigators.

Familiarize yourself with the system and its personnel.

Carefully review your organization's security policies, procedures, and programs (consult with your security personnel).

Review the audit policies and procedures (consult your auditors).

Carefully assess your overall policies and procedures.

The ability to adequately assess a problem is second in importance only to the ability to detect and/or identify that problem. The assessment should be meticulous, factual, and in line with the above basic investigatory principles; if it is, it will prove of great value to the police. Management, because of its familiarity with the organization's needs and policies, is adequately equipped to perform this function.

INVESTIGATORY TIPS

When conducting an in-house investigation, you will often be confronted with an array of charges and countercharges. It will often prove necessary to check out the validity and veracity of the many statements made to you by witnesses and suspects alike. In so doing, you can tap a pool of readily available resources. Some of the better known are:

State/local prosecutors
Court records (civil, domestic, and criminal)
Credit card companies
Telephone companies
Assessor's records
Tax collector's office
Recorder's office
Marriage license bureaus
Schools (college, professional, etc.)
Law enforcement sources

Neighbors, friends, and associates
Financial institutions
Bonding companies
Government agencies
Credit reporting agencies
Utility companies
Birth records
Automobile records
Police records
Directories (city, professional, etc.)
Hotel and airline records
Brokerage records
Newspapers and periodicals (especially professional types)

When preparing to interview a suspect or witness, keep in mind that your interview report could prove of extreme value in the event that there is a criminal prosecution. Statements made to you by the party you interviewed can later be used to construct the edifice of a criminal case. Thus take the process seriously, and keep these basic facts in mind:

Always use a notebook, and (whenever possible) also use a recording device.

At the beginning, inform the suspect or witness that he or she is free to leave at any time, and is not being detained; also state that the witness's cooperation is greatly appreciated.

We all have a tendency to take down too much information. Concentrate on pertinent material, and record only that information that is important to your investigation.

Take clear, legible notes. Your interview record will prove of little value if no one can read it.

Avoid using shorthand, special symbols, or abbreviations. These will only serve to make your record difficult to understand.

Ensure that all your entries are accurate and reflect only statements given by your interviewee. They should also be pertinent to the case at hand.

Have your notes typed and allow the interviewee to review them; once this has been done, ask the interviewee to sign and date the typed statement at the bottom of the last page. Make sure that both you and one of your associates also sign it.

Include in the above statement a clause that the interviewee signed it voluntarily.

As an added precaution, be sure that whenever you interview a suspect you always have another official with you. This will ensure that, should the case go to trial, the testimony you give will not simply be just your word against the suspect's word. Two witnesses carry greater weight with the courts than one only.

There are several additional checks you should consider when conducting the investigation. These are as follows:

Determine if the audit functions are independent of the activities under investigation.

Review the extent of staff compliance with authorized policies and procedures.

See if there are procedures for comparing financial information with statistics and trends for the industry.

Check the organizational procedures for the authorization, approval, execution, and recording of transactions.

Review procedures used to evaluate the performance of key EDP personnel.

Check the organizational policy statement on conduct.

Determine if the organizational structure is clearly defined.

Determine how responsibility is assigned.

Check if there was appropriate supervision and review.

As is pointed out in other parts of this book, many of the jurisdictions have been slow in enacting computer crime legislation. However, there are some laws that could have possible application, under specific conditions. Among the more widely used are:

Securities laws.   These could have application if a computer is employed to puff up the earnings, assets, and other property of a publicly held corporation.

Tax laws.   These would apply if a computer is employed to evade the payment of taxes.

Mail fraud statutes.   Where the United States mails are employed in furtherance of a computer fraud, these laws may apply.

Embezzlement.   If there is an abuse of trust by someone in a position of trust, the crime might be considered embezzlement.

Wire fraud. Where the wires are used in furtherance of a computer caper, these laws might apply.

Larceny. If there is a taking and carrying away of another's property (for example, the taking of software, hardware, and any other EDP system component), larceny may be involved.

Vandalism. This will come into play where there is an attack against the EDP system.

Arson. This occurs if there is a willful burning (fire).

Theft of services. This applies where there is unauthorized use of the system.

Burglary. This will come into play if there is a breaking and entering into the computer center.

The investigation of a computer caper can prove costly, time consuming, and even frustrating. It requires a pooling of organizational resources, and coordination with the authorities. Equally, if not more important, is the "selling of the case" to government prosecutors. Once the investigation is completed, you must convince the prosecutors that it has merit, in other words, that the probability of success is high.

If you cannot sell the case, the thief will walk free; you may sue, or dismiss the suspect (if he/she is an employee), but there is little else you can do. The prosecutorial function is vested in government, but you can influence that process. You can often do so by following these simple guidelines:

Jurisdiction. Whenever possible, select a prosecuting attorney who has demonstrated both a willingness and an ability to handle computer-related prosecutions. You will find that, in some jurisdictions, prosecutors are overworked and thus reluctant to involve themselves in complex, time consuming cases.

Timing. The public and the press take a greater interest in white collar crime when the economy is depressed. Selling your case will prove much easier during this period. Attempt to bring your case into a jurisdiction (if possible) where white collar crime prosecutions have become fashionable.

Preparation. Be prepared to outline the facts and evidence in your case in simple, lay language. Most prosecutors have neither the time nor patience to study computer science; in addition, ask for a personal meeting with the prosecutor. You will find it easier to answer all questions and assure the prosecutor of your commitment to the case, if done personally.

Format. The manner in which you present your case can make the difference between prosecution and nonprosecution. In selling your case, avoid technical jargon. Use easy-to-understand language. Paint the case in terms of "good versus evil," and explain why it is in the interest of the public to bring the criminal to court.

Visuals. A picture is worth a thousand words. Whenever possible, use films, slides, and other visual aids to detail the case. It makes your presentation more interesting; it also serves to simplify some of the technical jargon. You will not have to explain what terminals, programs, and such terms mean; the prosecutor will be able to see them. Slide presentations can prove especially valuable.

Patience. Avoid abrasive conduct. Answer all questions put to you in a soft tone; avoid the appearance of arrogance. Do not "look down" on the prosecutor, even if some questions appear to be simplistic. Remember, you need the prosecutor; he/she has more than enough business already.

The investigation of computer capers is everyone's business; it requires a total organizational effort. Management, of necessity, plays a role; in addition, it must assist in identifying and investigating these crimes. To do so, it must be sensitized to the underlying principles of criminal investigations.

SCREENING EDP PERSONNEL

It is not uncommon for an organization to find itself victimized by an employee who has a past criminal record. For example, an oil company hired a computer consultant who had embezzled funds from his previous employer; the "old urge" came back, and he took his new employer for more than $100,000. A government agency was taken for more than $40,000 in a computer caper; a background investigation would have revealed that the dishonest employee had been involved in a larceny at his previous employment.

Preemployment screening is a valuable tool; when used correctly, it can prove invaluable in screening out potential criminals. No organization would allow known felons access to its vaults, yet many allow them access to their computers. The price they pay is often high.

The objective of screening prospective EDP employees is not to discriminate; rather, it is to determine their suitability as regards ethics, character, work habits, education, and experience. Good employees pose few problems. Screening merely serves to provide the employer with information; it can serve to identify potential computer criminals. It should not be employed to serve the personal whims and binges of management; to do so would be illegal.

There are a number of guidelines you should follow when screening applicants for EDP positions. The guidelines are simple, inexpensive, and although not foolproof, can serve you well. Your preemployment inquiry should consider:

1. *Birth.* Place, date, hospital, parents, and other information related to the applicant's birth will help you screen out criminals who have established phony identities. The large influx of illegal aliens, many with phony or counterfeit documents, adds fuel to this problem.

2. *Education.* It may surprise you to know that a sizable number of applicants often do not have the credentials they represent themselves as having.

3. *Employment history.* Ask for dates, locations, and names of supervisors; check them out. Many a caper could have been prevented if the prospective employee's past work history had been fully verified.

4. *Government employment.* Check this out by contacting the prospective employee's supervisors and references. However, be cognizant of the fact that privacy laws limit what disclosures they can make.

5. *Professional groups.* If the prospective employee belongs to any, these can provide you with useful information.

6. *Character and conduct.* Check this out with law enforcement sources, past employers, educational institutions, landlord, neighbors, credit bureaus, and others. However, be cognizant that access to criminal records varies from state to state.

7. *Interview applicant.* This can prove most helpful. Question the applicant as regards the following:

    a. Family, employment, and educational history.

    b. Health history (with an eye for emotional instability and/or use of drugs/alcohol).

    c. Social activities (with an eye for gambling and related involvements).

    d. Past contacts with the criminal justice system.

    e. Involvement in litigation (whether a target of lawsuit).

    f. Review of character, integrity, and ethics.

    g. Dealings with criminal elements.

    h. Life-style (whether living beyond his/her means).

    i. Names of references who are acquainted with the applicant.

    j.   Professional groups applicant is involved with.

    k.   Marital and family situation.

8. *Privacy safeguards.* There are a multitude of Federal/state privacy laws and regulations that can open you up to a lawsuit if you violate them; be cognizant of their requirements. Generally, avoid any questions that deal with:

    a.   Race, sex, and ethnic background.

    b.   Union-related areas.

    c.   Fraternal and political associations.

    d.   Applicant's political views.

9. *Records.* Request the applicant to provide you with copies of school records, diploma, military discharge papers, birth certificate, and other documents. If the prospective employee has them, he/she should certainly be able to produce them; if they have been lost, copies can readily be obtained for a minimal fee.

10. *Residences.* Get a history of all places the applicant has resided in for the last ten years, especially the name of the landlord, dates resided at those locations, and the monthly rental paid.

11. *Conviction record.* Ask for this and also query the applicant as regards all past arrests (even where conviction did not result).

12. *Investigations.* Check to see if the prospective employee was the target of a civil/criminal investigation. Have the applicant list the agencies that investigated him/her (both civil and criminal).

13. *Civil/administrative litigation.* Ask if the applicant was ever a defendant/respondent in a civil/administrative action. Ask also who brought the action, and why it was brought.

14. *Truth determinants.* If the position in question is a sensitive one, you may have the applicant submit to a polygraph or similar test. However, employ only experienced and ethical examiners; in addition, check state/local laws on this, since many states regulate the way these tests are administered.

The successful detection and investigation of computer-related crimes can play an important role in preventing them; few computer criminals will risk loss of employment or a criminal prosecution, if they know that the likelihood of being caught has increased. Unlike street criminals, computer criminals are usually rational in their approach to crime; they do not like taking risks.

CHAPTER **10**

Coordinating
with Law
Enforcement

A New York company informs the police that a former employee stole one of its programs, and sold it to a competitor; the program is said to be very valuable. The police, however, decline to investigate; they advise the victim to consider bringing a lawsuit. A California student is charged with stealing more than $500,000 in valuable equipment belonging to an electronic firm; the victim was ripped off with the aid of its computer. The thief is convicted of grand theft, but receives only a 60 day jail term and three years probation; the victim never recoups its losses, and the prosecutors decline to press for restitution.

A Texas firm informs the local police that its computer communication lines have been tapped; it is assured that the matter will be fully investigated. However, two years have passed, and the victim has yet to see any progress in the investigation. In a separate case, a computer manufacturer assists the authorities in a "sting operation"; the thieves later ask the court to dismiss the charges on the grounds of entrapment.

The above cases illustrate both the frustrations and the dilemmas that the victims of computer capers face. If they decide to press for prosecution, they often find that the police and prosecutors are reluctant to pursue the case with vigor; oftentimes, the case simply dies in the bureaucratic maze.

Computer crimes are not the forte of law enforcement. It is only too common for the authorities to advise a victim to "see its lawyers." Even if they decide to press the case, the victim is often frustrated by lengthy and time consuming investigations; it is not unusual for some investigations to drag on for years. In addition, members of the victim's staff often find themselves spending many months educating the police; it is often the victim, rather than the authorities, who takes the lead. Further, valuable time and resources are expended in trials that never seem to end.

Even if a conviction should finally result, the criminal often escapes punishment with a "slap on the wrist." Incarceration is the exception rather than the norm in computer-related criminal prosecutions. While the average bank robber faces the prospect of a 10 year prison term, the average computer thief, if convicted, often pays only a small fine and is placed on probation. Some computer criminals have even gone on to become consultants to the very organizations that they previously victimized.[1] Needless to say, such an environment is not conducive to prosecution; the victim often feels frustrated and isolated. Yet without the victim's cooperation, the authorities can do little; at present there is a need to better coordinate efforts between law enforcement and the victims of computer crime.

NEED FOR PROSECUTION

Even the best of computer security measures are not foolproof; as a growing number of sophisticated professional criminals turn their attention to computer crime, deterrence will increasingly play an important role. Yet our present police forces are not trained to uncover and investigate computer capers; the odds favor the criminal. The likelihood that a computer crime will be discovered is probably one out of 1000. Given this reality, deterrence presently plays only a cosmetic role. It is safe to say that today's computer criminal enjoys free reign.

Our present police/prosecutorial forces are ill-equipped to address the threat of computer crime; in large part, this is because we have failed to provide them with the needed training and resources to address the problem. In both America and Europe police/prosecutorial efforts have been concentrated in the area of traditional crime; for many years, we never even sensitized them to white collar crime. It is as though we trained students in medicine, but never introduced them to the nervous system; little wonder, then, if the doctors could not treat many of its maladies. Thus the patients are the ultimate losers.

The backward nature of our law enforcement agencies in the area of computer crime requires greater coordination between the public and pri-

---

[1] The author was surprised to learn from one of his clients that it had retained the services of a disgruntled programmer who had ripped off his employer's computer.

vate sectors, between the victim and the authorities. The victim is thus called upon to both assist and coordinate its efforts with the authorities; the organization can no longer be simply a bystander.

Most victims—even sophisticated businesspeople—often do not understand the workings of our criminal justice system, yet it is necessary that they do. A grasp of how the system works can prove of invaluable assistance to both the victim and the authorities. It can make the difference between a successful prosecution and one that never materializes. Understanding how law enforcement operates, thinks, and what its objectives are is a must for modern management; it may ensure that it will better serve its organization's needs. Today's managers can no longer keep their eyes closed to the criminal justice system; safeguarding assets and property is a managerial responsibility.

LAW ENFORCEMENT IS ILL-PREPARED

When I am before a business or professional group, I am often surprised to find how little our better educated members of society know about the working of the criminal justice system; they have, unfortunately, abdicated that responsibility to the legal profession. While we train our modern managers in the latest managerial techniques for improving the efficiency and productivity of their organizations, we teach them little or nothing about the operations of our criminal justice system. In an environment where white collar crime is replete and organizations are victimized daily for millions of dollars, it would behoove management to understand the workings of law enforcement.[2]

In a word, modern management must get involved in the criminal justice system; it must coordinate its efforts with the authorities if computer crime is to be contained. It must understand both the strengths and frailties of the criminal justice system; it must also work to improve the system's efficiency. Yet today's MBA knows as much about this world as nineteenth century physicists knew about nuclear physics.

In fairness to management, however, it should be pointed out that law enforcement does not know, and understands even less, the daily problems afflicting the world of modern management. The average police officer has had little or no training in the workings of the business world; nor has he/

---

[2] It is not only management, but also those who train and educate them that must share the responsibility. "When was the last time," a friend once asked me, "that a business school taught a course in white collar crime?" He made his point.

she been trained to investigate economic crimes. These are usually the province of small and underfunded specialized units.[3]

A study of computer-related crimes by the Association of Chief Police Officers of England, Wales, and Northern Ireland found that law enforcement was ill-prepared to combat computer capers. Its survey found as follows:

United States.   Here efforts were being made to train police forces in this area. Much of the progress in combatting computer crime, the study found, had been carried out here.

Japan.   For many years, Japan's police forces had not viewed the problem as being serious; however, they had begun to focus on it.[4]

Hong Kong.   This colony was facing an increase in computer crime, and efforts were being made to train members of the Royal Hong Kong Police Force (Fraud Squad) in this area. Some squad members had already been sent to the United States for training.

West Germany.   This country closely followed the United States in its efforts to train specialized police forces in this area. The Federal Office of Criminal Investigation had been given the task of directing West Germany's efforts in this area.

Switzerland.   Surprisingly, the study found that the Swiss police forces were not very concerned about computer crime. However, because this nation is an important banking center, with highly automated payment systems, efforts were underway to train some police units in this area.

Canada.   Canada's computer crime problems were found to be similar to those of the United States. Some training had been introduced for its police forces at the Canadian Police College in Ottawa.[5]

Sweden.   Some training is being offered in this area at the Police Academy of Solna; the authorities were aware of their problem and were among the more advanced in this area.

Australia.   This nation faces considerable computer crime problems; efforts were being made to train some police units in this area.

Great Britain.   Surprisingly, Great Britain was one of the more back-

[3] The Federal Bureau of Investigation (FBI), for example, assigns fewer than 20 agents to its white collar crime unit in New York City.
[4] At a Washington, D.C., meeting with high-ranking Japanese police representatives, I was told that they had neglected the problem but were making efforts to train some specialized units.
[5] I have had occasion to meet with members of the Canadian law enforcement community, and they share many of the same problems found in America.

ward European nations as regards efforts to train its police forces in this area. The Association's study concluded that: "the United Kingdom is the only country in Western society not yet training its police specifically to investigate computer-related crime."[6]

In summary, it can be said that law enforcement, both in the United States and overseas, is ill-trained and lacking in a cohesive strategy to play an important role in the war against computer crime; in addition, communications between the world of business and that of law enforcement are, at best, poor. Both constituencies speak different languages; neither has made an effort to speak the other. The void perhaps represents the class differences in the constituencies of these two groups—especially in Europe. Yet unless they work together, and coordinate their efforts and strategies, time is on the side of the computer criminal.

EXISTING MECHANISMS

The present criminal justice system is an outgrowth of nineteenth century criminology. Modern police forces, funded and supported by the public treasury, first made their appearance in early nineteenth century England. Prior to that time, police functions were handled by a system of private watchmen. When the modern public police apparatus took shape, both in the United States and in England, its members were trained solely to address the problem of traditional crime. The primary task of the modern police officer became one of keeping the street criminal at bay. White collar crimes were viewed as private disputes; they were left to private litigants to resolve in the civil tribunals. This underlying dogma continues to permeate the mentality of many in leadership positions within the law enforcement community.

It was not until well into the twentieth century that government turned its attention to the problem of white collar crime. Illegal trade practices had become prevalent by the late nineteenth century; a huge public outcry had ensued. In response to this public pressure, the U.S. Congress and the state legislatures enacted legislation that established regulatory mechanisms; for example, the Federal Trade Commission, Interstate Commerce

[6] It may surprise the reader to know that the police forces of France, Italy, and Israel fare no better than those of Great Britain. Law enforcement is still in its infancy as regards the problem of computer criminology. It may take many years to train the requisite forces both in America and Europe; whether we have the requisite time remains to be seen.

Commission, and other regulatory bodies were an outgrowth of this public outcry.

The function of these regulatory bodies was, however, simply to discourage abuses by the private sector; they were not criminal investigatory bodies. No thought was given to training the traditional police apparatus in the investigation and prosecution of white collar crimes. In part, the business community itself was opposed to this; it feared that it might become the target of these revamped units. In addition, the public at large also feared that training the police forces in this area would detract from their efforts to handle street crimes. Thus the police apparatus changed little in the computer era.

In the 1940s, traditional criminology came under its first serious siege. In part, society owes Edwin H. Sutherland a debt of gratitude for the changes that were to follow; he lambasted the traditional perception of crime. He pointed out the dangers of white collar crime—now made easier by modern technology. The mass communication revolution, and the advances of computer technology had gone largely unnoticed by traditional criminologists. Their concern was—and continues to be—with crimes committed by the lower strata of society, namely, street crimes.

Criminal acts by the professional and affluent classes of society often went unnoticed; little wonder then that the evolving law enforcement apparatus failed to come to terms with the challenges of white collar crime. This partly explains its failure to embrace and adapt to the changing winds of computer criminology. In large measure, this has changed little even today. For every course being taught on white collar crime, there are dozens dealing with traditional criminology.[7]

It should be pointed out that, at least in the United States, the political structure played an important role in shaping the structure and dynamics of law enforcement. While homogeneous and centralized nation-states like France evolved national police agencies, the United States spawned small and localized police forces. At present, there are more than 40,000 such police forces. These, in turn, are supplemented by several hundred Federal regulatory and criminal investigative bodies.

America's present law enforcement apparatus has been rightly described as being a "patchwork of small, often inefficient police agencies, working at odds with each other." Cooperation between them is often the exception rather than the rule. Each agency is jealous of its "turf"; it guards it with fierce tenacity. It opposes any changes that it perceives as being a

---

[7] Teaching courses on computer crime continues to be regarded as taboo.

threat to its jurisdiction; it also opposes efforts by sister agencies to expand into areas it perceives as expanding their bureaucratic "empires."[8]

The prosecutorial system in the United States has fared no better; it, too, has been described as a patchwork of small, ill-equipped agencies, whose jurisdictions are confined by their geography. At the local level, we find several thousand prosecutorial agencies; these take the form of district attorneys, state attorneys, county attorneys, and attorney generals. Cooperation among these agencies is often the exception rather than the norm; for example, city and county prosecutors have traditionally been opposed to efforts to give state attorneys general criminal jurisdiction.[9] Thus in some states, the statewide prosecutor has only civil jurisdiction; all criminal cases must be referred to the local prosecutorial offices. Needless to say, this does little to promote efficiency.

At the Federal level, the prosecutorial burden falls on the shoulders of the U.S. Department of Justice (DOJ) and its United States Attorneys; the latter are located in more than 90 Federal judicial districts, and handle all local Federal prosecutions. The Federal prosecutorial machinery is also complemented by an array of regulatory bodies, for example, the Securities and Exchange Commission, the Federal Trade Commission, and many others. These, however, unlike DOJ, have only civil jurisdiction; they must refer all criminal cases to DOJ for prosecution. Traditional rivalries and disputes between DOJ and these regulatory agencies, however, often result in no criminal referrals; thus many white collar criminals escape Federal prosecution because of these prosecutorial quirks.

The law enforcement apparatus that has emerged, both at the Federal and state/local level, is highly decentralized, often ill-trained and ill-equipped to handle white collar crimes, and reluctant to meet the challenge of computer crime. The prosecutorial "turfs" have been defined, the "pecking order" has been firmly established, and incentives to modernize are, at best, minimal. America's prosecutorial machinery is more concerned with quantity than quality; the "body count game" has come to dominate prosecutorial policies. Simply put, prosecutors are more interested in simple and easy cases. They want to demonstrate to their constituencies that they are "doing battle"; the easier the battle, the better. "After all," a prosecutor once told me, "the public doesn't understand anyway."

The business community, however, both within the United States and abroad, can and does exert a powerful influence on politics and government. Yet these powerful constituencies have traditionally paid scant at-

---

[8] For many years, the FBI saw efforts by the U.S. Secret Service to train its own agents in computer crime investigation as a possible threat to the FBI's jurisdiction.
[9] The state attorney general has statewide jurisdiction.

tention to the criminal justice system. The attitude of the businessperson, especially in the United States, has been one of "leave it [criminal justice system] alone, if it leaves you alone." As long as law enforcement poses no threat to the businessperson's interests, he/she chooses to neglect it; it is a forgotten institution. Computer crime, however, is beginning to change this isolation; if the business community wants law enforcement to play a more aggressive role in this area, it must get involved. It must better coordinate its efforts with local and Federal law enforcement; it must also push for law enforcement's modernization. The age of the computer is upon us; the electronic revolution is upon us. The business community, both here and abroad, can and should play a role in shaping tomorrow's police forces.

UNDERSTANDING MODERN CRIMINOLOGY

The function of the present criminal justice system is often defined by the underlying precepts and ideologies that form the core of its foundations. It can be simply defined as that of "maintaining the peace." Like its European counterpart, it does this in three ways:

1. *Punishment.* The old Biblical adage of "an eye for an eye, a tooth for a tooth" still governs the underpinnings of modern criminal justice systems. In brief, criminals are apprehended and punished for their antisocial behavior. As regards computer criminals, however, punishment plays little or no role; electronic thieves are rarely apprehended. Even when discovered, criminal prosecution is not always the norm. Oftentimes, prosecutors shy away from these cases. Victims must resort to their own actions, for example, a lawsuit for damages against a thief, or dismissal from employment, if the thief is an employee of the victim.

2. *Incarceration.* Since antiquity, criminal conduct has often been dealt with by incarceration. By limiting criminals' freedom of movement, society hopes to limit their antisocial behavior. However, societies have traditionally been concerned with crimes by the lower classes; that is, street crimes. The present criminal justice system continues to adhere to eighteenth and nineteenth century policies concerning traditional crimes. Computer criminals are an unknown quantity in this equation; thus they often escape incarceration through a lenient sentence. Most often, computer thieves are placed on probation; courts are more concerned with street crime.

3. *Rehabilitation.* Referred to as the third pillar of the criminal justice system, rehabilitation emphasizes the need to reform criminals. The objective is to change their antisocial behavior. This concept found strong

support with nineteenth century criminologists; they viewed the criminal as a creature of habit. Change those habits, they said, and you change the individual; twentieth century criminology continues to espouse this view. However, the rehabilitative programs and institutions established in the last 40 years have been geared to modify the behavior of street criminals. The white collar criminal was left in a penal limbo; no efforts were made to rehabilitate this type of felon. As the class of computer criminals grows (this is directly connected to the growth and use of computer technology), penologists will have to address the rehabilitative needs of this class. At present, there are no programs to modify the antisocial conduct of the computer criminal.

However, not all antisocial behavior is a violation of criminal law; it may be unethical, but not necessarily illegal. This often escapes the attention of those who have little or no knowledge of the workings of the criminal justice system. Law enforcement often turns away from complex and time consuming cases; it is part of human nature to pursue the "course of least resistance." There are occasions, however, when law enforcement officials will decline to investigate a case because it falls into this "gray area"—the conduct may be unethical, but probably not illegal.

In the area of computer crime, the issue of what constitutes criminal conduct is further clouded by the lack of criminal statutes specifically directed at computer-connected antisocial behavior. However, there are some guidelines that can assist the layperson in identifying computer-related criminal acts. These are:

The conduct in question must be voluntary and intentional.

It must have been committed by someone who is legally capable of committing it (the insane are proved to be incapable of engaging in criminal conduct).

There must be a law, rule, or regulation that specifically makes the conduct in question illegal. Currently, when faced with computer-related abuses, prosecutors are forced to "shop around" for a law that makes the conduct illegal. In large part, this is because many states have yet to enact computer crime legislation.)

There must be a state instrumentality that has been assigned the task of investigating or prosecuting the illegal conduct in question. (Under our Federal system, law enforcement functions are specifically divided among numerous Federal and state/local police agencies. Thus a law enforcement agency may decline to pursue a case for lack of jurisdiction.

For example, the FBI does not have jurisdiction over illegal acts committed in intrastate commerce. These cases are left to the local police.)

Law enforcement action is discretionary. (The decision to investigate or prosecute a case is left to the discretion of police agencies. After having assessed a case, they can refuse to act if they believe the case "lacks merit." The authorities have thus exercised their "prosecutorial discretion" and the victim can do little to change their decision.)

To ensure that this police/prosecutorial discretion will not be abused, the victim would do well to understand the workings of the criminal justice system; this will ensure that its management speaks the same language and understands the politics of the game. However, managers should also be aware that "prosecutorial discretion" is often a catch-all phrase for refusing to handle complex and difficult criminal cases, such as those committed by computer criminals.

In those instances where an individual commits an illegal act, and even admits to having done so, a finding of guilt may not always suffice. The act must have been committed willfully and intentionally; the defendant must have known what he/she was doing. Thus a computer criminal, even if discovered and prosecuted, still has available various defenses that can be raised at the trial. These defenses are used to demonstrate that the culprit lacked the necessary criminal capacity (mens rea) to commit the illegal conduct. Thus you might need to anticipate the following potential defenses:

Mental culpability. The law requires that a defendant be in control of his/her actions at the time of the alleged offense. It must be shown that the accused freely chose to take the steps charged.

Mistake of fact. An individual is relieved of any criminal liability if a mistake negates the mental state required for the commission of the illegal act. For example, if a man enters a neighbor's house thinking it is his, he cannot be convicted of burglary.

Mistake of law. This is treated like a mistake of fact, and is a valid defense where it can be shown it negates the required criminal intent, but a mistake regarding the existence of a law prohibiting a specific act is not in itself a defense. This principle is embodied in the old saying that "ignorance of the law is no excuse."

Entrapment. In any prosecution for an offense, it is an affirmative defense that the defendant engaged in the proscribed conduct because he/she was induced or encouraged to do so by a public servant or someone acting in cooperation with a public servant, who sought to obtain evidence against the defendant for the purpose of criminal prosecution, and that the methods used to obtain such evidence were such as to create a substantial risk that the offense would be committed by a person not otherwise disposed to commit it. However, conduct merely affording a person an opportunity to commit an offense does not constitute entrapment. Thus, if a victim engages in the above, the defense of entrapment could be employed by the defendant; basically, the defendant is telling the court that he/she was tricked into committing the illegal act. The main thrust of this defense is to deter acts by the police or their agents that may cause the commission of an offense by someone who is not ordinarily disposed to commit it. This defense, however, will prove of little value to a person who regularly engages in illegal enterprises. Further, it is universally recognized that certain types of offenses, such as narcotics selling, prostitution, promoting gambling, and the like, would not be prosecutable without some undercover work by law enforcement officials, since the "victim" almost never complains. As long as the undercover conduct does not overstep the bounds prescribed above, the defense is not available. However, active efforts or instigation by a private person, not acting as an agent of the police, is not entrapment. Any business that participates in a "sting operation" or other efforts to assist the authorities should be on guard for this defense.

Infancy. In many jurisdictions, a person less than 16 years of age is held not to be criminally responsible for his/her conduct. In any prosecution of a juvenile, lack of criminal responsibility by reason of infancy is a defense. This defense has already been raised in computer-related crimes where juveniles have been involved; for example, a juvenile who accessed and erased a company's data banks was tried as a juvenile and not an adult.

Renunciation. Prior to the commission of the crime that the defendant facilitated, the defendant makes a substantial effort to prevent its commission. This can be used as a defense in computer crime prosecutions.

Intoxication. This may negate a required mental element of the offense.

Drug addiction. With the widespread use of social drugs in the white collar workforce, this could be used as a defense.

Insanity. This can also be used as a defense.

The criminal justice system is often neither just nor a system. It is a motley of laws, rules, and regulations; many of these are either antiquated or self-contradictory. It has been compared to a game; understanding its rules can often ensure success. Management would do well to understand the rules and politics of this system; it can make the difference between computer criminals being sent to jail or being set free.

HOW CRIMINAL LAW FUNCTIONS

The diversity of the American legal system has given rise to a multitude of laws. Foremost and oldest of these is the common law. It consists of rules and concepts that took root in medieval England; these were later transplanted to the American colonies. The common law is based on customs, traditions, and judicial interpretations (how the courts have interpreted the cases they have heard); it continues to carry weight in state/local courts. The common law, however, fails to address the problem of computer crime.

Many of our laws, especially at the Federal level, are statutory. They have been codified; these are statutes that the Congress or the state legislatures have passed. As regards computer crime, more than a dozen states have enacted computer crime laws. However, many jurisdictions continue to rely on the old criminal statutes to address the problem; this means that prosecutors often face the arduous task of making the crime fit the statute. In part, this is one reason why law enforcement officials are hesitant to tackle computer capers; they are unsure how the courts may interpret the law. One prosecutor put it this way: "I have enough to keep me busy. I don't need to experiment."

Laws, in general, fall into one of two categories: civil or criminal. The former deal with such things as contracts, wills, domestic disputes, and other concerns involving private parties. Civil laws are enforced in the courts by the private litigants themselves; they are not the concern of the public authorities. Criminal laws, however, are the province of the state; these deal with conduct that has been made illegal either by statute or the common law. For example, mail fraud and murder are both illegal acts; the former is a statutory crime and the latter a common law offense. Criminal acts are punishable by both fines and imprisonment; they are enforced by the state.

A criminal act can be one of two types: mala in se; or mala prohibita. The former are offenses that are inherently wrong; the latter are considered wrong because of some specific statute that was enacted to outlaw that conduct. Mala in se crimes are offenses that society considers inherently dangerous; it has outlawed them for its protection. State computer crime laws are mala in se; unlike mala prohibita offenses, computer crimes require an intentional and voluntary act.

Another area of the criminal justice system that often confuses the layperson is the establishment of punishment. Crimes are classified for purposes of punishment as being either felonies or misdemeanors. The former are offenses for which the penalty can be imprisonment for more than one year; they also carry with them fines. Murder, rape, burglary, and arson are examples of felonies. Some crimes, however, can be both; for example, larceny can be either a felony or a misdemeanor. Many state larceny laws have a cut-off point; if the thief steals more than $100 in property, for example, it is considered a felony. If the sum is less than $100, it is considered a misdemeanor in many states.

Most state computer crime statutes make it a felony, often punishable by a small fine and up to five years imprisonment, to use a computer as a vehicle for a criminal act. However, some of these statutes have also adopted the traditional cut-off point; thus some computer capers can be felonies, while others are misdemeanors. For purposes of a prosecution under one of these statutes, if you can demonstrate that the loss exceeded several hundred dollars, you may be able to convict the defendant of a felony; the deterrent will thus be greater.

CONVINCING THE POLICE

Simply discovering you have been the victim of a computer-related fraud is not enough for prosecution. Under the criminal justice system, you must also convince a government investigative agency (police) that the case has merit. If the police are not convinced it does, they will turn it down by simply telling you that the "evidence is inadequate." When it comes to computer capers, some police forces may prove only too happy to turn your case down.

There are several important steps to every police investigation; understanding these can prove most helpful to a victim. It may induce the authorities to take the case. The first important step in every police investigation is the inquiry. At this stage, the authorities simply seek to ascertain:

What happened
The resulting losses, harm, and/or damage
When and how it happened
Potential suspects
Actual and potential victims
Potential violations of the law

The victim should be prepared, even before the police arrive on the scene, to address these. Simplifying the case for the authorities and pointing out the merits of the case may ensure that they will take greater interest in pursuing it.

Once the police are swayed to pursue the case, the investigation then becomes formal. At this stage, the police will want to ascertain such things as:

Motives behind the criminal act

Impact of the act

Motives of potential suspects

Whether there was involvement by more than one person

Role played by insiders (dishonest employees)

Whether a position of trust was abused

Whether the victim has experienced previous similar problems

The evidence at hand

Custody over the evidence

Relevance and materiality of the evidence

Be prepared to assist the police with the above; also make it known that your experts and staff are ready to assist. In addition, identify industry experts who can provide the police with information and other assistance.

Even if the police decide to embark on a formal investigation, there is no guarantee that they will pursue the matter to prosecution; formal investigations often come to a full stop. Limited resources and changing priorities can play a role. Additional inducements may be necessary, especially where the case appears to be complex, time consuming, and the police already have their hands full. These inducements should take the following form:

The case should be comprehensive. Gather as much evidence as possible before you approach the police, and present it clearly to the police; be sure to consult with experts, lest you destroy important evidence or investigative leads. Make sure that a crime has in fact occurred; ensure that it is not the result of an error or malfunction of the system. Also determine the size of the loss.

It helps if the case has sex appeal. The loss should be sufficiently high to make the police feel it is "worth their while"; in addition, the case should be presented in an interesting and simple to understand manner. The authorities are always drawn by the potential news media appeal of a case.

Try to use simple "packaging." If the case appears complex and time consuming, the police may be turned off. Present the evidence in a fashion that is simple, direct, and meaningful. Public servants like to be "spoon-fed." There is little or no inducement for bureaucrats to work long and arduous hours.

You should be ready to prosecute. Assure the authorities that you are prepared to back them all the way, that you will provide witnesses and experts to assist them at trial. If you come across as being lukewarm, this may only serve to alienate the police. They do not want to spend limited resources on a time-consuming investigation, only to be left alone halfway upstream.

Give credit. Make sure that the investigators know you appreciate their efforts; do not hesitate to bring this to the attention of their superiors. Everybody wants to be appreciated; government bureaucrats are no different from their corporate counterparts.

Identify potential suspects. Prepare a list of who these are, their addresses, job descriptions, relationships to your organization, and other characteristics known to you.

Describe crime. Detail for the police how and when the crime was carried out, role of suspect(s), the type of crime (theft of data, unauthorized use, etc.), extent of losses, and other pertinent information.

It is also recommended that you maintain good contacts with your local law enforcement agencies. Inform your key supervisors as to what each of these agencies can do, whom to contact at each agency should the need arise, and the type of assistance each agency can provide. Management often has little or no grasp as regards how law enforcement operates, its policies and needs. Understanding how you can assist them can prove invaluable; oftentimes, success comes from understanding the needs of the other side.

UNDERSTANDING PROSECUTORS

Once a suspect is arrested and charged with an offense, it is the government that bears the burden of proving—beyond a reasonable doubt—that the accused committed the crime in question. The government must convince the court that the defendant did in fact commit the illegal act; it must detail how and when the crime was carried out. In the case of computer capers, this has not always proven easy; in fact, given the complex nature of some of these crimes, the prosecutor runs the danger of confusing the court with many technical details.

In addition, the prosecutor must also charge the defendant with a specific crime; the accused must be told in writing—in the form of an indictment or information—what it is that he/she is alleged to have done wrong. In other words, the defendant cannot be kept in the dark, expected to guess what he/she has done that constitutes a criminal act. In brief, the government bears the burden of detailing its charges to the accused, so that he/she may prepare a defense.

The government also bears the burden of demonstrating to the court's satisfaction that the defendant, beyond any doubt, committed the illegal act. The defendant need only appear at the trial and rebut—if he/she so wishes—the government's evidence and witnesses. The defendant does not have to prove innocence; the burden of proving the defendant guilty beyond a reasonable doubt rests upon the prosecutors. The government must prove, to the satisfaction of the court, all of the charges that it has alleged. In complex financial frauds, this is not always a simple matter; it can prove both expensive and time consuming.[10]

The government faces a number of difficulties in prosecuting complex computer crimes. Some prosecutors will openly tell you that they are not "excited" by the thought of having to prosecute a complex computer caper. The basic problems the prosecutors face are:

Detailing the case.   This must be done in a fashion that is simple and easy for the court to understand. In part, this will depend on the prosecutor's ability to simplify the case and unravel its intricate facts in a simple manner for the court; it will also depend on the sophistication of the court. Since the defendant can request a jury trial, a complex computer caper can confuse a jury of laypersons. The government's witnesses can also play an important part in educating the court and detailing how the caper was pulled off; they can play an important part in educating and assisting the prosecution in preparing its case. Victims, too, can play a key role in this area.

Legal arsenal.   The charges against the defendant must be specified in detail; it must be shown that the conduct in question fits the elements of the crime. For example, if the charge is mail fraud, the prosecutors must show that the defendant used the United States mails in furtherance of the fraudulent scheme. If it cannot be so demonstrated—which can be a too common occurrence—then the court may dismiss the charges.

---

[10] In the majority of computer crime prosecutions to date, the defendant often confessed to the crime and pleaded guilty to a lesser charge at trial. In large part, this is because many of the computer criminals discovered to date have been amateurs.

Since computer capers do not always fit the elements of the traditional criminal laws, this can pose a problem for prosecutors.

Evidentiary concerns.   The government must have the evidence and be able to introduce it at trial; this is not always easy. For example, let us suppose that the accused in a computer caper submitted to a polygraph examination, and the results indicate a strong possibility that the accused committed the crime. This may mean little, however, since these test results may not be allowed into court; courts are reluctant to allow such evidence at trial on the ground that it is not sufficiently trustworthy. Likewise, let us suppose you want to introduce a computer printout in evidence; this may also be difficult since it is not an original document, and the defense may object on the ground that it is not best evidence.[11] Thus getting the evidence admitted is not as easy as it appears.

Witnesses.   The manner in which a witness testifies—and what he/she testifies about—are dictated by various evidentiary rules and procedures. For example, a friendly witness cannot be asked a leading question (i.e., a question that suggests an answer). In addition, government witnesses are open to cross-examination by the defense; the accused can question them as regards their testimony. Witnesses can also have an impact on the court through their bearing, the manner in which they answer questions put to them, and their ability to communicate. Thus witnesses in computer capers should be knowledgeable and familiar with the problem.

Experience.   The level of experience that a judge (and jury) has had with white collar and computer crimes will also affect the outcome of the trial. If the judge (and jury) have had little or no experience with such crimes, the prosecution will face problems. The government may face evidentiary obstacles with a court that lacks an understanding of these crimes; even if conviction does result, the defendant may escape with a "slap on the wrist" (i.e., a mild sentence). Unfortunately, few courts have had any experience in this area; judges are more concerned with street crimes.

Defense.   The impression the defendant and the defendant's counsel make on the judge (and especially the jury) will also be a factor in the outcome of the case. If the judge (or jury) dislikes the defendant, the court could find for the government even though it did not fully grasp

---

[11] This rule prohibits the introduction in evidence of documents that are copies of the original. The rule requires that the original be produced, or that the court be convinced that the copy is an accurate reflection of the original document. The best evidence rule has its roots in the old common law.

the evidence presented it; emotions can sometimes play an important role in criminal prosecutions. However, if the defendant projects an "honest image," this too could affect the outcome. Since courts are accustomed to dealing with street criminals, the polished appearance of a computer criminal could sway them.

Prosecutors face a difficult task in the computer area; courts are swayed by the human element perhaps even more than they are by the law. Judges and juries are, after all, only human. In addition, courts neither understand computer crimes nor view these as serious problems. "Society," they will tell you, "is more threatened by street crime." Thus the victim bears two burdens: convincing the prosecution as regards the merits of its case, and educating the courts as regards the real threat that computer crime poses. As we increasingly become a computerized society, the task will become easier; however, until then, the victim bears part of the responsibility of bringing the computer criminal to justice.

WHAT INFLUENCES PROSECUTORS

Prosecutors, both Federal and local, are political animals; they are often responsive to the pressures and needs of their constituencies. It is the public who, in large part, dictates what their policies will be; the average citizen neither understands nor is concerned with computer crime. It is street crime that has caught the public's attention. Armed robberies are easy to grasp; the harm is visible. The public can sympathize with the victim.

Computer rip-offs, however, often victimize organizations; few citizens will weep upon learning that a corporation or government agency has fallen prey to a computer criminal. Frankly, the corporate world evokes little sympathy; much of the public views it as corrupt. For some, the computer criminal evokes memories of Robin Hood. The computer crime symbolizes the defeat of technology, the supremacy of the human spirit. One prosecutor was blunt: "I lose little sleep over corporate rip-offs."

This, then, is the environment of the prosecutor; they owe their jobs to the community they serve. Unless there is something to be gained, prosecutors may be reluctant to sacrifice sparse resources, possibly alienate their constituency, and embark on a battle where victory is not assured. Like the police, prosecutors often want to be "spoon-fed." They want an easy victory; if the victim can help achieve this, prosecutors will give strong consideration to the case.

Prosecutors, when reviewing a case, are also swayed by a number of other factors. These often deal with the human element. For example:

Age of accused. If the culprit is a teenager (as an increasing number of computernicks are), few prosecutors will want to be bothered. Juveniles make for bad politics. Juvenile proceedings are often closed to the public, and judges are often lenient with young felons. The prosecutor may then conclude that there is no perceived public interest in the case; few citizens will view the teenage computer criminal as a threat to society.

Sex of accused. Judges prove to be more lenient with female felons; female computer criminals stand a better chance of avoiding incarceration than do their male counterparts. Some prosecutors may thus reason: why spend limited resources and personnel on a case if in fact the felon will (at best) receive only a "slap on the wrist."

Previous record. An accused without a prior criminal record is not viewed as being a threat to the community. It is the recidivist who attracts the prosecutor's primary concern—especially the "violent repeater."

Charge. If the laws at hand are ill-suited for the case under scrutiny, most prosecutors would rather walk away from the case. There is little or no incentive to tackle a tough case; prosecutors have more than enough business. "Why take a test case," a prosecutor told me, "which may only set a precedent which can later be cited against me in a similar case." The law must fit the crime snugly.

Witnesses. The more, the merrier. Prosecutors want tight and shut cases. They are not—nor can they afford to be—gamblers. They are under constant public scrutiny and the public has been conditioned to equate success with a large number of successful prosecutions.

Confessions. If the suspect has confessed to the crime, few prosecutors will turn the case away. However, professional criminals are too well versed in the criminal justice system to cry their hearts out; amateurs are not. Thus the majority of convictions in computer-related capers have involved amateurs.

Strength of evidence. The stronger the evidence, the more solid the government's case. Prosecutors, when handling computer-related capers, are concerned with such things as the hearsay and best evidence rules and other evidentiary procedures. Prosecuting "invisible crimes" can prove more difficult than handling crimes where the evidence is simple, visible, and easily understood by the court.

Complaining witness. If the victim is a powerful constituent (for example, a large corporation or other big employer), the prosecutors will be more likely to take some action. In addition, the reputation of the victim may also come into play; prosecutors do not want to become the pawns of corrupt corporations. The victim's reputation for veracity, reliability, and its past record will also have an impact on the prosecutor's decision-making.

Size of loss.   The greater the loss, the greater the "sex appeal" of the case. Few prosecutors will take much interest in a computer caper involving small losses; for example, some Federal prosecutors have an unwritten rule: they will not take on a case unless the losses exceed $100,000.

Resources of accused.   The weaker the accused, the greater the likelihood of prosecution. If the suspect is a corporate competitor, with adequate resources to drag the case out for many years, the prosecutorial machinery may come to a grinding halt. Prosecutors are human; they want easy victories. The point of least resistance will catch their fancy first; it is the amateur computer criminal, who has spent the ill-gotten gains, that will attract them first.

Probability of success.   Winning is the name of the game, and prosecutors (like all lawyers) are trained to win at combat. If the chances of succeeding are high, then all other factors will play a secondary role. An easy victory has strong prosecutorial appeal.

Prosecutors are the doorkeepers of our criminal justice system. Even the best of police efforts will be to no avail if the prosecutor refuses to act. A prosecutor may decline a case by simply falling back on "prosecutorial discretion"; in the final analysis, it is the prosecutor who is the key actor in the criminal justice arena, the one whose views and perceptions of the case will, more often than not, determine whether the computer criminal walks to prison or to freedom. Thus, what a prosecutor looks for in a case can make the difference between a successful prosecution, and none at all. Understanding prosecutorial decision-making can prove of extreme value.

OUTDATED LAWS—NEED FOR NEW LEGISLATION

Even the best investigative and prosecutorial tools are nullified if the criminal justice system lacks adequate laws with which to charge a defendant. An adequate legal arsenal is gauged by the ability of a society's prosecutorial machinery to deter criminal attacks, but criminals will not be deterred by antiquated laws. In the area of computer-related crime, the prosecutor's arsenal is somewhat deficient.

The key weapon in the Federal prosecution of computer capers has been the mail fraud statutes. However, these will not come into play unless the

United States mails are used for the purpose of executing or attempting to execute a fraud, or a scheme to obtain money or property under false pretenses. Thus a computer criminal who makes no use of the mails could easily evade prosecution under the mail fraud statutes. In addition, the postmarked envelope(s) used in the mailing(s) will be needed as evidence that the mails were in fact used; if these are not available, it will be difficult to make a mail fraud case. At best, the mail fraud laws are of limited application.

If a criminal uses the wires in interstate or foreign commerce in a computer-related scheme to obtain money or property under false pretenses, it may be possible to prosecute under the Federal wire fraud statute. A criminal, however, could escape prosecution by simply not using the wires in furtherance of the scheme; in addition, it is no simple matter for the prosecutors to prove that the wires were used. The statute, however, has been employed with some success in a handful of computer caper prosecutions.

The Federal theft statutes are also of limited value, since these apply only to the theft of public money, and often apply only to agencies and corporations in which the Federal government has a proprietary interest. Although government computers would be covered if they were used to steal public funds, those in the private sector would not be covered by these statutes.

Another potent law in Federal prosecutions is the arson statute. It could be used, for example, if a computer facility within a Federal enclave were set on fire, but would be of limited value to the private sector. In addition, although vandalism has been a problem for EDP systems, arson has not.

The conspiracy statute can be employed where two or more persons conspire to defraud the Federal government. It provides for fines of up to $10,000 and/or imprisonment of up to five years. However, the shortcomings of this law are obvious in its reading; it comes into play only when two or more individuals are involved. It is of little value in prosecuting computer capers involving only one individual.

It is a felony to transport and/or receive in interstate or foreign commerce any stolen goods, securities, money, fraudulent state tax stamps, or articles used in counterfeiting. These Federal laws provide for up to $10,000 in fines and/or up to 10 years imprisonment. These statutes are also of limited application in cases involving the transportation and/or receipt of stolen hardware/software. The stolen computer components must cross state or national lines; it is not sufficient for the thief to merely introduce them into interstate or foreign commerce. These laws will prove of little value in cases involving intrastate thefts.

The bank fraud statutes make it a crime to manipulate the records of a Federally regulated financial institution; if a computer were used to carry out the manipulation, these laws would come into play. However, the bank fraud statutes cover only officers, employees, and agents of Federally regulated financial institutions. When the computer caper is committed by an outsider, these laws would prove of limited applicability.

Application of the bank robbery statute may also prove of little value; this statute applies only to one who forcibly takes, or takes with intent to steal, money, property or anything of value from a Federally regulated financial institution. Persons found forcibly taking anything of value can be prosecuted under this law. However, computer capers involve no forcible taking; the crime is often invisible, and the victim may not even be aware that it was ripped off.

Title III of the Omnibus Crime Control and Safe Streets Act makes it a Federal crime to willfully intercept any wire or oral communication; the Act defines "intercept" as the acquisition of the contents of any wire communication through the use of any electronic, mechanical, or other device. One of the Congressional objectives for passing the Act was to safeguard the privacy of an individual's wire and oral communications; however, the Act would not apply if computer communication lines were intercepted. The Act is directed at safeguarding the privacy of oral communications, and not the flow of data between computers.

The Foreign Corrupt Practices Act has been touted as being of some value in computer capers—especially where EDP systems are used to make illegal payments to foreign officials. The Act, however, remains untested in this area; proving that an EDP system was employed to make foreign payoffs will not prove an easy matter.[12]

The Right to Financial Privacy Act makes it illegal for an officer or employee of a financial institution to provide an outsider with access to or information as regards a customer's account. The Act could have application in those cases where the account data is computerized; however, the law comes into play only when the outsider is a government official. It does not cover private parties. Thus it would be of little or no value in cases involving the theft of data by private individuals.

It has been suggested that the Bank Protection Act might possibly prove effective in prosecuting computer capers. The Act requires that Federal financial regulators promulgate rules establishing adequate security procedures. The Senate Report that accompanied the Act recites several reasons for its enactment; these deal with burglaries, robberies, and deaths suffered by bank employees. This law would prove of little value to non-financial institutions, since computer crimes do not result in injury or death to bank employees, nor do they involve violence.

---

[12] It could have possible application when electronic fund transfer systems (EFTSs) are used in foreign payoff, kickback, and bribery schemes.

At the state level, the legal arsenal fares no better. Computer capers committed in intrastate commerce are handled by local prosecutors. However, local prosecutors are—like their Federal counterparts—limited in the criminal laws available to them to handle computer-related frauds, thefts, and abuses.

The statute most often used by local prosecutors is that of larceny.[13] Larceny is committed when: with intent to deprive another of his/her property or to appropriate the same to himself/herself, a person wrongfully takes, obtains, or withholds such property from an owner thereof. The elements necessary for a larceny prosecution are as follows:

Nature of property. This includes money, personal property, or "any article, substance or thing of value."

Ownership of property. This includes any person who has a right to possession thereof, superior to the thief's.

Taking or obtaining. Unless stated otherwise, the thief must obtain dominion and control of the property and carry it away.

Intent. The thief must: exercise control over property permanently or for so long as to acquire the major portion of its economic value, or dispose of it under such circumstances that it is unlikely that an owner will recover it.

The local larceny laws, however, would not prove effective when dealing with insiders or others who enjoy rightful possession of the hardware/software. They also would not apply to the copying of software, or the theft of data. Prosecutors would also face the problem of assessing value; this is important for purposes of charging a defendant with grand as opposed to petit larceny (in many states the cut-off point between the two is $100). However, demonstrating the value of a program, mailing list, marketing plans, or other data can prove difficult.

The local conspiracy laws are also of limited application in computer capers. As with their Federal counterparts, an individual is guilty of conspiracy only when: with the intent that conduct constituting a crime be performed, he/she agrees with one or more persons to engage in or cause the performance of such conduct. Thus an individual cannot be convicted of conspiracy unless at least one other person is involved; in addition, an overt act must be proved to have been committed by one of the conspirators in furtherance of the conspiracy. To prove a conspiracy, the testimony of one of the conspirators is often needed.

---

[13] However, local prosecutors will tell you that the larceny laws are of limited application in computer crime cases.

The theft of services is a misdemeanor in many states; these laws usually cover the following:

Unlawful use of credit cards
Dodging restaurant or lodging charges
Dodging transportation charges
Dodging telecommunication charges
Dodging metered charges
Obtaining utilities without supplier's consent
Using equipment or labor

The theft of services laws, however, would prove of little deterrent value in cases involving computer capers. Even if convicted, the defendant often stands to pay only a small fine and a suspended sentence (up to one year); further, one New York court has already held that the theft of services laws do not cover the unauthorized use of a computer.

The knowing possession of stolen property, with intent to benefit one-self or another than the owner, or to impede its recovery by the owner, is a crime in many states. These fencing laws are directed at middlemen who deal in stolen goods. However, they would prove effective only as regards criminal fences. Proving that the defendant knew the property was stolen can be difficult. The fencing laws have proven of little value, as the black market in high technology goods amply illustrates.

Robbery is a synthetic crime composed of: menacing, attempted assault or assault, plus larceny. It involves a forcible stealing. For example, the defendant uses or threatens the immediate use of physical force upon an-other for the purpose of one of the following:

Preventing or overcoming resistance to the taking of the property or the retention thereof immediately after the taking.

Compelling the owner or another person to deliver up the property or otherwise aid in the commission of the larceny.

However, unless there is a forcible stealing of computer hardware/soft-ware, the robbery laws would prove of no value.

Burglary often requires a breaking and entry, into a dwelling of another, and with the intent to commit a felony therein. The local burglary laws, however, have limited applicability in computer rip-offs, except for those cases where the rightful owner of the hardware/software is burglarized.

Arson is the intentional or reckless damage to a building, by intention-ally starting a fire or causing an explosion. The local arson laws, however, are of little value in computer-related prosecutions, unless the building in which the computer is housed is set on fire or otherwise damaged. The arson statute might have applicability in cases of sabotage or vandalism.

Criminal mischief involves damaging any property belonging to another. These local statutes can be employed in cases where the computer hardware/software is vandalized. To date, however, they have not deterred the computer criminal.

A person who renders criminal assistance to one who has committed a felony may be an accessory after the fact. "Rendering criminal assistance" includes, among other things: harboring, warning, providing means of escaping discovery, or suppressing any physical evidence with intent to hinder discovery of a fugitive who the defendant knows or believes is being sought for the commission of a felony. These laws will prove of little value in computer rip-offs, since the key problem is one of detecting the rip-off and identifying the suspect; few computer felons need to become fugitives. Given the fact that they receive only a "slap on the wrist" when convicted, they have little to fear from the authorities.

Embezzlement is the fraudulent conversion of personal property by a person to whom it was entrusted either by or for the owner. Whereas larceny is an offense against possession, embezzlement is an offense against ownership; the embezzler starts with lawful possession. These local laws have been used with some success in computer capers pulled off by bank tellers, clerks, and other insiders who stole money entrusted to them.

Forgery is the fraudulent making of a false writing having apparent legal significance. The requisites of the offense are: that the writing be of such a nature that it is a possible subject of forgery, that the writing be false, and that it was made false with intent to defraud. Forgeries usually involve writings that purport to be negotiable instruments, deeds, mortgages, bills of lading, wills, written contracts, or receipts. For forgery, it is not sufficient for the writing to tell a lie; the writing itself must be a lie. The forgery laws may prove effective in prosecutions involving "ghost employee" schemes, where the computer is programmed to issue checks to friends and relatives of the criminal. At the Federal level, the U.S. Secret Service has employed the forgery laws with some success, but they prove of no value in direct payment rip-offs.

Counterfeiting is the unlawful making of false money in the similitude of the genuine. Under modern state statutes, it is a felony. Closely associated to such misconduct is the fraudulent making of false foreign coins "current in the United States" or any false "bond, certificate, obligation, or other security of any foreign government," or any false "bank note or bill issued by a bank or corporation of any foreign government." These laws, however, will prove meaningless in a cashless society; the duplication of "electronic blips" cannot be said to be counterfeiting.

More than two dozen states have enacted computer crime legislation in response to the above concerns. Many of these bills are modeled after the first Federal computer crime bill (S.1766), first introduced in the 95th Congress. S.1766 provided for fines of up to $50,000 and/or up to five years imprisonment, for anyone who used or attempted to use:

> . . . a computer with intent to execute a scheme or artifice to defraud, or to obtain property by false or fraudulent pretenses, representations, or promises, or to embezzle, steal, or knowingly convert to his use or the use of another. . . .

The bill went on to define "property" as being:

> . . . anything of value, and includes tangible and intangible personal property, information in the form of electronically processed, produced, or stored data, or any electronic data processing representation thereof, and services.

S.1766 would have closed many of the loopholes found in our traditional criminal laws. It is these loopholes that often make it possible for the computer criminal to escape prosecution. S.1766, however, was not enacted into law.

Many of the computer crime prosecutions that have resulted in convictions have done so because the defendant—oftentimes an amateur criminal, not well versed in the ways of the criminal justice system—chose to plead guilty to a lesser offense. However, with the influx of professional criminals to the computer area, the drawbacks of the present Federal and state/local criminal laws may seriously hinder efforts to prosecute computer capers.

PROCEDURAL AND EVIDENTIARY CONCERNS

Law enforcement, unfortunately, is also faced with procedural and evidentiary-related problems when dealing with complex computer crimes. One area of special concern to the authorities is that of search warrants. The law requires that for a search warrant to be lawful:

It must be as specific as possible as regards the records to be seized.

It must be as specific as possible regarding the time period in question.

It must limit the number of persons whose records are sought.

It must be specific about the location to be searched.

The affiant must be a credible source.

When dealing with computer capers, the authorities may find it difficult to ensure that the search warrant will be specific as to the things to be seized and as to the time of the seizure. In many cases, the authorities may not even know what it is that they may want to seize, nor will they always be able to disclose the number and names of the persons whose records they seek. In addition, they may also be unable to be specific as to the location they want to search. The search warrant thus can face serious legal challenges for being overbroad—in essence, for constituting a "fishing expedition."

In computer crime investigations, the authorities will find it necessary to call on the services of computer experts to assist them in both drawing up the search warrant and in assisting searching for the records. Law enforcement may also find it necessary in some cases to actually shut down the EDP system so that they may conduct their search; this, however, can prove costly and may open the government to civil litigation should they cause damages to the system or its users. EDP systems are sensitive, and can easily be damaged.

When dealing with searches of EDP systems, there is always the possibility that the evidence seized by the police may be damaged or mishandled; if the evidence is to be employed in a prosecution, it cannot be tampered with. If it is altered, modified, or otherwise damaged, the defense may object to its introduction into evidence. For example, if programs or magnetic tapes seized by the authorities are altered or otherwise tampered with—even inadvertently—their evidentiary value will be lost.

Needless to say, the victim should take steps to ensure that its staff is readily available to assist the police, but otherwise it should not interfere with their investigation or tamper with the evidence. Rather, if you have identified valuable evidence, allow the authorities to handle it; they know what the courts want better than the average layperson. The private sector can best assist by cooperating and lending its support and expertise.

Additional procedural-related problems can arise as regards the issuance of subpoenas. These can be challenged by the defense on the grounds that they are overbroad (constituting a "fishing expedition"). Like search warrants, subpoenas must be specific as to persons and records sought; computer experts should be employed by the authorities in drawing them up. You might consider providing your expertise and assistance; limited resources may make it difficult, especially for local police agencies, to retain the services of experts.

The area of electronic surveillance can also pose problems for the authorities. In order to obtain a wiretap order, the authorities must first indicate to the court that:

There is probable cause that an individual(s) has committed, is committing, or is about to commit a crime.

Communications about that offense will be obtained by surveillance.

Those communications will occur at the specified time.

Normal investigative procedures have failed.

To withstand a challenge to its wiretap order, the government must ensure that it is specific as to communications, place, and time. In addition, there is also the potential that in using a wiretap, the authorities may also come across other illegalities, or simply invade the privacy of other system users. Whenever possible, make it known to the police that you are prepared to assist them in this area.

Law enforcement agencies are also faced with evidentiary-related problems in the area of complex computer prosecutions. The present evidentiary rules in many of our states make it difficult to introduce in a trial computer-generated evidence. Local prosecutors face such defense objections as the best evidence rule (which calls for the introduction of the original document into evidence) and the hearsay rule (which excludes oral or written statements made out of the court). Evidence must thus come in under one of the exceptions to these rules. In the case of local prosecutions, introducing computer-generated evidence in a trial can prove to be an acrobatic feat. At the Federal level, however, the new federal rule of evidence has somewhat relaxed these rules at least as regards printouts; these are treated as original records. Thus, given the fact that computers are open to malfunctions, errors, and fraud, the courts have shown a reluctance to admit computer-generated evidence in a criminal trial unless they are convinced as to its authenticity and reliability. It should be added that there is ample justification for this position.

Procedural and evidentiary-related problems as regards computer-connected investigations and litigation will not be easily resolved; the judicial apparatus moves slowly. It may very well be that computer technology may make it necessary to radically reform the manner in which we address litigation. The outcome will depend in large measure on public pressure and the judiciary's willingness to adapt to the changing environment.

TRIAL AND AFTER

Under the Anglo-American legal system, the judge acts as referee. He/she is called upon to decide what evidence will be admitted in a trial, the procedures to be pursued, and often to render a decision on the outcome of these proceedings. Some experts fear that our present judicial apparatus is ill-equipped and ill-prepared to deal effectively with litigation connected to computer technology. Computer crimes will increasingly call for a level of technical expertise that our present judiciary may find difficult to address. Present antitrust litigation amply illustrates this problem.

Critics of the present judicial establishment charge that computer-connected prosecutions will call for both intellect and energies that many of our judges lack; a hardpressed judiciary, bogged down in many of our cities with large backlogs, may also lack the resources to address the problem. Use of computers to assist the judiciary in the difficult task that faces them may prove to be a partial solution; however, whether a tradition-bound institution can sufficiently break with its past to embrace the new remains to be seen.

It should also be borne in mind that America's judicial apparatus is highly fragmented; it is made up of Federal, state, county, and municipal judges. These vary dramatically in both quality and quantity. In addition, most of our judges are accustomed to hearing simple and traditional criminal cases; their exposure to computer-related prosecutions is, for the most part, nonexistent. Complex computer litigation is out of their purview, yet computer technology and the advent of the cashless society have bought these to their doorsteps. The floodgates may burst yet.

Computer facilities are presently located mostly in our large cities, in large part because corporations made these their homes. However, with the growth and use of computer technology, and the corporate trend to move their headquarters into suburbia, EDP facilities will be constructed in all regions of the country: urban, suburban, and rural. Judges in sparsely populated areas, as well as those in our large cities, will increasingly be called upon to hear and decide prosecutions related to this technology. There is a dire need to educate and train judges in the legal nuances of this technology; increased resources will be needed for the judicial machinery.

Compounding the problem of judges is that of our juries. A Maryland case amply illustrated the problem. The case was a simple computer fraud, involving the theft of data. However, Federal prosecutors were fearful that the jury might not understand the technical evidence presented in the trial, that in its confusion, it would find in favor of the defendant. The jury eventually found for the government, simply because it "did not like the defendant." The law played a secondary role.

However, prosecutors stand to face serious problems when confronting juries with these new technological crimes. A group of laypersons may prove unable to grasp the intricacies of complex computer capers. As we move into the cashless society, traditional crimes will become increasingly outmoded; computer capers are the wave of the future. These changing criminal patterns may overwhelm our juries; the intricacies of complex electronic capers may well be beyond the ability of the average citizen to comprehend. We would do well to study the possibility of establishing high technology courts to address these demanding prosecutions; these courts would be manned by a judiciary that is trained in this area. There is precedent in this in the present specialized Federal courts.

Confinement is a last resort; courts often use this only in those cases where the defendant is a recidivist, or one who poses a serious threat to society. Judges and parole boards, when deciding whether to release an individual, look at his/her prior history: employment history, role and status in the community, history of involvement with drugs, prior crimes the individual may have committed, nature of the present crime, and other social/personality traits. This is the traditional penal approach to rehabilitation; the present model is geared (and evolved) to deal with the street (traditional) criminal.

However, some experts ask whether the present penal model can address this new class of (electronic) criminals. Is incarceration the best option available to society when dealing with the computer criminal, or are there other options we should perhaps explore? The truth is that we really do not know how to address the problem; as we increasingly become an electronic society, we should turn our attention to this growing class of criminals.

Computer crimes will increasingly make it necessary for us to revamp our penal system. Personnel in our penal facilities will have to be trained to deal with this class of criminal; our counseling, training, and halfway house programs may have to be modified. Sentencing and parole guidelines may have to be altered. Hard-core computer criminals—especially professional types—may prove especially troublesome. Unless we commence to address the problem, there is a real possibility that with the growth of electronic crime, two types of penal systems may emerge: one for traditional criminals, and the other for computer criminals. Such developments could have a profound impact on our society's democratic fabric.

Our present criminal justice system leaves much to be desired. In many respects, it is outmoded; but it is the "only game in town." We have none other. It needs to adapt to the changing criminology; it is here that the victims (and potential victims) of computer crime can play a role. By coordinating with law enforcement, understanding its needs and politics, and bringing their weight to bear, they can have an input. Victims can assist in the modernization of our criminal justice system. By so doing, they will best prepare it to combat the computer criminal.

CHAPTER 11

How and When
to Use Experts

A study by the General Accounting Office of the U.S. Congress found that: a clerk for the Transportation Department used its computers to steal $800,000; several employees at the Agriculture Department who obtained unauthorized access to the agency's computer banks used the confidential data to perform outside consulting work; and several Internal Revenue Service employees entered fictitious returns into a computer to collect tax refunds.

Not to be outdone, a hospital employee bilked his employer in a computer caper to the tune of $40,000. A multinational corporation fears that a competitor may have sabotaged its computers, and an advertising agency alleges that someone rigged its computer to spin out more than $20 million in bogus revenue.

Unlike traditional thieves, the computer criminals make use of a very sophisticated technology to rip off their victims. In many cases, the victims may not even be aware that they have been taken; the police are often ill-prepared to investigate those crimes. Even many of the corporate giants lack the needed in-house resources to prevent and detect these invisible capers; relying on in-house security personnel alone may not be adequate.

The computer crime expert has thus become an increasingly important component of the war against the electronic thief. Neither government nor the private sector can do without the services of these experts; technological crimes make it necessary to use these resources. However, knowing when and how to select an expert may not always prove easy. Who to select, the type of contract to enter into, and how best to manage the expert requires that management itself understand the role of experts as well as when and how to best use their talents. As crimes by computer become more sophisticated, the need for experts, both in the private and public sectors, will increase.

WHY THE NEED?

Computers have been employed by criminals in numerous ingenious ways to rip off both business and government. The techniques may vary from the simple to the highly complex. For example, experts might be used to unravel how thieves use computers to:

Reroute freight, cargo, or rolling stock.

Tamper with fuel allocations.

Carry out illegal betting schemes.

Keep records of personal businesses.

Play games.

Pull off complex financial frauds, create phony assets, embezzle funds, or steal payrolls.

Alter corporate records.

Destroy or steal a competitor's marketing plans, programs, mailing lists, or other valuable business-related data.

Issue phony bills, collection notices, or other bogus paper instruments that are used to deceive.

Computers can be either the targets of criminals or the vehicles for the commission of a crime. An expert can assist in identifying and understanding whether the computer was:

The object of the unlawful act. Here the objective of the criminal is to destroy, damage, or hold for ransom the computer, any of its components, the data stored within it, or the system itself.

The subject of the illegality. The computer is employed to store illicitly gained assets or data with the purpose of using them later.

The instrument of the thief. In this instance, the computer is used to fabricate records, assets, or payments for nonexistent services and nonexistent employees.

The symbol of the crime. The computer is used to create phony records, which may then be used to deceive the victim.

The above can prove of extreme value to both investigators and prosecutors.

HOW THE EXPERTS CAN HELP

Computer crime investigations can pose a problem for both in-house security personnel and also public law enforcement. Both the private and public sectors, unfortunately, have neglected to develop investigatory resources and tools in this area. The expert, however, should be able to assist in:

Detecting the crime. Because computer-related crimes are often invisible (for example, they may involve the manipulation of data), their detection can prove difficult for laypersons; their discovery is usually accidental. However, even when discovered, it is no easy matter to detail how the crime was committed, or to prove who did it. The expert can prove invaluable in both detecting the crime and zeroing in on suspects.

Compiling evidence. Our criminal justice system is oriented toward prosecuting paper-based (visible) crimes. However, because many computer-related crimes often take the form of manipulating "electronic impulses," the investigator faces a host of evidentiary obstacles; paramount among these is the problem of seizing and preserving the physical evidence. The hardware and software, unless properly handled, can be damaged, thus destroying the evidence. The expert, however, can assist by identifying the evidence, assisting in the search and seizure, and also in preserving the evidence.

Addressing inadequate laws. Only a minority of the states have computer crime statutes on their books—the Federal government does not. Law enforcement is forced to rely on traditional criminal laws to prosecute computer crimes. This is not always easy; it has been compared to forcefully fitting the foot in the shoe. The expert can assist the authorities in both identifying and fitting the elements of offense into one of these traditional criminal statutes.

Technical know-how. Computer technology brings with it its own jargon. The expert can be instrumental in simplifying the nature of the operation so that a layperson can understand how the crime was committed.

The expert can also play several additional roles, proving instrumental in:

Identifying the extent of the losses (this is not always easy).

Detailing how the crime was committed.

Explaining the time, effort, and level of sophistication needed to commit the crime.

Coordinating with the police.

Discovering any other computer crimes.

Uncovering the jurisdictional lines involved in the offense.

Zeroing in on any remote computer terminals or telephone hookups that may have been used.

Determining if the crime was an inside job.

Detailing the level of technical skill needed to commit the crime.

Uncovering potential motives.

Assisting law enforcement in identifying the suspect.

Gathering and preserving the needed physical evidence.

Zeroing in on the audit trail.

Ensuring that the evidence stored in the memory core and magnetic tapes is not altered, destroyed, or tampered with.

Assisting prosecutors in gaining the admission of printouts and magnetic tapes (these are viewed by the courts as copies and originals) in evidence at a trial.

Outlining the technical nature of the crime.

In a highly complex industrial society, the expert assumes an important role. In the area of computer criminology, the expert can be instrumental in assisting both victim and the authorities; it should be remembered that the police are often no better prepared than the victim to address these crimes.

WHO THE EXPERTS ARE

The growing complexity of computer technology may make it necessary to call on more than one expert for assistance. Not all experts are "experts" in every facet of computer crime. The type of expert you need may vary with the nature of the offense; in addition, it will also be necessary for the expert to retain the services of others. However, in general, an expert is someone who has one or more of the following attributes:

Has special skills or knowledge in a particular field

Is a specialist

Possesses special authority

Is trained by practice

Is experienced

Has a peculiar knowledge on certain subjects

When selecting an expert to assist you, be sure that you have selected one that matches your needs. Oftentimes, dissatisfaction with the expert stems from hiring the wrong person for the task. Match your expert to the task at hand; for example:

Applications programmer. This expert should be employed to design, develop, debug, install, maintain, and document applications programs.

Communications engineer/operator. Use one of these experts to advise you in the areas of communications equipment, including concentrators, modems, and line switching units.

Computer scientists. This expert is of value in matters dealing with electronics and programming.

Security specialist. Use this expert to evaluate, plan, and assist in implementing and maintaining a physical and personnel security program.

EDP auditor. This specialist can prove valuable in reviewing and determining the integrity, adequacy, performance, and security of a computer system.

Facilities engineer. Use one of these experts to inspect, repair, modify, or replace equipment used in your computer operation.

Peripheral equipment operator. This is an expert who can review data input and output functions.

Programmer. This specialist can assist in reviewing the design, writing, and testing of a computer program.

Programming manager. This person is valuable in checking the design, development, and maintenance of computer programs.

Systems analyst. Let this expert review and analyze your system's requirements, specifications, and design activities.

Systems engineer. This specialist can check the design, testing, and repairing of system's devices and components.

Technical engineers. This expert can test, diagnose, assemble, and disassemble the system's components.

Forensic scientists. This person's services are valuable in analyzing the software, hardware, printouts, or the physical evidence.

Document examiner. This is an expert who can determine from which computer printer a particular printout came.

Experts come from a number of sources. Who their employer is often determines the value of their services. They can come from:

The private sector.   These experts are usually retained by a private organization or person to assist in either establishing a security program or in investigating possible illegal acts. The expenditures are borne by the contracting party.

The government sector.   These specialists are provided by a government agency to assist the victim in investigating the potential crime; because the expert is a government employee, the findings will be referred to the agency and not the victim. The latter exerts no control over this expert.

The victim organization (or person).   In this case, the victim itself provides its own expert(s) to assist the police in their investigation. The expert works for and is paid by the victim. Increasingly, it is becoming necessary for victims to retain their own experts.

The manufacturer.   In some cases, the computer manufacturer or service organization may provide its experts to assist the victim in the investigation. The expert is an employee of the manufacturer or the computer service organization.

The court.   The expert is appointed and paid for by the court, and is therefore the court's agent and under its control.

SELECTING THE RIGHT EXPERT

A large organization, oftentimes, has some expert resources within its own staff. Smaller firms, however, are forced to look for outside assistance. Irrespective of the size of your organization—whether it be a corporation or government agency—you should call on the services of an expert whenever:

The case is too complex for the in-house staff.

Your in-house personnel lack the needed technical expertise.

The in-house resources are stretched too thin.

Your security office requests such assistance.

The case is of an extremely sensitive nature.

Physical and budgetary considerations make it necessary.

Local police/prosecutors lack the capability and needed resources.

Whenever you select an expert to assist your in-house staff, always consider a number of factors, among them:

Cost.   Is it worth the expenditure?

Need.   What level of expertise do you need?

Sophistication.   What is the level of sophistication of the caper, and how sophisticated an expert do you need?

Personality.   Can the expert get along with your in-house staff?

Competence.   Is the expert a specialist in the specific area your case involves?

Funds.   Have you budgeted for the expert?

Laws.   Does the expert meet the licensing and registration provisions of the jurisdiction?

An expert's qualifications are often a key element in the selection process. There are two reasons for this: first, if your case ends in civil litigation, the expert's credibility on the witness stand will depend in large part on his/her credentials; and second, if a criminal prosecution ensues, the authorities will call on your expert to assist them. The weight of the government's case may easily hinge on your expert's qualifications.

Thus, when selecting an expert, check the following:

License or certification held.

Academic credentials.

Level of training.

Continuing education.

Books and articles authored.

Any teaching and lecturing.

Professional associations connected with, and office held in them.

Professional recognition in the form of awards.

Prior consulting.

Level of ethical conduct.

Professional reputation in field.

Quality of previous services.

Professional bearing and demeanor.

Work habits.

Ability to articulate a position.

Mannerism.

Personal behavior.

Ability to get along with others.

Level of trustworthiness and integrity.

Presence before a jury.

BIG VERSUS SMALL

A question I am often asked at my lectures is whether an organization should select a large as opposed to a small firm of experts. There are advantages to both; size is not always an indication of talent. In fact, some of the worst and more expensive experts have found safe havens in large firms. When faced with the problem of size, consider the following:

Advantages of large firm.   It can handle the larger projects, and also has more technical resources and staff to draw upon. It also may be able to provide more support services.

Advantages of small firm.   It can achieve a higher level of interaction with the client, red tape is minimal, and its reaction time is less. It also has a smaller overhead and can pass these savings to you.

Specialized services.   Most firms tend to specialize. Thus, when selecting a firm, specialization rather than size may be the determining element.

The above considerations should also be weighed against your organizational needs and resources.

Another perennial question I am asked is: "Where and how can I find the expert I need?" To this, there are no easy answers. The computer security industry is still in its infancy—the first computer caper surfaced in the mid-1960s. However, there are some general sources you should contact, among them:

Trade associations

Professional groups

Police (Federal, state, and local) agencies

In-house security personnel

Licensing and certification bodies

Professional contacts

Manufacturers/vendors

Service organizations

Other victims
Universities and colleges
Research centers
Noted authorities

Selecting an expert in the computer crime area is not always an easy task. However, the above guidelines should make your task easier.

The expert can and should be used in a number of functions. He/she can assist in the following computer-crime–related investigations:

Cases involving the malicious destruction of hardware or software.
Industrial sabotage, espionage, extortion, and vandalism.
Frauds involving the computer.
Diversions and theft of property through the use of the computer.
Unauthorized use of the computer.
Development and implementation of a security program.
Preparation of a civil or criminal prosecution.
Outlining patterns of computer abuse in a given industry.
Developing a profile of the computer felon.
Identifying complex computer-related abuses.
Outlining the organization's vulnerabilities.
Assisting in the drawing up of a search warrant or subpoena.
Interviewing and interrogating witnesses and suspects.
Anticipating potential defenses at trial (civil or criminal).
Assisting in pretrial discovery.
Advising on cross-examination of the other side's experts.
Giving technical testimony in trial.

MANAGING THE EXPERT

Once brought on board, the expert should be integrated within the organizational framework. However, because the expert is an outsider and because of professional and personality considerations, this may not always be easy to accomplish. However, there are some general guidelines that can assist you in managing your expert; these are as follows:

1. Assign to someone on the staff the specific responsibility for guiding and directing the expert.

2.   Set out in writing the level of compensation to the expert. This should include:

    a.   Fee arrangement
    b.   Work schedule
    c.   Deliverables
    d.   A payment plan

3.   Specify the preexisting standards and specifications to which the work product should adhere.
4.   Establish quality controls.
5.   Review and approve all work products.
6.   Always take note of security considerations.
7.   Check out your expert's credentials.
8.   Consider Federal, state, and local laws and regulations.
9.   Establish a good working relationship with the expert.
10.   Encourage an atmosphere of trust.
11.   Integrate the expert within the team.
12.   Detail specific duties and obligations in a written agreement.
13.   Specify in advance the scope of the expert's tasks.
14.   Be specific as to the expert's role.

The services the expert is to provide should always be set out in writing; this should include the terms and conditions of your agreement. The agreement should incorporate, among other things, the following:

A provision regarding the periodic reporting requirements.

A provision that the consultant keep confidential any information that he/she comes across in this line of work (e.g., trade secrets or confidential marketing plans).

A provision that corrective action will be taken in the event of nonperformance, unsatisfactory, or late performance.

A provision for the modification of the agreement.

Specification of the nature and extent of the work to be performed.

A schedule for performance of services.

Specific deadlines for deliveries of work products.

The name of the official who will provide guidance and direction to the expert.

The level of compensation.

A provision that payment will depend on acceptance of the work product.

A provision that an official will be assigned to specify satisfaction after completion of each task.

The financial arrangements should always be set out in writing; avoid verbal agreements. The agreement should consider the following:

Period of time for which you will need the expert's services.

Place where the work will be performed.

In-house resources available to the expert.

Whether the training of in-house staff is part of the expert's services.

Acknowledgment by the expert that he/she has reviewed the project in its entirety prior to its commencement.

Definition of the problem, scope, and the objectives of the task.

Details of the estimated cost of the project.

Specification of the project timetable.

A provision for timely completion of the project.

Specification of the role of each expert.

Do not expect the impossible from your expert. Oftentimes, an organization that has been victimized—or fears that it may be a potential target—places unrealistic expectations on the expert. This often causes friction between the two sides and may even result in litigation. Consider the following:

Avoid unreasonable demands.

Do not expect miracles or overnight successes.

Be sensitive to the morale of the in-house staff.

Expect no more or no less than you would from your doctor.

Insure that the expert does not become a fixture within the organization.

Keep the expert's role simple and at arms' length.

Do not be oversold.

Always consult with your staff.

Invite recommendations by your in-house staff.

Afford the expert the needed cooperation.

Do not make the expert your scapegoat.

Reserve to management all final decisions.

MATCHING EXPERTS AND TASKS

Before you go out and retain the services of an expensive expert, there are
two questions that should come to mind: first, do you really need an expert
for the task; and second, is this expert the right person for the task? The
first is not always difficult to answer; the second can pose a problem. Match-
ing the right expert to the task may not always prove easy. However, there
are some simple guidelines that can assist you; these are as follows:

> *Detecting crimes.* For these tasks, you should employ EDP auditors,
> data base managers, forensic scientists, computer security specialists, or
> experienced computer crime investigators.
>
> *Understanding systems.* Retain the services of EDP auditors, security
> specialists, systems analysts, data base managers, programmers, com-
> puter users, and/or manufacturer/vendor representatives.
>
> *Coordinating with police.* Employ systems analysts, EDP auditors,
> electronics engineers, data providers, and/or experienced computer
> crime investigators.
>
> *Interrogating the suspect.* Assign this task to experienced computer
> crime investigators, EDP auditors, and/or computer security specialists.
>
> *Preparing for litigation.* Use EDP auditors, experienced computer
> crime investigators, forensic scientists, and/or security specialists.
>
> *Detailing the operation.* Retain computer scientists, programmers, sys-
> tems analysts, and/or EDP auditors.
>
> *Investigating the crime.* Make use of manufacturer/vendor represen-
> tatives, EDP auditors, forensic scientists, and/or experienced computer
> crime investigators.
>
> *Zeroing in on criminal.* Employ experienced computer crime investi-
> gators, systems analysts, EDP auditors, and/or security specialists.
>
> *Identifying and collecting evidence.* Use data base managers, pro-
> grammers, operators, forensic scientists, security specialists, EDP audi-
> tors, systems analysts, and/or experienced computer crime investigators.

LEGAL CONSIDERATIONS

Whenever you open your data processing center to an expert, remember
that you are also opening up your organization, its clients, trade secrets,
plans, decisions, and other valuable data to outside scrutiny. Thus there are
a number of legal considerations that you should be cognizant of; these

oftentimes are imposed by Federal, state, and/or local laws and regulations. A failure to abide by these could result in legal liabilities.

The manner in which you employ and utilize the talents of the outside
expert is, oftentimes, dictated and regulated by law. From the start, both
you and your expert should have a full understanding of these obligations.
Once retained, the expert becomes your agent; his/her acts can open both
of you to a lawsuit. Thus, in writing, inform the expert of these obligations.[1]
Among other things, this document should consider:

1. *Potential disclosures.* These can open your organization to a lawsuit under one or more of the following:

   a. Trade Secrets Act
   b. Federal Privacy Act
   c. State privacy laws
   d. Fair Credit Reporting Act
   e. Right to Financial Privacy Act
   f. Family Educational Rights and Privacy Act
   g. Medical statutes and regulations
   h. Statutes and regulations dealing with arrest records

2. *Violations of special privileges.* There are a number of privileges
under the law that enjoy special safeguards; violating these could open
your organization to a lawsuit. These include:

   a. Attorney/client privilege
   b. Doctor/patient privilege
   c. Psychologist/client privilege
   d. Clergy/penitent privilege

3. *Abuses of confidential data.* Such conduct is often prohibited
under:

   a. Federal, state, and local laws
   b. State trade secret laws
   c. Federal and state privacy laws and regulations

4. *Privacy considerations.* Since the expert will have access to trade
secrets, confidential financial files, and other privacy-related data, it should
be clearly stated that the information should not be misused. In addition,

---

[1] It is also a good idea for you to have the expert sign some type of statement,
whereby he/she acknowledges these obligations.

you should inform the expert that, in order to limit any potential legal exposure, you may have to:

a. *Screen the expert and/or his/her staff.* This would be to insure that the expert is trustworthy and of good character. Among the things you would look for are the following:
Previous experience with sensitive cases.
Potential conflicts of interest.
Personal and professional ethics.
Trustworthiness.
Respect for privacy of others.
Previous history of unauthorized disclosures or abuses.

b. *Specify security guidelines.* In writing, detail your security guidelines and the need for compliance with them by the expert and/or his/her staff. These guidelines should detail the following:
Access to confidential data should only be on a need-to-know basis.
The expert should provide an affidavit, agreeing not to abuse/misuse any data.
The expert will assign a person from his/her staff to insure compliance.
The expert's activities and contacts will be monitored.
The expert will comply with periodic checks of the work.

5. *Breach of contract liability.* The expert should also be informed that any breaches of the contract by the expert or his/her staff will make the expert liable for any counsel and court-related expenses that you incur.

6. *Liability for negligence.* State that any injuries arising out of the expert's conduct or that of his/her staff will make the expert liable for all resulting damages.

7. *Definition of legal exposures.* The specific responsibilities and obligations of the expert should be set out in writing. The written agreement should incorporate provisions dealing with:

a. Any illegal acts carried out by the expert and his/her staff.
b. Misuse/abuse of the confidential data.
c. Liability for privacy invasions.
d. Liability for unlawful disclosures.
e. Liability for breaches of special privileges.
f. Liability for violation of any Federal, state, and/or local laws and regulations.

EMPLOYING THE EXPERT IN LITIGATION

Oftentimes, because of the technical nature of computer crimes, the expert can play a key role in detailing and explaining the fraud to lawyers/prosecutors. Use of experts in criminal prosecutions has become increasingly common and necessary; few such prosecutions could be carried out without their services.

The role of experts in a criminal litigation is multifold. They can serve various functions; among these, they can:

Detail the illegal conduct.

Demonstrate how the security measures were bypassed.

Demonstrate how the system was compromised.

Detail key findings of the investigation.

Provide litigation support.

Provide expert testimony.

Assist in developing an overall theory of the case.

Advise on known patterns of computer crime.

Suggest questions for cross-examination.

Provide general support in preparing for trial.

Provide technical assistance.

Testify before a grand jury.

Interpret evidence.

Assist in preparation of subpoenas.

Assist in the indexing of case evidence.

Explain intricacies of a case.

Analyze evidence.

Authenticate the physical evidence.

Assist in anticipation of defense strategies.

Lay foundation for admission of computer-generated evidence.

Answer hypothetical and factual questions.

Advise as to questions to ask on redirect.

Review trial strategy.

Assist in preparing exhibits.

Assist in preparation of witnesses.

Review transcripts of testimony.

Assist in rehearsal for cross-examination.

Screen and review other side's evidence.

Assist in drafting opening statement.

Assist in identifying competence of opposing expert witnesses.

However, if you plan to have your expert testify at the trial, check out all credentials. Quiz the expert regarding:

1. Educational qualifications:

   a. Basic background in computer area
   b. Advanced degrees held
   c. Special training courses, seminars, or other studies taken

2. Teaching experience (if any):

   a. Name of institution(s)
   b. Number of years
   c. Academic rank
   d. Subjects taught

3. Professional experience:

   a. Apprenticeship(s)
   b. Years of active experience
   c. Associations with government agencies, police departments, and the like
   d. Positions of responsibility
   e. Court appearances
   f. Specific experience in subject matter of present testimony

4. Proof of authorship:

   a. Lectures
   b. Articles in learned journals
   c. Books on specialty

5. Honors or recognition.
6. Membership in professional groups:

   a. Offices held
   b. Length of membership

If the expert does not qualify regarding the above, his/her expertise may prove of limited value for purposes of testifying at the trial.

The assistance of experts in computer crime cases is not a luxury; rather, it has become a necessity. Many computer capers have become too complex and sophisticated for the lay in-house security staff to handle. In addition, knowing how to use and manage an expert, what to expect from him/her, and how to integrate the expert's input in an investigation or prosecution can play a key role in preventing crimes by computer. The expert is an indispensable tool in any successful computer-related security program, investigation, and/or prosecution. Learning how and when to best employ this resource could prove of immense value to your organization.

CHAPTER 12

Basics of
Risk Assessment

A California company had spent several hundred thousand dollars on its new EDP system, only to find that a rainstorm put it out of operation. A New York company found its operations crippled when fire damaged its computer center, while a government agency found that lightning had damaged its tape library.

The above serve to illustrate a common, and often little spoken about EDP-related problem: planning for disaster recovery. Every organization is vulnerable; all EDP systems can suffer a setback. The unexpected can and does occur; only by planning for it will you ensure your system's survivability. Planning to meet potential threats and risks head on will ensure that your organization will pick up the pieces and continue to function.

ASSESSING POTENTIAL THREATS/RISKS

Risk assessment or analysis entails determining the probability that your EDP system will survive when faced with specific threats/risks. It is a vehicle that can be employed to anticipate potential losses from some adversity; if properly utilized, it can serve to analyze specific threats. It will also identify those system components that are most vulnerable. Every organization, large or small, should plan for such threats/risks; it should also determine its ability to recover its EDP capability.

In planning for EDP-related disaster recovery, management should first, among other things, consider the following:

Environment. This involves reviewing and analyzing threats to the environment in which your EDP system operates. Not all environments are the same. For example, the problems management faces in a high crime urban environment differ radically from those it would face in a rural setting.

Personnel. The quality and quantity of the people who operate your system will vary. This should thus be considered, keeping personnel-related problems in mind.

Communications. Review the type and extent employed by your system.

Storage. The ability of an EDP system to recover will depend on the available stored reserves.

Practices. Review the procedures employed to operate your system. You will find these vary from organization to organization.

Industry. Not all industries have the same needs. The resources needed to recover will, in part, depend on your industry.

Laws and regulations. Since these may dictate the types of safeguards and plans that you can implement, be careful to check them out. A disaster recovery plan is worth little if laws prohibit its implementation.

Once you have made a determination to implement a disaster recovery plan, you should next consider:

Objective. Even before you embark on the plan, be specific as to what is expected of it; in addition, all participants should be told from the beginning what their function, role, and end product should be. Well-defined objectives will ensure a well-functioning plan.

Scope and resources. Determine the extent of your needs and organizational resources needed to meet them; also what your plan will cover, who it will cover, and the zeal of your commitment. Give also some consideration to the threats and risks you anticipate.

In-depth planning. Your recovery plan should be well thought out, adequate preparation should be made, resources should be set aside, and all serious obstacles should be considered.

Project manager. All recovery plans should have an overall manager to oversee, coordinate, and supervise the needed operations. Determine and assign that task to a specific individual; someone must be responsible for ensuring the proper functioning of the plan.

Team effort. Select only those individuals who can make a contribution to the plan; they should bring with them some form of expertise. The team members should be highly qualified, knowledgeable, and committed to the project; halfhearted attempt can stop your efforts in their tracks.

Necessary documentation.   Provide all participants with written documentation as regards your EDP system.

Adequate support.   Provide your recovery planning group with all the cooperation and resources it will need. This may involve overcoming some opposition from other departments; the recovery planning group must be assured of the necessary organizational support and backing.

Knowledge of the system.   Be sure to include in your group individuals who are familiar with your EDP system. Be sure to involve, minimally, auditors, security officers, and EDP managers.

Weighing benefits.   Give serious consideration to whether the resources, work-hours, and other related expenditures are really worth the benefits. Avoid the "overkill" approach, and use your energies wisely.

Additionally, your disaster recovery plan should be comprehensive in its analysis. It should address both intentional and natural phenomena that pose a threat to your system. You may decide not to implement safeguards as regards these potential risks; that is a policy question. You should, however, give them consideration in your planning stage.

The planning group should analyze, at the minimum, the following potential threats/risks to your system:

Criminal acts.   These can take the form of sabotage, vandalism, or some other illegal conduct; they are committed knowingly and willfully by one or more persons.

Accidental conduct.   This results from human error, negligence, or failures in the system caused by some system malfunction.

Acts of God.   These are natural occurrences viewed as being outside the scope of human intervention.

Fire.   This can be either intentional or accidental.

Flooding.   This can also be intentional or accidental.

Defects in plumbing.   Bursts in the pipes can cause severe floodings.

Power.   Failures or other irregularities can shut down your system.

Air conditioning.   Consider the costs of standby systems in case of a breakdown.

Ventilation outage.   Consider backup equipment, its cost, and/or spare parts to fix the original.

Magnetism. Since this can affect data stored in the system, determine if any machinery or equipment in the area produces magnetic fields.

Electrostatic fields. Determine if atmospheric conditions in the area can cause such problems.

Radio frequencies. Since radar and high-powered transmitters can blow out microcircuit chips, consider using inexpensive screens to guard against them.

Line interferences. Guard against faulty lines.

Line failures. Take these into consideration and provide for backup.

Ionic problems. Atmospheric ions can interfere with the health of your EDP staff.

Program failures. Anticipate intentional or accidental changes, deletions, malfunctions, or destruction of the software.

Hardware failures. Weigh the replacement cost, maintenance costs, and leasing costs.

Access codes. Consider the possibility of their accidental loss or theft.

Data loss. Consider procedures to safeguard the data.

The ability to anticipate threats/risks to your EDP system, will determine whether your EDP operations will continue to operate successfully or shut down. It can sometimes make the difference between organizational survival or disaster; in the age of computer technology, few large organizations could long survive if their EDP systems ceased to operate. Thus determine the potential threats/risks to your system and attempt to address them.

OBJECTIVES OF THE RISK ASSESSMENT

Risk assessment may be defined as a vehicle for analyzing the vulnerabilities, applications, assets, and threats to the EDP system. It is also employed to determine the potential losses the system can suffer as a result of an array of potential threats. In addition, it reviews the probability that any of these events will occur. Thus the role of a risk assessment analysis is to:

Define the potential risks to the system.

Estimate the probability that these risks will materialize.

Determine the system's exposure to these risks.

Implement effective controls to address these risks.

Carry out a cost-benefit analysis of these potential problems.

The risk analysis should also encompass several other matters. Among these, it should:

Analyze the time, effort, and resources both available and necessary to address the problems.

Determine your assets.

Analyze your applications.

Carry out a threat and vulnerability assessment.

Identify, define, and review your controls.

Identify, select, and maximize those controls.

The risk assessment should also incorporate a detailed analysis of your assets. This analysis should:

Identify the value of the property.

Assess the costs of recovery.

Estimate the value of the system resources.

Include all EDP assets.

Make an inventory of all assets.

Determine the costs that can result from the potential losses.

Weigh the replacement costs.

Consider the repair of any damage suffered by the system.

Analyze the replacement of the lost assets.

Consider the restoration of services.

Consider the relocation of the facility.

As regards the threat and vulnerability analysis, it should:

Identify the sources, scope, methods, and outcome of potential threats.

Estimate the probability of each occurrence.

Identify potential weaknesses in your system.

Analyze all types of threats and vulnerabilities.

Identify potential exploitable vulnerabilities (technical, physical, and administrative).

Identify your existing defenses.

Identify the necessary controls.

Limited resources, however, place limits on an organization's ability to detect and identify the vulnerabilities of its EDP system. But you can nevertheless take steps to minimize the potential threat of loss. These should, whenever possible, be taken:

Prior to the approval and design of your system.

Whenever there are any significant changes to the physical facility or hardware/software.

At periodic intervals (commensurate with the sensitivity of the data processed and the importance of your system).

To establish contingency plans (to provide you with reasonable continuity should your system fail to operate in a normal fashion).

In developing appropriate countermeasures to address the many threats to the system, you should consider the following:

You will never be able to address all of the threats faced by the system.

The human element will introduce unpredictable factors into your equation.

You will only be able to address specific and limited numbers of threats to the system.

Those in charge for operating the system should be well versed as regards their specific responsibilities.

Management should be knowledgeable as regards the system.

You should consider the geographic location in which your system is situated.

You should remember the possibility of the threat repeating itself.

You should be certain you have assigned some monetary value to the loss (take into consideration inflation and its replacement value).

You should determine specific threats to specific components of the system.

You should set priorities as to which system components (programs, assets, structures, etc.) warrant the greatest consideration.

You should zero in on those security measures and controls that are most effective for the dollar.

Your system should be reviewed and tested periodically; update the potential risks and the magnitude of the damage that your system could sustain without disruption. Also prepare a list of individuals and resources that you can tap. The risk analysis should also define the magnitude of the disastrous event that could put your system totally out of operation.

A systematic risk assessment ensures that you have reviewed and analyzed all potential eventualities, that you have also explored potential solutions to these problems. It is a valuable vehicle for identifying the vulnerabilities and potential risks to the system, as well as the safeguards your system will need to continue its operations. See Table 1.

TABLE 1   THREAT ASSESSMENT MATRIX[a]

	Acts of God	Criminal Acts	Accidental Acts
Data security			
Software security			
Hardware security			

[a] Details potential threats to the EDP system from three key sources: acts of God, which include all types of natural phenomena; criminal acts, which include such things as thefts of data, fraud, espionage, sabotage, and so on; and accidental acts, which include such things as errors in the input, accidental destruction of the software, hardware failures, and others. By drawing the above matrix, and analyzing your system's potential vulnerabilities, you are sure to better prepare for potential threats to its integrity and continuing viability.

GUARDING AGAINST INTRUDERS

Guarding against intruders constitutes an effort to measure the potential losses that can result from numerous human-connected threats. These risks are often measured in terms of cost, inconvenience, impact on the ability of the organization to continue providing its services, and also its ability to survive these threats. Every risk assessment involves three basic steps; it assesses: the value of the asset to the organization; the value of the asset to the intruder (where the threat is caused by human intervention); and the probability that the threat will materialize.

The value of an asset to the organization is often measured in terms of:

Replacement cost
Extent of the losses of services

As regards the value of an asset to an intruder, this can take any of various forms. For example:

Economic benefits that accrue to the intruder.

Value of the stolen property.

Extent of the unauthorized use of the system.

Psychological gratifications to the intruder (for example, fulfillment of a need for revenge for some perceived wrong).

Espionage by a competitor.

Since threats can materialize, you should take steps to estimate the probability that an intruder will attempt to exploit vulnerabilities or weaknesses in your system. The probability can be determined by analyzing:

Past attacks involving the system

Criminal history of system personnel

Statistics computed by insurance companies

Industry history

Industry projections

ASSETS AND APPLICATION ANALYSIS

Once the risk assessment analysis has been completed, you should turn your attention to the assets analysis. The latter entails the preparation of a list of all the equipment in your EDP center; the analysis should also include the purchase and replacement costs of the equipment. At the minimum, the analysis should incorporate the following:

A list of all your key assets.

Details on how these can be replaced in case they are destroyed.

The replacement cost of each asset.

Whether similar items are available.

The time necessary to repair or replace the damaged or lost equipment.

Available substitutes in case it is not possible to replace the lost equipment.

Cost of replacing the lost or inoperative equipment.

The economics of leasing equipment.

Having completed the above, you should then carry out an application analysis; this entails identifying and ranking application programs. These are important to the system and must be protected. Your analysis should review and determine the need for security of the application programs; it should also prioritize the risks.

The application analysis should consider, minimally, the following:

Impact from the loss of the programs
Impact of a modification of the programs
Needed recovery time
Ability to recover
Extent of recovery
Cost effectiveness of recovery
Replacement cost of the programs
Leasing costs
Availability of replacements

Potential threats and losses to your assets and application programs can result from the following sources:

System errors and failures
User input errors
Network/communications outages
Fires, earthquakes, lightning, floodings, and severe storms
Thefts/frauds
Power fluctuations or interruptions
Denial of service
Unauthorized manipulations
Unauthorized use
Vandalism/sabotage
Labor-related problems
Civil disturbances
Air conditioning/heat failures

CONTINGENCY PLANNING

Having studied and analyzed the myriad of potential threats to your EDP system, you should next turn to contingency planning to address, at least partly, these problems. One of the basic functions of every contingency plan should be to ensure that:

There will be no unauthorized use, alteration, modification, or destruction of the data.

There will be no unauthorized denial of the data to authorized individuals.

There will be safeguards to ensure the credibility, reliability, and integrity of the data.

The contingency plan should also address efforts by intruders to:

Hamper the system's operations.

Employ the system for illegal purposes.

Modify, alter, delete, or in any other way manipulate the system.

Make disclosure as regards confidential data stored in the system.

Additionally, the contingency plan should anticipate and prepare for:

Expected losses.

Costs resulting from these losses.

Undesirable events.

Determination of the value of each potential loss.

Institution of appropriate responses.

High risk events.

Establishment of priorities for organizational resources.

Planning for every contingency also entails a vulnerability assessment of the contingency plan itself. This is a listing of significant vulnerabilities, hazards, or weaknesses your system faces; it should, at the minimum, incorporate:

1.   A detailed listing of potential threats and hazards to, or weaknesses inherent in your system, such as:

    a.   Storms, earthquakes, and other natural phenomena

    b.   Riots, bombings, and other civil disturbances

    c.   Loss of needed services

2.   An identification of potential vulnerabilities to your system's:

    a.   Data collection/conversion

    b.   System hardware/software

    c.   Application program design

d. Physical/personnel security
e. Terminal/communications security

The contingency plan(s) should be made known to the key personnel at your EDP system; users should be informed as to their respective responsibilities in the event that the system loses its capability to function. The plan should also:

Be tested periodically through the use of drills and exercises.
Provide for the documentation and communication of responsibilities.
Provide for the monitoring of all alarm sources.
Assign specific responsibilities for making decisions.
Train employees in emergency procedures.
Identify critical tasks.
Identify alternative processing sources.
Plan for the ability to run the critical jobs.
Identify key resources needed for continued operations.
Identify alternative sources needed for system recovery.

Any contingency plan is only as good as the preparation that went into it. However, no plan is foolproof. It is always difficult to predict potential human behavior, natural phenomena, and mechanical malfunctions. The more complex the EDP system, the greater the margin for error; we live in an imperfect world and we work with imperfect information. Thus your contingency plan may not always reflect the real needs of the system. If, however, the plan addresses, at least minimally, the system's basic needs, then it has served part of its function.

DISASTER RECOVERY PLANNING

Disasters may be the outcome of either human or natural phenomena; they can be both unpredictable and unexpected. They can strike anywhere and any organization. It is thus necessary to prepare for such eventualities. The purpose of a disaster recovery plan is to see that necessary steps are taken, well in advance, to ensure the successful continuation and survivability of your EDP operations and capabilities.

A disaster recovery plan is more than simply a piece of paper; it should be an important management function. It should consider the needs of the people who operate the system, and be cognizant of the politics, special interests, and legal environment in which it must be implemented. A monolithic approach to the problem is neither possible nor desirable; the recovery plan should be sufficiently flexible to both address the needs of the EDP system and adapt to the changing environment.

Once you have analyzed the potential threats to your EDP system and considered various contingency options, consider the need for a disaster recovery plan. The size of the commitment, in terms of resources, personnel, and management involvement, will vary from organization to organization. In part, this will depend on:

The size of your organization
The complexity of the EDP system
The tasks assigned to the system
The geographical location of the EDP facility
The history of previous disasters
Industry practices

However, before embarking on such a plan, ask yourself the following:

Do you feel such a plan is needed?
What steps have other organizations taken to address the problem?
Consider the costs of implementing such a plan.
Consider the resources needed to implement the plan.
Test the plan while it is still in its paper stage.
Consider less expensive options.
Weigh management-related issues and other problems as they relate to the plan.

Bear in mind that such plans, if implemented, can be costly; shop wisely. Check on what others in your industry are doing, and compare different plans. If you decide to adopt a plan, then select one that suits your specific organizational needs. Remember that disasters do not always strike someone else; they can also strike your EDP system.

CHAPTER 13

Function
and Role
of Security

A clerk takes his employer in a computer caper for $500,000, while a dissatisfied programmer sells valuable software belonging to his employer to one of its competitors. An operator accidentally sets fire to his company's computer center.

The above cases serve to illustrate that events, of both intentional and accidental natures, can victimize an organization; none is immune. Thus every organization should be concerned with assessing and addressing its security needs—especially those of its EDP system. It should also identify and fully define those needs, and take adequate measures to detect, prevent, and recover from criminal attacks directed at the system. It should also be prepared to anticipate and address unexpected attacks and potential future problems as they relate to its EDP system.

No modern organization can long safeguard its EDP system without adequate security. It should be borne in mind, however, that because of the rapid advances in computer technology, even the best of security systems must be often reviewed, upgraded, and tested. The role of computer security is not only to safeguard the system from present problems, but also to anticipate and protect it from potential future attacks. It behooves the modern manager to understand the role of computer security.

DEFINING YOUR SECURITY NEEDS

Computer security goes by many names; numerous efforts have been made to define it. Among other things, computer security constitutes an effort to protect the data stored in an EDP system, its software/hardware, communication links, output data, and the very integrity and ability of that system to function. It reflects an organizational effort to safeguard the accuracy, reliability, and dependability of the overall system and its components, as well as the data it processes and stores. A diagram of computer vulnerability is shown below.

Many organizations will tell you that they have implemented security measures for their EDP systems; unfortunately, these measures are often merely cosmetic. To be adequate, there are four important areas that a meaningful computer security program should, at the minimum, address. These are as follows:

1. *Data security.* This refers to safeguards involving the information stored in the system. These measures are aimed at guarding against and/or preventing accidental disclosure and misuse of data by either unauthorized or authorized persons. It constitutes an effort to safeguard the data from unauthorized alterations, deletions, modifications, and other changes, also to safeguard it from theft and abuse.

2. *Software security.* This refers to safeguards enacted for the purpose of safeguarding the instructions given to the computer for the handling and processing of data. It seeks to prevent and deter the modification,

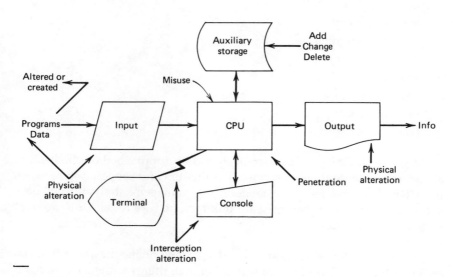

Areas of computer vulnerability. Various stages of a computer operation are vulnerable to criminal attack. The system is also open to electronic penetration by sophisticated criminals. (See "Computer Crime," *FBI Law Enforcement Bulletin,* July 1979.)

alteration, destruction, and copying of system programs. The threat can come from either accidental or intentional acts, by either authorized or unauthorized persons.

3. *Hardware security.* This encompasses safeguards that are directed at the computer's handling and processing equipment. Its objective is to ensure that the equipment is not destroyed (either accidentally or intentionally), modified, stolen, sabotaged, vandalized, employed in a criminal scheme, or damaged in any fashion.

4. *Communication security.* This involves efforts to safeguard the telephone/teleprinter circuits (public or private) employed to transmit data back and forth between the various computers, or between computers and remote terminals. The safeguards are aimed at preventing unauthorized access to the system (for example, the copying, alteration, modification of data and software). It constitutes an effort to ensure that the system's communication lines are employed only by authorized persons in a lawful manner.

However, because an EDP system faces a variety of potential threats and illegal acts, a comprehensive security program will be needed. In devising such a program, be sure to integrate personnel with the following functions:

Auditing
Physical security
Computer programming
Legal
Insurance
Personnel security
Forensic science
Management

To prove effective, your program should be approached on the basis of a team effort; there should be close coordination and cooperation between the EDP personnel and management; top management should not be a spectator. In devising your security program, be sure to take into account several important factors:

1. *Assets.* You should carefully identify and define the assets that you seek to safeguard. Take into consideration such things as their location, replacement cost, and replacement sources. Among these, you should list the software, hardware, and data.

2. *Threats.* Review and enumerate all the potential threats that your

system faces. These can often take three forms; the more common are the result of natural occurrences, such as fires, floods, and related natural hazards. The second category to be considered takes the form of intentional acts; these can result in thefts, sabotage, vandalism, fraudulent modifications, espionage, and other misuses of the system. A final category takes the form of accidental acts; these result from human error, for example, software or data entry errors, accidental destruction or modification of data or software, hardware or software failures, and data transmission failures.

3. *Expenditures.* Because an organization has limited resources and workforce, foolproof security is not possible; nor is it technically feasible, irrespective of what consultants and manufacturers will tell you. Management should approach the problem in a realistic fashion when preparing its security program; it should aim for acceptable and obtainable levels of security. It can do no more; it should also be forewarned that security carries with it many indirect costs. These should be budgeted for; they include expenditures for:

a. Guards
b. Periodic audits
c. Updating the program
d. Electromagnetic detection
e. Use of consultants
f. Enciphering equipment
g. Potential lawsuits
h. Bonding of personnel

4. *Exposure matrix.* In considering your security model, be sure to list all threats to the system, in order of priority. Your model should define the various classes of threats faced by the system, the priority you assign to each, and also a listing of all the assets you realistically expect to safeguard.

Thus, when defining your security needs, assess what these are, the assets you seek to safeguard, and the priority you assign to each. Be realistic in addressing your needs; attempt the possible, and not the ideal. Set realistic goals, take note of your resources, and shop wisely. In addition, make sure that top management is committed to your efforts.

OBJECTIVES OF SECURITY

Every security program ideally attempts to attain three objectives; these are as follows:

Prevention.   This means keeping an unwanted act from occurring.

Detection.   This involves learning that an unwanted act can take place.

Recovery.   This implies minimizing the impact of an unwanted act.

In addition, when devising your security program, consider incorporating four types of controls; these are:

Physical.   This implies surrounding the EDP facility and its contents.

Administrative.   These deal with the use of the computer facility.

System accuracy.   These are constructed into the software.

Legal.   These are aimed at safeguarding the organization from lawsuits and ensuring compliance with laws and regulations.

To ensure adequate security, you will need to both consider and, in one fashion or another, incorporate all of the above controls in your program. The manner in which you employ these, the resources you allocate to each control, and the commitment to each will depend upon your organizational needs and resources. Regardless of how you decide to employ these four controls, you would be ill-advised to dismiss their role.

CONSTRUCTING A MODEL

When constructing your security model, you should be careful to consider a number of other important factors. The weight and resources accorded each will vary from organization to organization, but it would certainly serve you well to review them nevertheless.

The security concerns that should be reviewed for your model are as follows:

1.   *Identification.*   This means identifying those who use the system. This can be done, for example, by a password, security code, and/or identification tag/card. These should be changed periodically; remember also to include in your system threat monitoring capabilities. These will serve to pinpoint the time and location of any suspicious attempts to gain access to the system.

2.   *Authorization.*   This implies that only those who have a right to use the system will be allowed to do so. It places limitations on what an authorized person with access to the system can do once within it; for example, it may limit a user to only reading, adding to, or deleting from a file.

3.   *Privacy.*   Data should be rendered unintelligible to unauthorized

persons. This can be carried out through the use of cryptographic transformation, concealment systems, and various other methods. Many of these methods often fall into one of the following five categories:

a. *Coding.* Replaces one or more words in one language with a word from another language.

b. *Compression.* Entails compacting the data files. This is carried out by removing repeated consecutive characters or by packing more than one character into a single character's worth for storage space.

c. *Substitution.* Involves replacing letters of one alphabet by one or more letters of another.

d. *Transposition.* Changes the order of letters in a message without changing the alphabet.

e. *Composite.* Involves applying a sequence of elementary transformations.

4. *Audit trails.* These include internal controls and journaling. The latter creates logs of information about transactions and file actions; these should assist in tracing specific transactions, reconstructing damaged files, and analyzing questionable activities within the system.

5. *Backup techniques.* These recovery efforts address damages to the hardware, software, or data. They include:

a. Compatible computer(s).

b. System programs.

c. Master files.

d. Transaction files.

e. Other facilities and services.

f. Forms.

g. Skilled personnel.

6. *Technical considerations.* The following should be considered in your model:

a. Similar organizations with multiple installations.

b. Organizations in the same industry.

c. Organizations within the same geographic area.

d. Computer manufacturers.

e. Service bureaus.

7. *Construction.* Many times, the location and contruction of the computer center can play an important role in safeguarding the EDP sys-

tem from abuses and illegal activities. The types of materials used in its construction can prove important in addressing threats and other related concerns. For example, the EDP facility should always be located away from walls and windows; it should always be above the ground floor, so as to limit the potential damage from water.[1] In addition, use fire resistant materials whenever possible; combustible materials should always be kept away from the center.

8. *Physical measures.* The objectives of these are identification and authorization. They constitute passive defenses against unauthorized personnel gaining access to the system. They often take the form of sign-in logs, badges, authorized entry lists, key lock systems, intruder detection devices, guards, and other related safeguards. They are directed at both people and objects, for example, intruders or packages containing explosives.

9. *Administrative measures.* These ensure that the system is employed only in accord with management's objectives and directives. They outline measures that system personnel should take to properly operate the system.

10. *Personnel policies.* These ensure that those people who have contact with the system do so in accord with the directives of management. They also serve to ensure that undesirables and other individuals who pose a threat to the system are prevented from so doing. System personnel should be made aware, at the commencement of their employment and thereafter, that EDP security plays an important role in safeguarding the system, that it is not a game, nor does it constitute an overreaction by management. Personnel should also be made aware of available emergency procedures and equipment; they should be issued identification cards with their photos, signatures, and dates of expiration marked on them. Duties should be rotated whenever possible; for example, personnel in computer operations should not also be employed in programming functions. In addition, no one person should have authority for processing a job from beginning to end.

Depending upon the nature and size of your organization and its business, there are a number of other basic security tools that you should consider employing in your program. The value of these will vary with each organization; they are, however, worth considering:

Alarm systems.- These should be employed at points where visitors and personnel enter the facility. They should also be equipped with hidden means of activating them.

---

[1] These considerations are addressed in greater detail in other chapters of the book.

Visitor controls.   Unescorted or unidentified visitors should be promptly challenged. All visitors should be required to show positive identification before being allowed entry.

After-hours access.   Maintain a log, and whenever possible, have cleaning and maintenance personnel escorted by a guard or supervisor. Guards should also make periodic checks of the facility.

Restrooms.   These should be locked to limit unrestricted public access.

Maintenance closets.   Keep these locked at all times.

Telephone and electrical equipment rooms.   They should be kept locked. Access to them should be allowed only to escort maintenance and telephone personnel.

Identification badges.   These should have a photograph of the bearer and a handwriting sample of his/her signature, also the date of expiration. Automated card readers or push button door locks should be used whenever possible, to allow entry only to authorized personnel. In high risk situations, it is advisable for all EDP personnel to wear their identification badges while on the premises.

Fire protection.   Detection and suppression capability should always be provided. Extinguishers should be readily available and the staff instructed in their use.

Safe room.   It should not be accessible from the outside, and should have a sturdy door and lock. In addition, it should not be identifiable as a safe room.

Emergency supplies.   These should be maintained at the facility, and key personnel should know their locations.

Publicity releases.   You should always be prepared for the eventuality that you may suffer an unwanted act. Always be prepared to address the press.

Incoming mail.   All incoming mail should be screened and packages should be checked.

Parking spaces.   These should be identified by number, and the parking lot itself should be periodically checked.

SAFEGUARDS AGAINST OUTSIDERS

The threat of unauthorized outsiders misusing your EDP system is both real and growing. The rising interest shown by professional criminals in this area amply illustrates the problem. At the minimum, your computer security program should both deter and identify attacks by outsiders.

The threat of the intruder can be addressed through a series of available safeguards. These are as follows:

Perimeter barriers (both natural and structural)
Perimeter entrances
Protective lighting
Intrusion alarm systems
Fence vibration or screen detection systems
Motion detection systems
Photoelectric or infrared alarm systems
Microwave systems
Strain sensitive alarm systems
Closed circuit television systems

When addressing the threat of the intruder, also consider the following:

Local population
Dissident or terrorist groups
Discontented individuals
Visitors who may engage in covert sabotage

When planning for the location of your EDP facility, there are a number of factors to consider. Among these, check the following:

Site location. It is always preferable to construct it in an isolated area.
Regional considerations. Some areas of the country are more likely to harbor militants, terrorists, dissidents, and other antiestablishment elements that may threaten your EDP system.
Constructing a facility. Consider how attractive your site may be to saboteurs.
Security versus productivity. Your review should also consider the impact of security on productivity.
Attackers. What resources, expertise, technical know-how, and other tools can potential intruders draw upon in the area you have selected as a site for your EDP center.

Computer security has become a catch-all phrase; it is often employed to include a gamut of tools for the purpose of securing EDP systems. However, none of these will prove effective unless top management cooperates. Top management has both a role and responsibility in this area; among these, it should:

Take an active role in the development and implementation of security.
Assign to an independent group or individual the specific responsibility for overseeing security.
Require the group or individual to report directly to it.
Be involved in the design stages of the system.
Be involved in the evaluation tests.
Ensure that sampling spot checks are used periodically.

Computer security should be employed wisely and with an eye on economy. Do not spend more than you have to; understanding the function and limitations of security can prove of assistance to management. An adequate review of your existing system should serve to best define your needs; once you have done so, consider the various tools at your disposal. In so doing, remember that the art is still in its infancy, and not all security measures may be suited to your needs.

CHAPTER 14

Instituting
a Security
Program

A boxing promoter was convicted of embezzling more than $20 million from a California bank; he did it with the assistance of the victim's employees and its computer. A 34-year-old claims representative with a Federal agency was charged with embezzling more than $100,000 in a computer ghost beneficiary scheme, while in a separate case, four computer "freaks" were arrested for the theft of computer manuals belonging to a telephone company. The manuals outlined how portions of the system's telephone service could be shut down.

Meanwhile, several students at a California college discovered a simple method for penetrating computer systems. The technique, it is feared, could open banks, research institutions, government agencies, corporations, and others who employ computers to store sensitive information to computer rip-offs. It is feared that a group of individuals arrested in California may have used related techniques to penetrate an airline computer system; they used it to reserve prepaid tickets for themselves. Meanwhile, Pentagon specialists fear that sabotage of the National Military Command Center's computers could render the United States helpless to foreign nuclear attack.

The above cases serve to illustrate that computers are vulnerable to criminal attack, in addition, that many computer-related capers can be easily prevented through the use of adequate computer safeguards. These safeguards should address the three key areas of every EDP system: people, equipment, and data. Damage or loss to these is often the result of fraud, theft, and/or malicious acts. Adequate computer security, however, can and does play a role in preventing such losses, but remember that even the best safeguards are only as effective as management's willingness to both implement them and enforce compliance.

SHOPPING FOR A PROGRAM

A scrutiny of the professional literature will easily disclose that, if anything, the area of computer security is inundated with a multitude of recommended programs. These range from the simple to the complex; from the inexpensive to the very costly, and from the pragmatic to the "trendy."

The problem of management is thus one of defining its realistic EDP security needs, and doing so at a reasonable cost. There are two principles to keep in mind when shopping for security:

1. *Do not be oversold.* The computer crime scare has led some organizations to embark on massive and costly security programs, which are often unnecessary.

2. *Shop wisely.* The computer security industry has proliferated in the last several years to the point where, unfortunately, charlatans have also made their way into the field. Do not be swayed by promises that cannot realistically be carried out; always get at least a second opinion.

Computer security does help; at its best, it will serve to deter or catch the "small fry." Its value as regards professional thieves and crooked top management is more limited. After all, how do you tell the head of your organization that he has no access to the computer center? Thus do not expect miracles from EDP security; it is a tool that, when employed wisely, can assist. It is not a cure for all types of computer-related problems, nor is it a substitute for prosecuting computer criminals.

The objective of every EDP security program is, at the minimum, to safeguard the system and all of its components from unlawful and accidental acts. Its function is to ensure that the system continues to be reliable, accurate, and viable. Security, however, suffers from the same flaws that plague its architects; it will reflect the human shortcomings of its designers. In designing it, bear this in mind: at best, your program will exact a price from the criminal, who will thus have to decide whether the benefits are really worth the anguish. A security system serves to raise the "ante."

There are no guarantees in the security game; there is often a great gap between the real and the ideal. This middle ground is what you should aim for; it constitutes the possible. Thus, when devising your program, consider the following:

Make unauthorized entry to the system sufficiently difficult.

Make efforts to minimize the impact of criminal attacks or attempts.

Enhance the system's ability to detect sabotage, unauthorized use, modifications, threats, and other deviations from the norm.

Ensure that the system will function in a cohesive, predictable, and reliable manner.

Make sure that data in the system will have an identifiable origin and use.

Ensure that authorized users will have access only to that data to which they are entitled.

Guard the communication links in the system against electronic interception.

Safeguard the privacy and confidentiality of the data stored in the system.

Secure the system from external/internal manipulations.

Ensure the continued operation of the system.

Screen undesirable employees.

Project a "tough image" for the organization.

Be sensitive to employee-related problems.

Augment your fraud detection capabilities.

Enhance the system's ability to take corrective actions.

An EDP security program should also evaluate the sensitivity of each system application, particularly those that will process sensitive data or that will have a high potential for loss. For sensitive applications, specific controls should include policies and assign responsibilities for:

Defining and approving security specifications prior to programming the applications or changes (prior to the approval of any security specifications, consider the views and recommendations of the individuals responsible for the security of the system).

Conducting and approving tests of the system prior to using it operationally. (The function of the design reviews should be to determine whether the proposed design meets the approved security specifications. The results of the design review should be fully documented.)

Conducting periodic audits and evaluations of the security safeguards (audits and evaluations should be performed at time intervals commensurate with the sensitivity of the information processed).

Establishing guidelines for acquiring and operating computer facilities, equipment, software packages, or related services (these guidelines should be reviewed and approved by officials assigned the responsibility for security).

Ensuring compliance with current Federal, state, and local laws, rules, and regulations.

Basic EDP security is divided into two important components: physical and personnel. Physical security deals largely with the construction, location, storage, communications, and important operations of an EDP system. It encompasses the hardware and software of the system, as well as the connecting terminals and communication lines employed to transmit the data. In an age of growing crime and political terrorism, physical security has increasingly come to play an important role.

However, physical security by itself is like an automobile without gasoline; it must be complemented by personnel safeguards. These address the human threat; it is the people problem that often hampers the effectiveness and integrity of an EDP system. Your security program should seek to safeguard the system from the dishonest and careless employee; it is the insider who currently poses the greatest threat to your system. Security should also be concerned with the threat of the outsider, for example, customers, competitors, and others.

Employee-connected security measures, however, can pose a dilemma for many organizations—especially for those in the private sector. In an effort to safeguard the privacy of those it services, or to maintain the effectiveness of the system, an organization may be forced to infringe upon the privacy of its own employees. This could serve to open the organization to a lawsuit from an employee who feels his/her privacy rights may have been abused or violated.

Physical and personnel safeguards must be constructed with the legal environment in mind; they may require a team approach. Security, EDP, legal, and other experts will have to be consulted; in addition, these safeguards must be balanced against the other needs and priorities of the organization. You should also consider the legal environment in which you operate—especially if yours is a regulated industry. Implement only those safeguards that are needed, keeping in mind, however, that your resources are limited.

ESTABLISHING SECURITY

The level of sophistication of a computer security program will depend upon both the type of system and the organization it is designed to safeguard. It is neither realistic nor wise to make broad general statements as regards the security needs of a system; however, there are some basic measures that have application to most EDP systems. In reviewing your security needs, consider measures that are most appropriate for your system.

Employee Security

Most of the computer capers that have surfaced to date have involved an insider. This person's role is often that of lone thief; sometimes the insider has been a part of a conspiracy. The security measures most often employed to protect an EDP system from dishonest employees take the following forms:

Ensuring that management is sufficiently sensitive to its employees.

Briefing security managers on Federal and state/local laws and regulations regarding employees.

Screening prospective employees to ensure that they have not been involved in prior criminal activity.

Conducting background checks for employees in sensitive EDP positions.

Conducting periodic background checks for all employees with access to the computer facility.

Immediately informing supervisors of any serious employee-related problems.

Bringing disgruntled employees to the attention of their appropriate supervisors.

Establishing a program for handling employee-related problems.

Hardware Security

The physical equipment used in data processing is also open to criminal attack. Unauthorized usage of the system is a perennial problem, especially by dishonest insiders. Recommended safeguards should take the following form:

Checking incoming work against the authorized users list.

Conducting periodic spot checks to detect and minimize misuse or abuse of the system.

Reviewing maintenance activities.

Verifying all periods of downtime.

Monitoring the system's operations to ensure compliance with your security program.

Correlating meter hours with utilization hours.

Identifying all terminals.

Checking all changes, repairs, and modifications.

Software Security

The system's programs, procedures, and rules are also open to criminal attack and abuse. Programs can be erased, altered, and manipulated. Security in this area should encompass some of the following:

Carrying out periodic checks.

Using keywords or passwords whenever possible (these should be changed periodically).

Employing scrambling and cryptographic devices.

Employing only reputable software systems experts.

Verifying and recording all modifications.

Recording all unauthorized attempts to access the system.

Investigating all suspect activity.

Controlling and logging access by maintenance personnel to sensitive areas.

Consulting EDP auditors as regards appropriate tests and checks to be incorporated into the application programs.

Dividing responsibilities between two or more persons for the maintenance of programs.

Maintaining an audit trail of all changes to programs.

Separating program debugging from production activity.

Placing tapes in their containers when not being used.

Selecting only reputable contractors to clean your disk packs.

Maintaining detailed utilization records.

Controlling and documenting all program changes.

Having programmers give written (not oral) instructions to computer operators.

Containing a statement of ownership on all programs.

Separating responsibilities for writing, authorizing, modifying, and running programs.

Locating the tape library in a secure area.

Storing tapes away from magnets.

Preparing backup tapes and disks.

Constructing threat-monitoring safeguards into programs.

Keeping a log of all personnel who have had access to sensitive data banks.

Supervising vendor activities.

Requiring the security officer or a designate to verify all modifications.

Requesting vendors to screen employees who have access to sensitive data.

Constructing safeguards in operating systems to prevent unauthorized access to data bases.

Controlling and documenting all programming changes and maintenance.

Employing tests to validate outputs from critical reporting systems.

Access Controls

Access controls are procedures for ensuring that only authorized persons have access to the EDP system. These often take the following forms:

Controlling and documenting visits to the facility.

Establishing escort procedures to control the flow of visitors.

Briefing all employees as to their respective responsibilities.

Securing windows with alarm systems.

Considering the use of guard forces to secure access to the facility.

Limiting access only to authorized personnel.

Escorting unauthorized personnel on all occasions.

Clearing system personnel through background checks.

Segregating duties.

Determining if the computer facility has been the target of past criminal acts.

Determining if current access controls are adequate.

Employing keys and locks to control access.

Using admission badges to distinguish authorized personnel.

Escorting dismissed employees from the computer facility.

Directing system employees to question suspicious persons.

Using guards to respond to unauthorized entries.

Determining the likelihood that the system will be the target of criminals.

Segregating the file areas (so that only authorized individuals will have access).

Changing keys and locks at regular intervals.

Training personnel to challenge improperly identified visitors.

Briefing potential escorts on their responsibilities.

Ensuring all exterior windows near the street level are covered with expanded metal grills.

Screening the computer room from the street.

Manning the central computer facility at all times with two or more cleared personnel.

Not advertising the location of the computer center.

Training your security personnel to handle threats and extortionist demands.

Data Security

Data security ensures that the data in the system is protected from both intentional and accidental modifications, alterations, disclosures, or manipulations. These controls entail the following:

Monitoring all program changes.

Maintaining backup source data.

Recording and classifying all programs.

Investigating all stoppages.

Maintaining duplicates of all documentation.

Keeping updated inventories of all records.

Conducting checks to ensure accuracy of the backup system.

Filing duplicates in a separate facility.

Making periodic inventories of all duplicates.

Allowing only approved program changes.

Accounting for documents sent to the computer room for input processing.

Accounting for corrections on source documents for input processing.

Making corrections on source documents only at the originating department.

Retaining source records for a sufficient period of time.

Numbering vendor checks, payroll checks, and other negotiable items.

Numbering purchase orders and other important forms.

Logging the output and storing it in a secure fashion until routed to its authorized recipients.

Making storage areas fireproof.

Educating system personnel in data security.

Controlling user input.

Classifying data in terms of its value.

Segregating tapes, disks, and cards.

Monitoring output.

Securing the facility from outsiders.

Terminal Security

Terminal security controls are aimed at ensuring that only authorized personnel have access to points or devices at which data can either enter or exit the system. These controls often involve the following:

Safeguarding portable terminals from theft and misuse.

Employing passwords to identify spceific terminals and users.

Controlling access to keyword and lockword files.

Controlling terminal access.

Employing guards and physical barriers to control access to and from terminals.

Using machine-readable cards or badges to identify terminal users.

Changing password and individual security codes periodically.

Requiring terminal users to indicate at sign-off when they will next become active.

Programming the computer to disconnect terminals after a specific period of inactivity.

Limiting valid users access to specific files.

Programming the system to record unsuccessful entry attempts.

Monitoring time-sharing systems.

Testing the system for electronic interceptions.

Tape/Disk Security

Storage devices can be easily destroyed, copied, or stolen; in addition, the data stored in them can be altered, deleted, or erased. Controls are thus important; these should include:

Establishing accountability procedures.
Keeping tapes/disks clean and environmentally safe.
Filing them in an orderly fashion.
Allowing only authorized users access.
Placing them in secure containers when not in use.
Selecting only reputable individuals to service them.
Locating the library in a secure area.
Not storing them near magnets.
Preparing backups.
Marking them with a neat identifier.
Maintaining detailed utilization records.

Organizational Security

Organizational security measures are directed at ensuring both acceptance and compliance with the above security measures. They involve the following:

Making computer operations independent of other departments.
Limiting access by EDP personnel to cash and inventories.
Prohibiting EDP personnel from authorizing checks or purchases.
Requiring all EDP personnel to take their designated vacations.
Separating key responsibilities.
Requiring explicit permission to use computer equipment.
Investigating all unexplained stoppages, interruptions, and errors.
Reviewing security measures frequently.
Limiting access to the computer facility.
Sensitizing management to the importance of security.
Separating personnel functions so as to minimize the opportunity for collusion.
Coordinating with Federal and state/local police agencies.

Establishing contacts with professional organizations that specialize in security.

Ensuring employee compliance with the security program.

Ensuring the support and cooperation of top management.

Periodically upgrading the existing security program.

Identifying and reviewing your existing resources.

Budgeting for future and potential needs.

Ensuring your security program is in compliance with local/state and Federal laws and regulations.

The above safeguards will not be needed for all EDP systems, nor are they necessarily adequate for the more complex and sophisticated systems. However, they have weathered the test of time, and should prove of some value to those who are either establishing new programs or are upgrading their existing ones.

ADDITIONAL CONSIDERATIONS

There are several additional measures that you should consider when implementing (or upgrading an existing) computer security program. The value of these will depend on the needs of your EDP system; however, they merit consideration.

Environmental Controls

The objective of these is to safeguard the system from intentional, accidental, or natural harmful events. These controls are aimed at safeguarding the physical integrity of the system and/or its components. These measures should include the following:

1. Safeguards against water damage:

    a. Ensuring computers are excluded from areas below water grade.
    b. Insisting that overhead steam or water pipes (except sprinklers) are eliminated.
    c. Ensuring there is adequate drainage under the raised floor.
    d. Installing drains on floor above to divert water accumulations away from all hardware.
    e. Having adequate drainage to prevent water overflow from adjacent areas.

   f.   Ensuring all electrical junction boxes are under the raised flooring held off the slab (this prevents water overflow from adjacent areas).

   g.   Making sure all exterior windows and doors are watertight.

   h.   Protecting against accumulated rainwater or leaks in rooftop cooling towers.

   i.   Ensuring large plastic sheets are available to cover equipment for quick emergency water protection.

2.   Safeguards to secure the air conditioning system:

   a.   Ensuring the duct linings and filters are noncombustible.

   b.   Having a backup capability.

   c.   Ensuring the air intakes are covered with protective screening (and are located above street level).

   d.   Ensuring the air intakes are free of pollutants.

   e.   Making sure the air temperature and humidity in the computer facility are recorded.

3.   Ensuring uninterrupted electric power:

   a.   Having a backup.

   b.   Making sure the local power supply is reliable.

   c.   Checking the power source with recorders to identify electrical transients.

   d.   Having emergency lighting.

   e.   Ensuring the fire alarm system is backed up with battery power.

   f.   Testing backup power at regular intervals.

   g.   Having emergency power for all exits and within the computer center.

   h.   Ensuring emergency power offs are protected from accidental activation.

4.   Securing against accidental/malicious fire:

   a.   Flammable materials used in computer maintenance should be kept in small quantities and in approved containers.

   b.   Emergency crews should be able to gain access to the installation without delay.

   c.   Staying in touch with the local firefighting force.

   d.   Installing smoke detectors in ceiling, under raised floor, and/or in air-return ducts.

e. Testing smoke detection system regularly.

f. Holding periodic fire drills.

g. Cleaning regularly under the raised floor.

h. Having a readily available adequate supply of firefighting water.

i. Having battery-powered emergency lighting throughout the computer area.

j. Installing enough fire alarm pull boxes throughout the EDP facility.

k. Ensuring the alarm sounds at the local fire or police headquarters.

l. Training personnel in the use of firefighting equipment.

m. Making sure portable fire extinguishers are readily available in the computer area.

n. Ensuring emergency power shutdown controls are accessible.

o. Including the air conditioning system in the emergency power shutdown.

p. The building storing the computer should be constructed of fire-resistant/noncombustible materials.

q. Separating the computer room from adjacent areas by the use of noncombustible fire-resistant partitions, walls, and doors.

r. Storing papers and other combustible supplies outside the computer area.

s. Storing file tapes and disks outside the computer area.

t. Ensuring raised floors are made of noncombustible material.

u. Ensuring ceilings and support hardware are noncombustible.

v. Assigning personnel specific tasks in case of fire.

w. Making sure curtains, rugs, furniture, and drapes are noncombustible.

x. Restricting smoking in the computer area.

5. Guarding against natural disasters requires that the computer facility be:

a. Housed in a structurally sound building.

b. Resistant to wind, storms, and hurricanes.

c. Resistant to flood damage.

d. Resistant to earthquakes.

e. Properly grounded for lightning protection.

f. Remote from any earthquake faults.

6. Guarding against negligent conduct entails:

 a. Preventing the accumulation of trash in the computer area.
 b. Cleaning the equipment covers and work surfaces regularly.
 c. Washing the floors regularly.
 d. Cleaning off dust.
 e. Ensuring wastebaskets are of metal material with closing tops.
 f. Insisting that wastebaskets be dumped outside of the computer area to reduce dust discharge.
 g. Ensuring that the carpeting is of the antistatic type.
 h. Discouraging eating in the computer room.
 i. Using low fire hazard waste containers.
 j. Prohibiting smoking in the computer room.
 k. Using self-extinguishing ashtrays.

Threat Detection

Detecting threats entails being able to identify and monitor existing and potential threats to the system (or any of its components) before it is too late. In so doing, consider the following:

Brief security and operations personnel on how to deal with potential threats.

Establish a good liaison program with law enforcement agencies.

Train management to handle threats.

Maintain a monitor log of those who access data banks or any sensitive files.

Use a software security routine to monitor attempts by unauthorized users to access sensitive files.

Notify the operator routinely via the on-line console.

Provide a record of all such attempts via a printout at the end of the day.

Develop patterns that can help to track down possible suspects who misuse or have unauthorized access to vital data records.

Investigate all incidents to determine their cause and the corrective action to be taken.

File Security

File security safeguards are designed to ensure that the data in your EDP system is not subject to unauthorized use or destruction. They involve maintaining documentation standards that include:

Adequate explanations of codes, tables, and calculations.

Rejected record procedures.

Explanations of halts.

File sequence descriptions.

Control and balancing instructions.

Logic or flow charts.

Current listings.

Input/output formats.

Output samples.

User documentation.

Copies of test data.

Utilizing low fire hazard storage equipment for documentation.

Maintaining duplicates of all documentation.

Doing an annual inventory of all files.

Reviewing the documentation backup periodically.

Approving all changes in programs and documentation.

Having the internal auditors review all changes.

Reviewing the system documentation for compliance.

Having a documented retention cycle for the data files.

Maintaining data files within and under the control of the computer complex.

Classifying files in terms of sensitivity and value.

Keeping files in an area other than the computer room.

Filing/storing duplicate files in a separate building from the originals.

Storing programs in low fire hazard containers.

Keeping a current inventory of such files.

Holding a "dry run" to test the file backup system.

Monitoring and controlling all program changes.

Maintaining a record of items withdrawn from production file area.

Classifying programs according to a predetermined classification policy.

Keeping files in a fire-protected area.

Controlling access to files.

Using special low fire hazard storage containers for critical files.

Coordinating source document retention with the file reconstruction procedures.

Complying with legal requirements for file retention.

Educating users in a file security program.

Audit Safeguards

Audit safeguards seek to ensure the accuracy, validity, and credibility of the operations of the EDP system. These entail:

Having an overall audit control philosophy (as regards the computer system).

Employing computer usage and production controls.

Controlling user input to ensure receipt of all input data.

Maintaining the output to ensure compliance with standards.

Having follow-up procedures.

Establishing quality controls to verify proper execution of reports.

Ensuring that program changes are controlled.

Controlling conversions to ensure continuity.

Having adequate intrusion safeguards.

Having a backup for all programs, files, and hardware.

Ensuring the systems are auditable.

Having auditors included in the design of the system.

Time-Sharing Controls

These controls seek to ensure that only authorized users have use of the system, and that they use it only in an authorized manner. These controls should include the following:

Remote terminals should be available only to selected individuals.

Access to terminals should be controlled by doors, guards, and/or other restraints.

Terminals should be located so that each user's privacy is ensured.

There should be absolute control over portable terminals (so as to prevent their theft and misuse).

Passwords should be utilized to identify both specific terminals and users.

Passwords should be tamperproof.

Passwords should be changed at intervals (in accord with security guidelines).

Physical keys or access badges should be combined with passwords.

Software should be employed to restrict a given individual to specific data files.

Authority to add, delete, or modify files should be limited.

Access to the keyword and lockword files should be restricted.

Accurate records of all activity should be maintained against each data file.

Security-override procedures should be classified.

Use of override procedures should be monitored closely.

Scramblers and cryptographic techniques should be employed.

The time-resource sharing security system should be monitored.

The program debugging of the security system should be monitored.

Software safeguards for on-line operating systems and applications programs should be used.

Service Bureau Safeguards

These are recommended for all who use an outside computer service bureau. Their function is to ensure that the service installation is secure from potential threats and hazards. The following checks are recommended:

Determine if their location is in a high risk area.

See if access to their computer and file areas is controlled.

See if their customer work area is secure.

Check their fire or other threat potential.

Determine if they are responsive to your needs.

Check whether their staff is competent.

See if their couriers are efficient and trustworthy.

Ask if they screen employees in sensitive positions.

Check if their operating and control procedures are adequate.

Ensure the contract provides for recovery in case of losses.

Determine what controls they have to prevent erroneous results.

Check safeguards they have to prevent the inadvertent release of your data.

Review their controls for loss of a vital file.

Check if they are insured for liability.

See if they are financially sound.

Check their financial affiliations.

Review the loss potential of the work you are having processed.

Contingency Safeguards

To be adequate, a security program should consider and plan for numerous potential threats. When preparing your security program, provide for a contingency plan. This should include:

1. Specific responsibility for each functional area.
2. Detailed notification procedures that detail:

   a. Who calls whom
   b. Role of management
   c. Role of emergency crews
   d. Role of users

3. Backup sites.
4. Service personnel.
5. Criteria for determining extent of disruption.
6. Responsibility for retaining source documents and/or data files.
7. Identification of backup installation.
8. A backup computer that can handle the workload.
9. Testing of the system.
10. A regular maintenance schedule.
11. Monitoring for compliance.
12. Stocking of spare parts.
13. Purchase or lease of new or temporary equipment.
14. Purchase of computer time/services.
15. Hiring additional staff.
16. Acquisition of replacement tapes/diskpacks.
17. Provision for an alternate site.

As is the case with the other recommended computer security measures, these may not prove appropriate or necessary for all EDP systems. However, you stand little to lose by reviewing them; as regards a contingency plan, you would do well to consider one. Regardless of the size and complexity of your EDP system, you should prepare for the possibility that your system may fall victim to crime or natural disaster.

PERSONNEL COUNTERMEASURES

In the final analysis, computer-related frauds, thefts, and abuses are people problems; more specifically, it is often an organization's employees at all levels who pose a threat to the system. Even when outsiders are found to be involved, they often have the assistance of dishonest insiders. It is the latter who provide the former with the requisite specifics as regards the system's vulnerabilities; the threat of the dishonest insider should be taken seriously.

The insider's threat can take many forms. You should, however, be especially concerned with the following illegal acts:

Manipulations. These involve deleting, altering, modifying, or destroying data/software.

Thefts/abuses. These are usually directed at the hardware, software, and files, and can take the form of copying, misappropriating, or unauthorized use.

Sabotage/vandalism. These are physical attacks directed at the system or any of its components.

Espionage. This is directed at trade secrets, marketing plans, mailing lists, and other valuable data. As we increasingly become an "informational society," access to data bases will mean power. Industrial espionage should continue to grow; by all indicators, it appears to have a bright future.

It would thus behoove you to include within your computer security program countermeasures specifically designed to address the insider threat. These are simple, can be established at little cost, and they can go a long way in making your system secure. Consider including the following:

Screening. Oftentimes, "undesirables" are able to gain employment with an organization because of slipshod hiring practices. For example, a known embezzler was hired in a sensitive position by a government agency; he took his employer for $40,000 in a computer caper. A simple background check could have prevented the fraud; it would have alerted the employer to the potential threat. Use of credit bureaus, private investigators, and such can assist in screening personnel for sensitive positions.

Supervision. This is both a valuable and inexpensive tool in preventing employee-related frauds. If poorly applied, it can undermine other controls. It should include overseeing operations, improving employee morale, improving working conditions, minimizing employer-employee problems, and creating pride in the organization.

Coordination. In most cases, the diverse elements within an organization have little or no input in the EDP security program (both in its inception and enforcement). Each organization has a pool of diverse talent; it should draw on it. A coordination of resources can serve to enhance both productivity and security.

Planning. This should include not only EDP personnel, but also security personnel; this will serve to balance the overall planning and implementation of the security program. Unfortunately, long-term security planning gives way to short term budgetary concerns.

Additional countermeasures specifically directed at dishonest insiders could include the following:

Change in master memory records should not be handled by personnel doing day-to-day transactions.

Computer operating personnel should work separately from personnel who handle input, output, and programming.

Personnel who maintain records of all file updates should not be individuals who made the updates.

Control accounts for each type of master data by personnel should be maintained independent of the computer.

Personnel involved in computer usage, programs used, tape reference files, and start/stop times should be monitored carefully.

Computer personnel should log and be required to explain all stoppages or interruptions.

Personnel should be required to record all program changes, showing dates, and reference to other programs that might be affected.

All program changes (or new programs) should first be authorized by head of department.

Planning and programming personnel should not have access to tapes used for processing.

All operators in the computer room should be required to initial the operating log.

Personnel should be instructed to record all errors/deviations detected and action taken.

Require personnel to maintain a written history of each tape reel (use, contents, updating, etc.).

Control staff (and not the computer operators) should check the control totals.

All output that leaves data processing should first be reviewed by the control group.

222 INSTITUTING A SECURITY PROGRAM

Personnel countermeasures, if well thought out and vigorously implemented, can help stave off the dishonest insider. They are not foolproof; a sophisticated thief will find a way around them, but at least you will make it tougher to do so. This, in itself, can sometimes prove to be an adequate deterrence.

LIMITS OF SECURITY

Even the best of EDP security measures have their limits; in part, this stems from the ability and ingenuity of the computer criminal to circumvent these barriers. Every countermeasure gives rise to an adequate response; human beings ⟨criminals included⟩ learn how to adapt and respond to their changing environment. Security measures must thus keep abreast of these criminal adaptations.

Computer security must also comply with the legal environment in which the organization finds itself. Federal and state/local laws and regulations often dictate what tools, vehicles, and controls management can employ to deter and prevent criminal behavior. In addition, other institutions (for example, labor unions) often dictate how it will deal with its personnel. EDP security does not operate in a social vacuum; its architects must consider and weigh the social milieu in which they operate.

In addition, be on guard against the "expensive and trendy." Human beings are often impressed with new gadgets; for example, the energy shortages of the 1970s saw a proliferation of energy saving devices. Many of these were worthless, if not outright frauds. In shopping for security, do so intelligently and with economy in mind; the best things in life need not always be the most expensive. The various security measures detailed in this chapter should prove of value; be a wise consumer.

PART 3

Additional
Concerns

CHAPTER **15**

Potential
Legal
Liabilities

A retail chain was sued and charged with fraud by one of its competitors; the latter alleged that the defendant had purchased a valuable program from one of its former employees. A computer malfunction cost a financial institution $1 million in losses; a court held it liable for "botching up" a client's account. In a separate case, a computer user was held liable for damages caused to others as a result of a computer error; the court ruled that the user should have taken adequate precautions to insure the accuracy of the data.

With the growing proliferation and use of computers in all industries, the potential for computer-related legal liabilities is both real and great. Retail stores, financial institutions, computer users, and others have ample reason to be concerned. Computer-related litigation is on the increase; it can prove both costly and time consuming. Thus it behooves members of the business community to know how to avoid its potential legal pitfalls.

SOURCES OF LITIGATION

Much of the computer-related litigation has centered around computer errors, malfunctions, and abuses and misuses of the system. The targets of this litigation have included banks, retailers, credit card companies, public utilities, air carriers, credit reporting agencies, and many others. Every business and industry is a potential target of this litigation. You need not, however, be "open game" for lawyers. Identifying and understanding the potential sources of this litigation is a must for management; it can often eliminate or limit your legal exposure. Many of the sources of legal exposure can be either controlled or avoided by management.

Any mass technology that daily records and transmits information on millions of individuals and organizations runs the risk of error, malfunction, natural disaster, fraud, theft, abuse, or some other event that can often cause a loss to those it services. Losses emanate from any of the following parts of an EDP operation:

Stage at which data is collected
Type of data that is collected
How the data is collected
Manner in which erroneous data is corrected
How the data is updated
Who has access to the data
How the data is disseminated
Measures taken to safeguard the accuracy and integrity of the data
When and how notice is given to a customer/user
Legal duties and obligations imposed by the community

Much of the past litigation has centered around such things as the release of false or erroneous:

Financial/marketing data
Personal/medical information
Customer lists
Mailing lists
Credit reports
Pricing and inventory data
Product development data
Statistical findings
Projections
Bills
Electronic funds transfers

Litigation has also revolved around the theft or copying of programs and trade secrets. Industrial espionage—and the theft of high technology—has also spawned a multitude of lawsuits.

The activities that most often give rise to legal exposure, and those that you should be most concerned with, are:

1. *Natural disasters.* These can be the cause of litigation in those cases where an organization fails to adequately safeguard against such natural phenomena as:

    a. Fires
    b. Earthquakes
    c. Floods
    d. Lightning
    e. Other disasters

2. *Mechanical malfunctions.* An organization should take steps to insure that the EDP system is properly serviced.

3. *Personnel errors.* The staff should be sensitized to the need for data accuracy. The organization may be liable for the errors of its personnel.

4. *Negligence.* The staff's failure to take adequate and reasonable steps to safeguard the system from fraud, abuse, misuse, or breakage can open the organization to a lawsuit.

5. *Contractual disputes.* Your contract defines your duties and obligations. Be sure to abide by them.

6. *Strict product liability laws.* Some courts may hold your organization to a strict liability test. It matters little how the damage happened; only that it did occur and someone was injured.

7. *Electronic interceptions.* EDP systems are open to an array of sophisticated electronic interceptions. A failure to adequately guard against them could open you to a lawsuit. The ones you should guard against include:

    a. Wiretapping
    b. Electromagnetic pickups
    c. Browsing
    d. Between-the-lines entry
    e. Piggyback entry
    f. Trapdoor entry

8. *Fraud, theft, and abuse.* Gun manufacturers have been sued by the victims of crimes for failing to take adequate measures to safeguard their products. Store owners and the owners of residential buildings have been sued for failing to institute adequate safeguards. Crime by computer is a serious and growing business; it victimizes society to the tune of over $100

million. The news media makes mention of it daily; it can hardly be said that modern management is not aware of it. Thus a failure to enact adequate security measures could result in litigation.

Legal exposure from computer-related crimes could thus result from a failure to:

Safeguard the system from use by unauthorized personnel.

Secure the system from manipulations involving the theft or diversion of goods, merchandise, services, or other property.

Safeguard the system from the theft or the disclosure of valuable/confidential data.

Prevent use of the system to pull off financial capers (for example, embezzlements and "ghost employee" schemes).

Secure transmitted data from illegal interceptions.

In guarding the system, be on the lookout, among other abuses, for:

Theft of data
Unauthorized use
Vandalism
Sabotage
Espionage
Financial frauds
Theft or diversions of property

DUTIES AND OBLIGATIONS IMPOSED BY LAW

Computer manufacturers, vendors, users, and others would do well to beware. There are a multitude of laws, rules, and regulations that could be employed by injured parties to bring lawsuits for damages. The areas of greatest concern revolve around the law of:

1. *Contracts.* Agreements between two or more parties are often the basis for legal liability. To limit an organization's contractual exposures, its legal staff should see to it that its staff abide by the duties, obligations, and other responsibilities detailed in the agreement.

2. *Negligence.* Under the common law, a person who breached a legal duty or obligation owed to another was held liable for damages suffered by the latter as a consequence of that breach. The common law of

negligence has now been codified by many of the states; thus a failure by the staff of an EDP system to exercise adequate precautions can open its organization to litigation. Most negligence-related lawsuits center around:

a. Computer errors and/or malfunctions.

b. A failure by the EDP system personnel to exercise the needed diligence to remedy a problem.

The plaintiff needs, however, to demonstrate that he/she was injured because of reliance on the defendant's act(s).

3. *Privacy.* Computer technology makes it possible to disseminate voluminous data at the press of a button. Management bears the responsibility to see that the data stored and/or disseminated by its computers is accurate and is disclosed only to an authorized individual. An erroneous or unauthorized disclosure could cause a person or a company economic loss. For example, a police computer landed a Florida housewife in jail when it mistakenly identified her as an escaped convict. In a similar case, a gasoline company erroneously overbilled a customer by $200 without his knowledge; he was later denied credit for "failing to pay his bills." The courts have long recognized that individuals have a right to control information as regards themselves; they have a right not to be "placed in a false light." Acts that cause an individual anguish and distress are thus actionable; the disclosure of inaccurate or misleading information can be the basis of a lawsuit.

4. *Defamation.* Corporations and living persons have a right not to have false statements (either written or oral) made about them. If an organization disseminates false information about one of its customers, and that information impacts adversely on the reputation of the customer, the customer can sue for defamation. The only defense to a defamation suit is the truth; the fact that the disclosure was in good faith is not a defense.

There are also a number of Federal laws and regulations that could place additional obligations on organizations that operate in interstate/foreign commerce, and deal with Federal agencies (such as financial institutions). The ones of special concern, and of potential application to EDP systems, include:

Fair Credit Reporting Act. It has application as regards the accuracy and privacy of computer-generated data.

Equal Credit Opportunity Act. It requires that computerized credit files be current and confidential.

Tax Reform Act. It directs financial institutions to notify their customers when the Internal Revenue Service issues a summons for their computerized records.

Right to Financial Privacy Act.   It limits access to computerized customer records by requiring government investigators to produce a subpoena, summons, or search warrant for their release.

Bank Secrecy Act.   It authorizes the Secretary of the Treasury to order financial institutions to record the identity and activities of specific customers.

Electronic Funds Transfer Act.   It outlines the liabilities, duties, and obligations of financial institutions vis-à-vis their customers. It also provides criminal sanctions for some computer-related crimes and abuses.

Truth in Lending Act.   It requires timely and meaningful disclosure as regards credit costs.

Foreign Corrupt Practices Act.   It outlines measures for ensuring that computerized payment systems are not employed in foreign payoff, bribery, and kickback schemes.

OTHER LEGAL CONCERNS

Legal liabilities may also arise out of misappropriating "information and systems" belonging to another. For example, a vendor sued several former employees and a user for copyright infringement; it alleged that the defendants had misappropriated confidential "information and technology." Much of the litigation in this area centers around the misuse of another's software; lawsuits in this area are on the increase, and the law is fraught with many traps. You would do well to beware.

Potential litigation in this area can often arise from three areas of the law. Although the courts differ in the interpretations they give these laws, you should nevertheless be aware of them; they are as follows:

1.   *Copyrights.*   The objective of these laws is to protect the specific expression of an idea (not the idea itself) from infringement. However, bringing software within the protection of the Copyright Act of 1976 had proven difficult. This changed with passage of the Computer Software Copyright Act of 1980. Section 101 of the Act defines a program as a set of statements or instructions, to be used in a computer in "order to bring about a certain result." The Act also provides the owner of a computer program with the right to copy it or transfer rights in it, including sale and leasing arrangements. While copyright experts hold that the 1980 Act is drafted "poorly," suffice it to say that one who purchases software from

dubious sources should be cognizant of the potential legal exposures faced in this area.

2. *Patents.* These cover any new and useful "process, machine, manufacture or composition of matter" that is "unobvious." Whether the patent laws cover software remains in dispute. The Patent Office has, traditionally, been opposed to applying them to computer programs on the grounds that they grant monopoly rights over something that should be freely stored. Many courts have likewise held that programs are not patentable. The U.S. Supreme Court, however, has demonstrated a willingness to bring programs under the safeguards of the patent laws. This area of the law remains, at best, murky.

3. *Trade secrets.* Unlike the copyright and patent laws, these have no Federal statutory framework. These are state laws, decided on a case-by-case basis. To ensure their application, a plaintiff must demonstrate that:

    a. The matter being protected is actually used in its business.

    b. It is something that is not generally known in one's trade or business.

    c. It lends its owner a competitive advantage.

These laws would not be effective against a third party who develops the same program independently. However, an organization that purchases a copied or misappropriated program could find itself open to a lawsuit from the rightful owner of the program.

REGULATORY LIABILITIES

The American economy is a regulated one; the free enterprise system survives only on paper. Many of our key industries are regulated daily from the bureaucrats in Washington, D.C. Some of the more important regulatory concerns, especially for financial institutions, are as follows:

1. *Federal Deposit Insurance Corporation.* Its regulations can take the form of civil or administrative action for:

    a. Unfair or deceptive practices

    b. Use of deceptive advertising

    c. Limiting credit access

2. *Federal Home Loan Bank Board.* Its concern is with:

    a. Deceptive advertising regarding services

b.   Deceptive advertising regarding finances

3.   *National Credit Union Administration.*   It could bring action in cases involving:

a.   Deceptive advertising
b.   Deceptive representations

4.   *Comptroller of the Currency.*   It can exert regulatory powers as regards:

a.   Unfair or deceptive practices
b.   Misleading advertising
c.   Diversion of income
d.   Limiting access to competitors

5.   *Federal Reserve System.*   It regulates areas dealing with a failure to:

a.   Provide adequate disclosure
b.   Correct inaccurate data
c.   Delete unverifiable information
d.   Remove obsolete information
e.   Provide periodic statements
f.   Avoid unfair or deceptive practices
g.   Allow customers access to credit

LIMITING YOUR EXPOSURE

You need not, however, be open to all of these potential liabilities. There are measures that you can take to safeguard yourself from many of the legal trappings connected to the misuse or abuse of computer technology. These can take one or more of the following forms:

Personnel security.   These safeguards will serve to limit liabilities connected to EFTS frauds, thefts, abuses, and other unlawful acts.

Physical security.   This will serve to ensure the confidentiality and integrity of the data.

Software security.   This can curtail or eliminate system manipulations.

Communication security.   This will prevent electronic interceptions.

Education and training.   An adequate training program can limit computer-related errors and malfunctions.

Service and upkeep. These can limit breakdowns of the system and losses connected to natural hazards.

Sufficient liability coverage. This will cover your losses.

Legal awareness. Key EDP personnel should be sensitized to the legal and regulatory framework within which they operate.

The computer revolution is upon us. Banks, retailers, public utilities, carriers, brokers, and others can take action to avoid costly and time consuming computer-related litigation and regulatory enforcement actions. These, oftentimes, stem from the manner in which organizations collect, record, store, and disseminate information. By taking adequate safeguards in these areas, an organization can limit its potential legal exposure.

CHAPTER **16**

Theft of
High Technology

Acting on a tip from an informant, law enforcement agents arrested four men who were alleged to have stolen more than $70,000 worth of semiconductor chips; these were said to be valued at more than $600,000. Police had hoped that the arrests would lead to a break in a $3.4 million heist of electronic circuits. In another case, a former Exxon Corporation employee pleaded guilty to attempting to sell to a competitor detailed plans of an unreleased line of information on processing products.

An American businessman and several associates were arrested and charged with attempting to smuggle computers, fiber optics, and lasers to the Soviet Bloc. At the same time, a European businessman was charged with attempting to steal and sell to the Soviets a coded computer program, while six Japanese businessmen were arrested for conspiring to ship secret data on confidential computer documents and tapes stolen from IBM.

The theft of high technology has become big business. Losses are said to run into the billions of dollars annually. One international ring alone is said to have stolen more than $8 million worth of valuable high technology in a span of less than three years. The targets of these heists are computers, programs, terminals, semiconductor chips, lasers, fiber optics, and any valuable formula, pattern, device, or compilation of information. Computer technology, however, is of special interest to the "electronic underworld" because of the widespread use of computers in both the civilian and military areas. The motives for these thefts are both economic and political.

234

On the economic side, corporate competitors resort to high technology thefts for the purpose of gaining an economic edge over the victim. It is "cheaper to steal a product" than to develop and manufacture it. On the political side, the Soviet Bloc and other nations view these high technology heists in terms of military and industrial applications.

Through a network of "dummy" corporations, dishonest employees, criminal fences, professional thieves, and spies, the theft of high technology has become a serious and growing problem; dishonest employees play a key role in these electronic heists. No company—regardless of its size—is secure from industrial espionage. Its secrets, inventions, and marketing plans are the targets of both corporate and foreign spies; of special concern to the high technology firms should be the influx of Eastern Bloc spies.

TARGETS OF INDUSTRIAL ESPIONAGE

The "Bruchhousen network" best illustrates the manner and sophistication of the "high technology underworld." Through a series of a dozen American corporate fronts, the Bruchhousen gang is said to have smuggled millions of dollars of computers, semiconductors, communications gear, and manufacturing equipment to Austria and West Germany. From there, the smuggled equipment is said to have made its way to the Soviet Union. It took government investigators, working internationally, almost two years to finally close the pipeline. The kingpin of this "electronic network" escaped prosecution.

American high technology companies have cause for concern. Their inventions and trade secrets are open for the picking. The threat comes from both within and outside the United States. A sting operation engineered by the Federal Bureau of Investigation (FBI) is said to have nabbed more than a dozen Japanese businessmen. The seriousness of the problem has spurred the chairman of a U.S. Senate Subcommittee to write:

> We believe it is most important for us to receive from officials in the private sector who have responsibility for the security of sensitive information some specific examples of the types of problems American industry faces in this area as well as other input concerning the scope of the problem and possible solutions.

The severity of the problem convinced California legislators to pass tough legislation that is directed specifically at high technology thieves. Under the California law, any person who is convicted of "knowingly buying, selling, receiving, disposing or concealing" stolen semiconductor devices or computer equipment is guilty of a felony.[1] The statute carries a term of up to three years imprisonment. It also covers the forgery or unauthorized removal of a company logo from a microelectronic product.

The California law, however, is an exception to the norm; both at the local and Federal levels, prosecutors have to deal with antiquated laws. Even if conviction results, imprisonment is the exception rather than the norm; also, funds and training for government investigators in this area have been slow in coming. What makes matters even worse, the Soviet Bloc has also turned its attention to this area. Soviet agents, with their vast resources and contacts, have joined the electronic underworld; high technology firms—especially the smaller ones that cannot afford adequate security—have reason for concern.

WINDOW OF VULNERABILITY

Industrial espionage and the theft of a competitor's trade secrets are not new to the world of business. Medieval Venice made it its business to steal the inventions and secrets of her commercial rivals; she employed an army of agents for this purpose. The ancient Chinese guarded their inventions with an iron hand. Greed, lax security, and the ease with which these thefts can be perpetrated play a key role in high technology thefts. Simply put, it pays to steal another's trade secrets. Deterrence is often lacking; law enforcement efforts lack coordination. Our objectives are ambiguous; as a result, tomorrow's breakthroughs in computer technology may belong to other nations.

Summarizing the reasons for why the problem exists would require many chapters and extend beyond this book's limited scope. Simply stated, however, the problem stems from:

Lax corporate security.

Piecemeal and porous export controls.

Ill-trained law enforcement personnel.

Lack of coordination between the Federal and local police agencies.

Piecemeal Federal policies to address the problem.

Lack of deterrence. (Few of the high technology thieves ever go to prison. For example, several thieves convicted in a multimillion dollar smuggling operation of computers, lasers, and other electronic equipment merely received three year probationary sentences and fines of $25,000. They are said to be back in business.)

[1] California Senate Bill (SB) 862 became law on January 1, 1982.

The resources and manpower committed to address the problem have been inadequate. (For example, the U.S. Commerce Department's Compliance Division, partly responsible for policing the export of high technology equipment, has traditionally committed only a token number of its investigators to this area.)

Sophisticated techniques and vast resources are being employed by the thieves and foreign espionage services. (For example, the East German intelligence service is reported to spend more than $20 million a year on espionage efforts aimed at America's computer industry.)

Cooperation between the private and public sectors has been, at best, poor. (Computer manufacturers and other high technology firms fear this could eventually lead to regulation.)

There is need for laws that specifically address the problem. (Presently, law enforcement must resort to antiquated laws.)

New law enforcement strategies and policies are needed. (Old police strategies will not fare well against this class of criminals.)

Victims must be encouraged to come forth. (Often they are held in ridicule, and shy away.)

In addition, corporate security must be tightened. In one case, for example, three dishonest employees ripped off from their company valuable service manuals, computer hardware and software, test cables, confidential documents, circuit boards, and other valuable equipment; the losses were said to have exceeded $4 million. A simple background check of these individuals would have revealed that at least one of them had been involved in a similar case before. No such screening was ever conducted; in fact, one of the thieves occupied a very responsible position within the company. Simple security can play a key role in containing these thefts, but few companies are willing to expend the needed resources.

FOREIGN SPIES AT WORK

Some experts note that the present military hardware and technology of the Soviet Union has come to rival ours. In some cases, they add, it may even surpass ours. Our high technology lead may, we are told, soon become a thing of the past. America's computers, lasers, communication equipment, and other high technologies have, and continue to make their way to the Soviet Bloc and other foreign nations. Japan's Economic Council has stated that by the year 2000, Japan will replace America as the dominant economic power in the world. Through a sophisticated network of spies, professional agents, thieves, and criminal fences, the Soviet Bloc has robbed American companies of some of their more advanced technological innovations.

The transfer of high technology to the Soviet Bloc began in earnest in the early 1970s. With the rise of détente, the Soviet Bloc began to both purchase and steal our most advanced inventions and trade secrets. The modern Soviet military apparatus, experts note, was made possible largely by stolen American technology. The vice-president of a major electronics manufacturer has warned that "military critical technologies for future military systems are now making their way to potential adversaries." A high law enforcement official has observed that "they steal it, before we develop it."

The massive theft of America's high technology by the Soviets has seriously undermined not only our national defense, but also our technological lead. Technological breakthroughs made at the cost of billions of dollars in research have made their way to the Soviet Bloc at little or no cost. The theft of America's high technology, according to the Washington-based Institute on Strategic Trade, has saved the Soviets billions of dollars in research and development costs. Federal officials place the value of these heists at more than $1 billion annually.

In large part, the private sector has itself to blame. One corporate security officer told me that "we invite theft." Businesspeople, in search of new markets, often close their eyes to the need for security. For example, with the approval of both the Federal government and corporate America, Soviet officials have been permitted to visit and photograph high technology plants. They have also been permitted to link their computers to our data banks, making it possible for them to sift information on new products and patents at the press of a button.

The Soviet threat has increased; one business leader has warned that the "Western Alliance will soon face an enemy who possesses weapons of equal technological capability." The impact of high technology thefts by the Soviets is both commercial and military. It threatens our standing in world markets, and our ability to meet our national commitments. The theft of high technology carries with it a high price tag.

A quick glimpse alone will usually have little or no impact on the casual observer; after all, computer-related crimes and abuses are everyday occurrences. But the involvement of Soviet and other foreign intelligence services in this arena adds a new dimension to the problem. To cite only a few examples:

A Soviet buoy fished up off the coast of North Carolina is said to have been used to gather important data for antisubmarine warfare. It radioed the information back to the Soviet Union; it was all made possible by using stolen American technology.

A gang of international smugglers was charged by Federal prosecutors with conspiring to ship several million dollars worth of computers, semiconductor manufacturing equipment, and related technology to the Soviet Bloc.

West Coast gangs, consisting of American, West German, and Austrian citizens, are said to have smuggled millions of dollars in sophisticated computer and electronic equipment to the Soviet Bloc.

A Polish intelligence officer, while employed as a representative of the Polish American Machinery Corporation, paid an American engineer more than $90,000 for secrets dealing with a highly advanced computer-operated radar system.

High-speed computers, capable of assisting in the development of nuclear weapons, have already made their way to Eastern Bloc countries.

West German Customs officials have seized shipments of stolen microcomputer chips. The shipments were traced to an international criminal syndicate that had planned to smuggle them to the Soviet Bloc.

A network of American and West German citizens, working through dummy corporations, is said to have smuggled computers and classified communications gear to the Soviets. The ring operated through a network of more than 20 corporate fronts based in Western Europe.

The president of a California-based consulting firm has been convicted of conspiring to steal electronic secrets valued in excess of $10 million. He headed an industrial theft ring that diverted secret electronic designs to the Soviets.

A California-based company is under investigation for allegedly diverting more than $5 million worth of integrated circuits and computer manufacturing equipment to the Eastern Bloc.

A Swiss company is said to have sold sophisticated American-made computerized drafting equipment to Soviet agents.

Owners of a California firm were convicted of illegally exporting computers and laser optical mirrors to the Eastern Bloc through a network of European fronts. The equipment is said to have military application.

Canadian and Israeli citizens helped Soviet agents obtain more than $1 million in sophisticated computer equipment.

An Austrian company specialized in the sale of American computers and other equipment to foreign buyers.

A California businessman is said to have sold electronic equipment to Warsaw Pact nations.

A secret microwave receiver is said to have found its way to the Soviet Bloc.

Soviet agents, assisted by American citizens, are said to have stolen secret data on an American spy satellite.

An East European official is said to have paid an American engineer large sums of money for valuable trade secrets related to computer technology.

The motto among high technology thieves, it would appear, is that it "pays to rip off American companies." Some companies, however, are "willing victims." In their search for markets and economic advantages, some businesspeople have become willing accomplices of these thieves. The huge economic profits and technological advantages gained from these heists have also attracted spies of other nations. For example:

An American businessman and the managing director of a Pakistani company are said to have attempted to smuggle high technologies, needed in the construction of nuclear weapons, to Pakistan.

American businessmen are said to have illegally shipped military technologies to foreign governments with ties to terrorist groups.

British and American businessmen are said to have run a giant smuggling operation, using dummy corporations in Liberia, England, and the United States.

A West European company with access to American technology has assisted Third World nations in developing rockets with potential military applications.

An American businessman is said to have illegally diverted military technologies to Libya.

A high official at the U.S. Department of Defense has summarized the Soviet threat to our high technology:

Using agents, co-opting citizens, taking advantage of unsuspecting business men and women, moving goods through neutral and Third World countries, exploiting the weaknesses in our control system, they [Soviets] are gaining access to [our] technology on an unprecedented scale.

He went on to add that of special concern to them is our computer industry. A former Deputy Director of the Central Intelligence Agency has warned that:

the bulk of the new technology which they [Soviets] have employed has
been acquired from the United States.

The Soviets pose a credible threat to our high technology—and especially
to our computer industry.

MODUS OPERANDI

The theft and diversion of high technology by the Soviet Union has been
carried out by two of its best intelligence services: the KGB (State Security Committee), and the GRU (Chief Intelligence Directorate of the Soviet General Staff). Through a network of spies and corporate fronts,
KGB and GRU agents have smuggled computer chips, laser technologies,
and other high technologies to the Eastern Bloc. The KGB's strategy and
view of American businesspeople is best illustrated in one of its training
manuals, where the following observation is made: "[Americans] regard
money as the sole means of ensuring personal freedom and independence."
    The KGB is rated high in "spy circles"; even the best corporate secu-
rity efforts are not always sufficient to stop its well funded and experienced
pool of agents. Because we are an open society, the KGB often operates
with impunity.
    Of special interest to corporate security officers, especially those in the
computer industry, should be the KGB's modus operandi and chain of
command. Its espionage efforts are directed by:

First Chief Directorate. It oversees the more than 5000 KGB spies
who operate in the West.
First Department. It carries out the North American espionage
operations.
Service "T." It concentrates the KGB's efforts in the area of American
high technology.
Eighth Directorate. It is primarily responsible for the KGB's electronic eavesdropping operations.
Second Directorate. It monitors and recruits American businesspeople, tourists, and others.
Thirteenth Department. It handles sabotage.

The resources and personnel the KGB has committed in the United
States are impressive. They consist of the following:

Many Soviet government officials in this country are connected to the KGB, or are military intelligence agents.

The KGB is assisted by other Eastern Bloc agents assigned to the United Nations.

KGB agents are also assisted by Eastern Bloc students studying in American universities, and Eastern Bloc tourists and immigrants.

The major KGB bases of operation are Washington, D.C., New York, and San Francisco.

The number of KGB and GRU spies operating in this country is said to exceed 1000.

The Soviet San Francisco consulate is said to have a staff of 50 to 60 KGB officers and at least 25 GRU agents assigned to it.

Both KGB and GRU agents employ American and European business-people as agents.

At least $1 billion in high technology is said to have been illegally shipped to the Soviet Bloc from the United States with the assistance of KGB and GRU agents.

The KGB and GRU have set up a network of corporate fronts in Switzerland, Canada, and West Germany, to act as conduits for the shipment of stolen high technology equipment.

The KGB also makes widespread use of dishonest American and West European businesspeople, corporate employees, and others. The methods employed to recruit these agents often vary; sometimes they can be ingenious. For example:

A prime candidate is someone with access to military, diplomatic, or technological secrets.

Recruits are provided spying equipment.

They communicate with their Soviet contacts through secret "dead drops," intermediaries, or at select foreign cities.

American law enforcement agencies have cause for concern; they fear that the Soviets may have also placed moles in many of our high technology companies. The number of Soviet-connected high technology intelligence activities increases daily.

Equally important in the theft and diversion of American high technology is the Soviet military intelligence apparatus (or GRU). The modus operandi of GRU differs somewhat from that of the KGB. Although both agencies have proven adept at stealing America's corporate trade secrets, some experts give GRU higher marks. GRU operates as follows:

It is headed by a General.

Its foreign intelligence budget is larger than that of the KGB.

It is the agency that is credited with stealing the American secrets to the atomic bomb.

It often goes under its cover name "Military Department 44388."

Aeroflot (the Soviet airline) is said to be one of its fronts.

It controls some 30,000 ("Special Designation") agents, trained in sabotage.

Its budget for stealing industrial secrets from the West is said to be unlimited.

It is the prime supplier of technology to the Soviet military industrial complex.

The head of GRU is a member of the powerful Military-Industrial Commission (VPK).

Each year the VPK issues a "shopping list" of Western high technology equipment to GRU agents.

Thefts of high technology are referred to as "Line X" items.

The GRU school for spies is housed at the People's Militia Street in Moscow; the school's cover name is "Military Department 35576," and its official name is the "Military-Diplomatic Academy of the Soviet Army."

GRU agents, like their KGB counterparts, operate widely in both the United States and Western Europe under various covers. These disguises often take on various forms and can be difficult to detect. For example:

As journalists, academics, professionals, trade unionists, and United Nations employees.

Aeroflot employees.

Under the cover of the International Labor Organization.

At trade exhibitions.

Both GRU and KGB should prove of concern to corporate America. Their record in the area of industrial espionage is matched by few. The successes that their agents have scored not only in the United States, but also in Japan and Western Europe, have been impressive. For example:

Thefts of high technology have made it possible for the Soviets to develop the Typhoon-class and Alfa-class submarines. These are faster and can dive deeper than anything in the West's arsenal.

Laser equipment for use in space warfare was stolen by Soviet agents from American defense contractors.

Soviet agents have attempted to recruit French scientists.

Soviet agents stole the plans of the French Mirage-2000 fighter plane.

Soviet agents are credited with the theft of satellite data from an American company.

Soviet agents have had little difficulty in purchasing the needed technologies to operate their missile plants, missile launchers, and their Missile Design Bureau.

The Soviet espionage network is both well funded and coordinated. Its agents are professionals and are often assisted by dishonest corporate employees and professional criminals. Their task is facilitated by lax corporate security, and by a poorly trained and uncoordinated police apparatus.

ADDRESSING THE THREAT

Security alone, however, will not suffice to safeguard America's high technology from thefts. Even the best of security programs will not always stop a determined and sophisticated criminal. In part, to address the problem, we need:

Aggressive and well coordinated investigative/prosecutorial efforts.

Minimum mandatory prison sentences for convicted felons.

High fines and forfeiture laws.

A "get tough" approach to industrial espionage.

Better training for law enforcement.

Tighter corporate security measures.

Above all, a recognition of the problem.

The computer/telecommunications revolution has opened up new opportunities for criminals, who have been joined by foreign spies. Why should a corporate competitor or foreign power invest billions of dollars in research if it can steal someone else's findings with little effort? High technology thefts are a problem for both industry and government; legislation may be necessary to address part of this problem. Businesspeople, however, would do well to take a lead in the war against high technology criminals; they can do this by tightening security, pressing for prosecutions, and educating the public. Whether they are willing or able to do this remains to be seen. The outcome could decide whether America will continue to lead the computer revolution.

CHAPTER 17

Computers
as Tools
in Corporate
Takeovers

Two corporations trading on the New York Stock Exchange are locked in a cross fire of litigation. The smaller of the two seeks to stave off an $800 million tender offer for up to 75 percent of its stock; the target company also charges that computer sabotage caused the price of its stock to fall below its book value. In a separate case, the target of a takeover was not so lucky. By the time management discovered that someone had tampered with its computers, the price of the company's stock had dropped so dramatically that it became an ideal takeover candidate.

Acquisitions are not new to Wall Street, but the above cases illustrate that a company's computer can also become the target of an acquisition-minded company or group of investors. The computer saboteur can bring a potential takeover candidate to its "financial knees," the indirect result being loss of investor confidence in the company's stock.

Takeover battles can be, as a client once remarked, "very nasty and dirty." The computer simply offers the aggressor a new tool; it should be viewed as an electronic pressure tactic. A potential target, however, can take measures to safeguard itself; these can take the form of computer security and financial security. The former is addressed in other parts of the book; this chapter addresses the financial safeguards.

NEED FOR FINANCIAL SAFEGUARDS

Adequate financial safeguards can play a role in dissuading a predator
from your doorstep. Computer security can and does play an important
role in safeguarding the finances of your company, but more is needed.
Computer security alone will not stave off a predator, nor will it assist you
in identifying the potential predator. In addition, a determined and sophisticated criminal can breach most security systems on the market; no system
is foolproof.

Safeguarding your company from an acquisition-minded company will
entail enacting adequate financial security to dissuade an undesirable
suitor. These should always be employed in conjunction with computer
security; you should consider the following:

Make a determination whether you are an acquisition target.

Identify and understand the modus operandi of the potential predator.

Outline the necessary financial strategy.

Institute the needed financial safeguards.

Develop a plan to combat the takeover.

Adequate financial safeguards will go a long way in ensuring that even
if your computers are sabotaged, the aggressor will not find your company
an easy takeover candidate. The computer is the workhorse of the modern
corporation; destroy it and you have retarded the ability of the modern
manager to address the company's daily needs. Adequate financial safeguards will enable your firm to stave off a takeover attack, while efforts
are made to repair the computer sabotage.

CHARACTERISTICS OF POTENTIAL TARGETS

There are a number of Wall Street sources that, for a fee, will identify
potential acquisition targets for a predator; there are also a multitude of
experts that, for the right fee, will sabotage a company's computers and
thus facilitate its acquisition. By destroying its computers, the saboteur
hampers a company's daily financial viability; in turn, this has an impact
on the price of the target company's stock.

But you need not find yourself on the "gunsight" of a predator; there
are steps you can take to safeguard your company from an unwanted
suitor. However, you must first determine if your company is a potential
takeover target; this can be done by taking a simple "acquisition litmus"

test. If you find that at least 50 percent of your responses to the following questions are positive, then consider yourself a potential acquisition target. Check to see if your company:

Has a low price/earning multiple.

Has substantial borrowing capacity.

Occupies an important position in a new and/or growing industry.

Ranks above average in its distribution capacity.

Has understated assets.

Has a history of merger negotiations.

Has an absence of large holdings by management.

Has a high liquidity.

Offers a unique product or service.

Has been the target of an attempted computer sabotage.

If your company scores badly on the above test, then proceed with some additional checks. Consult your management regarding the following:

See whether there is any unusual trading activity in your stock.

Find out if your sources in the Wall Street community have heard anything on the "financial grapevine."

See if your computer(s) are amply secure from sabotage.

Determine whether there are any unusual price fluctuations in the stock.

Identify and determine the sizes of the concentrated holdings.

See whether there are major "suspect" stockholders.

See if any geographic concentrations are developing.

Check whether there have been past takeover efforts.

Identify suspicious block trades.

See if the Schedule 13D filings disclose suspicious activity.[1]

Make sure important stockholders are in your corner.

See if the trading activity has deviated from its norm.

If after your review of the above you are concerned, then proceed both to check for EDP-related sabotage and to tighten your EDP security. A

[1] These are filed with the U.S. Securities and Exchange Commission in Washington, D.C.

potential acquisition candidate has cause for concern; its EDP system, if vulnerable, can prove to be its "Achilles heel." In addition, proceed to identify potential predators and their techniques.

MODUS OPERANDI OF PREDATORS

Predators often differ in both their objectives and the techniques they employ; a vulnerable EDP system, however, can facilitate their task. Also, because a computer-related sabotage can prove difficult to detect, the computer is an inviting target.

You should keep in mind that the attempted acquisition may merely be a ploy; it may serve to disguise the predator's real objectives. Predators are sometimes interested in simply forcing the target company to buy back its stock at a substantially higher price, giving the predator a profit. If management refuses, the predator can apply added pressure by threatening a proxy fight; the mere threat often intimidates top company officials.

A predator's takeover strategy will vary from case to case. However, there are some identifiable patterns; the more common are the following:

The predator will often screen several potential takeover targets.

The predator will zero in on the most vulnerable target.

The acquisition target is often a company whose stock trades low.

The predator may embark on a plan to sabotage the target's computers.

Once this is accomplished, the predator will then commence to purchase large blocks of the stock as it falls in price (usually below book value).

In its Schedule 13D filings (with the Securities & Exchange Commission), the predator will state its reason for these purchases as simply "investment purposes."

Once a large percentage of the stock has been secured, the predator may request a meeting with the target's management.

At that and other meetings, the predator may request a seat on the Board or even liquidation of the target company.

The predator may also intimate that it is ready to sell the stock back to the target company at a higher price.

If management resists, the predator may attempt (or threaten) to run its own candidates for the Board.

The predator may run on a platform that calls for the liquidation, sale, or merger of the company.

Once it has selected and sabotaged the computers of a target company, the predator will often make an immediate effort to acquire the target, but the predator knows it is not guaranteed success. Thus to enhance the probability of success, it may resort to "mud throwing" tactics. These often take the form of:

Having private investigators "get the goods" on management.

Blackmailing key members of management.

Threatening to go to the authorities with revelations of corporate wrongdoing.

Turning disgruntled employees (especially EDP types) into informers.

Contacting former company officers for corporate "skeletons."

Further undermining the viability of the target's EDP system.

Threatening to embarrass, frighten, and cajole management.

The above techniques can often—especially when employed in conjunction with a computer sabotage—prove effective. Takeover battles should be treated for what they are—"corporate wars." The target company's survival and that of its management are often at stake. Steps should be taken long before the problem arises to ensure that the company staves off the attacker.

CONSIDERATIONS CONNECTED TO FINANCIAL SAFEGUARDS

A target company need not be helpless; it can deter or stave off a takeover attempt. The attacker can be "stopped in its tracks," but management must first institute the needed financial safeguards.[2] The safeguards are often simple and inexpensive. Before instituting them, however, you should be cognizant of the environment in which they must operate. You should first consider the following:

Legal needs. There are a multiplicity of state and Federal statutes, rules, and regulations that can have an impact on these financial safeguards. Make sure that the ones you are considering comply with the law.

Comprehensiveness. The safeguards should be both well thought out and fully suited to your company's needs. Avoid piecemeal and cosmetic approaches.

---

[2] These should always incorporate adequate computer security.

Timing.   Unfortunately, some firms wait until they become the targets of an acquisition to implement these safeguards. Be wise and plan well in advance.

Stockholders.   Because the implementation of your safeguards may require stockholder approval, consider how they may react. If the safeguards are viewed as serving only management, you will have stockholder problems.

Regulators.   Consider how the regulatory agencies (state and Federal) will react to these measures.

Expenses.   Money alone will not always buy the needed safeguards. Discard the notion that only the most expensive safeguards are the best. Be a wise consumer and consider how you can get the most for your dollar.

Image.   Consider how others in your industry may react to these safeguards.

Evolution.   Implement your safeguards in a well planned and timely manner.

It is important that the safeguards you select not only meet your company's needs, but also comply with the regulatory environment. However, always remember that even the best of these safeguards are only as good as their architects. Review and update them periodically; also be ready with a contingency plan just in case your safeguards are not adequate to contain an attacker. Computer security has an important role to play, but alone, it will not suffice in staving off an acquisition effort. You need complete security; it should encompass financial safeguards.

FINANCIAL TAKEOVER SAFEGUARDS

Securing your EDP system will ensure that your company's assets, trade secrets, marketing plans, client lists, and other valuable and confidential data is safe from theft, but takeover safeguards, when coordinated with EDP security, can ensure that your company will not be easily "swallowed up" in a takeover. When instituting any safeguards, however, remember that management is presumed to be acting both in good faith and in the best interest of the company (and its stockholders). Having considered this, proceed to review and implement the needed takeover safeguards.

Your financial safeguards should always reflect the unique needs of your company; these often vary from company to company. There are, however, some guidelines that have general application; these are:

Repurchase some of the company stock when the price drops.

Consider issuing a special class of voting stock.

Carry out an active stock options program.

Stay on good terms with the regulatory agencies.

Diversify the company's business.

Eliminate unnecessary liquid assets.

Use your employee benefit plan to purchase company stock.

Stay on good terms with the large stockholders.

Review your EDP security periodically.

Tighten computer security.

Keep the company laundry "clean."

Stagger the election of your directors.

Consider changing the state of incorporation.

Limit special elections.

Limit the right of stockholders to remove directors without cause.

Require a high proportion of stockholders to be present at the stockholder meetings.

Refer all "bad apples" to the regulators for action.

Secure your shareholder list.

Allow access to your shareholder list only on a "need-to-know" basis.

Guard against computer espionage.

Ensure that the transfer agent has taken adequate steps to safeguard your (computerized) stockholder list.

Split the stock periodically.

Ensure that a sufficient number of unused (but authorized) shares are available for issuance on a need basis.

Review the corporate charter and bylaws periodically.

Give directors authority to increase the number of members on the Board.

Maintain an updated list of all your stockholders.

Identify holders in nominee and broker's names.

Maintain good ties with brokers.

Maintain friendly relations with your creditors.

Provide for cumulative voting.

Ensure flexibility in the timing of your annual meeting.

Eliminate preemptive rights.

Conduct periodic reviews of changes in stock ownership.

Stay on good terms with other members of the industry.
Be alert to suspicious fluctuations in the price of the stock.

The above recommended guidelines can fend off unwanted suitors, but these must always be employed with adequate computer safeguards. Always remember that even the best computer security measures can be circumvented; no EDP system is ever totally safe. However, even if your computers are sabotaged in a takeover scheme, adequate financial safeguards can help stave off an unwanted suitor. Should all your defenses fail, however, be well prepared for an acquisition fight. Your "war plans" should be prepared and thought out well in advance.

FIGHTING TAKEOVERS

You should always be prepared for the possibility that your computer and financial safeguards may not be sufficient to stave off an unwanted suitor. Be cognizant of other measures available to you to defeat unwanted overtures. As with computer and financial safeguards, always review the legality, costs, timeliness, and other considerations that the takeover battle plans may have on your company. The best of battle plans, if illegal or ill-planned, will not serve you well.

Once you have analyzed and weighed your takeover war strategy, note that there are several defensive measures that your company should consider in order to wage a successful takeover battle. These should include:

Outlining management's position to the stockholders.
Seeking stockholder support.
Aggressively repurchasing the company stock.
Actively competing for all available stock.
Soliciting the support of the local community (for example, "if we are acquired, many local jobs will be lost").
Increasing the outstanding common shares.
Disclosing the takeover attempt.
Contacting the regulators.
Exerting political pressure.
Checking the accuracy and timeliness of the Schedule 13D filings.
Keeping your 14D information current.
Having your company divest itself of any assets or subsidiaries the attacker wants.

Proposing a merger to a powerful "white knight."

Proposing liquidation.

Explaining why the takeover will have a negative financial impact.

Filing for an injunction (for example, on the grounds that the attacker filed false/inaccurate information and/or made material omissions in the offering).

Filing an antitrust action.

Promptly informing the regulators of all violations of law.

Fighting requests for the stockholder list.

Filing a stockholder derivate action.

Seeking public support for your position.

Initiating legislation and/or regulations that will impede the attacker.

Acquiring a company that is a direct competitor of the attacker.

Initiating public demonstrations by the company employees.

Reducing the debit capacity.

Increasing the stock dividend.

Pursuing an aggressive public relations campaign.

Demonstrating your tenacity to carry on a prolonged battle.

Making it costly for the predator to pursue its plans.

Demonstrating widespread stockholder support.

Demonstrating support from labor unions.

Soliciting the support of pressure groups (for example, women's groups and minorities).

Having company employees lobby their elected officials.

Seeking the assistance of company creditors.

Assessing the real motives and objectives of the predator.

Determining the size of the attacker's holdings.

Reviewing the attacker's modus operandi in past takeovers.

Publicizing negative aspects of other acquisitions by the attacker.

When fighting a takeover, your company should play it tough; take the offense whenever possible. Take the battle into the predator's own camp; be aggressive and determined. You can accomplish this by taking to the offensive:

Acquire the opponent's stock.

Request its stockholder list.

Contact its key creditors.

Approach its large stockholders.

Coordinate your efforts with its competitors.

Computer sabotage as a tool in an overall takeover strategy is still in its infancy, but as companies increasingly come to rely on their computers for their daily operations, vulnerable EDP systems offer the predator an opportunity to bring a publicly held corporation to its knees. In addition, the detection of the sabotage may prove difficult; tying the attacker to it may prove impossible. Saboteurs can easily erase all tracks and vanish from whence they came.

Computer security measures can assist, but even these can be circumvented by a determined and sophisticated criminal. These must be employed in conjunction with financial safeguards and a takeover battle plan. Computer technology has opened new horizons for companies and investors in search of takeover candidates.

CHAPTER 18

On the Road
to a Cashless
Society

A housewife who learned about Electronic Funds Transfer Systems (EFTSs) from watching a television show ripped off a Maryland bank for more than $20,000 in a fraudulent electronic wire fund transfer. Thieves knowledgeable in computerized bank transactions stole nearly $2 million from a Florida bank in a sophisticated EFTS fraud. A California court convicted a computer consultant who had been charged with a $10 million illegal wire transfer. A large Washington, D.C., money market fund was ripped off by one of its employees for more than $1 million in a wire fraud; the thief evaded prosecution.

Increasingly, we are becoming an "electronic money" or cashless society.[1] Paper and coin money are giving way to electronic blips; rudimentary EFTSs have already made their appearance. Billions of dollars are transferred and recorded daily across states and continents by networks of computers connected by terminals, wires, and satellites. Thousands of computers are used to operate these electronic money systems, employing a workforce of more than 1 million men and women.

The cashless society is here to stay; its impact on our social, political, and economic institutions has only begun to be felt. Questions are already being raised about the ability of democratic societies to adequately address the many challenges of EFTS. The computer is its workhorse; herein also lies its weakness.

[1] Electronic Funds Transfer Systems (EFTSs) are often referred to as the cashless society.

UNDERSTANDING THE CASHLESS SOCIETY

The National Commission on Electronic Fund Transfers (EFTSs) has defined the "cashless society" as a payment system in which the processing and communications necessary to effect economic exchanges, and the processing and communications necessary for the production and distribution of services incidental or related to economic exchanges, are dependent wholly or in large part on the use of electronics. Others have described EFTSs as a class of related practices and technologies that employ electronic impulses, generated and interpreted by computers to debit and credit financial accounts. Each such debit or credit transaction is termed an "electronic funds transfer" (EFT). Electronic impulses, rather than paper or coin, are thus employed to effect economic transactions.

In its simplest form, the cashless society can best be described as an array of electronic financial services. Among the services most frequently associated with it are wire transfers, direct deposits, authorized payments, check verification, credit card authorizations, and telephone bill-paying systems. Point-of-sale systems (POSs), automated teller machines (ATMs), and automated clearing house facilities (ACHs) constitute more advanced forms of EFTSs.

These electronic financial systems transfer funds through the use of electronic impulses traveling over the wires and recorded by a network of computers. Without the computer, the cashless society would still be in the realm of science fiction. These electronic financial systems presently operate at the regional, national, and international levels. Today, EFTSs are found in many parts of the industrialized world.

OTHER PAPERLESS SYSTEMS

The computer revolution has also sparked the development of other paperless systems, very analogous to EFTSs. These other paperless systems are best illustrated by the Electronic Message Systems (EMSs) revolution. Still in its infancy, EMSs constitute additional shifts away from our present paper-based society; they also represent new vehicles for the cashless society. Rudimentary EMSs have already taken shape.

EMSs can best be defined as data transmission systems that employ electronic impulses, rather than paper, to effect the flow of information. These systems have come to embrace a wide range of services. Among the better known are the Electronic Computer Originated Mail (ECOM), Electronic Message Services (EMSs), and Intelpost. Proponents of the cashless society view these systems as eventual substitutes for the present postal, telex, and cable communicating systems.

ECOM

ECOM is a mailgram-type service that is run by the U.S. Postal Service. Messages are initially recorded on a magnetic tape or disk by the user; they are then transmitted on-line from the user's premises to each destination post office. At present, the system is limited to mass mailers; it may eventually link all of the nation's large post offices.

Upon destination, the messages are then converted into hard copy and delivered to the recipient by a mail carrier; deliveries are made within a day from the input time. ECOM also offers a variety of address and text editing features. The service, however, has become embroiled in a dispute between the Federal Communications Commission and the Postal Service; each views it as being within its jurisdiction. This has served to retard its growth.

INTELPOST

Similar to ECOM in its workings, INTELPOST is undergoing tests by the Postal Service. INTELPOST would provide an international computerized transmission service between users in this country and Europe.

EMSs

Fearful of losing its first class mail sender to private electronic message systems, the Postal Service has embarked on EMSs. The service provides for the electronic transmission of first class mail directly to the recipient's office or home; ITT, RCA, Western Union, and Xerox are currently developing their own private EMSs networks. The Postal Service is also experimenting with a more advanced form of EMSs.

SWIFT

Known as the Society for Worldwide Interbank Financial Telecommunications, SWIFT is a private international message service. SWIFT was created under Belgian law by a group of American and European financial institutions. It links over 500 institutions, both in America and Europe, into an international specialized EFTS/EMS service. It handles more than 100,000 messages daily, and has replaced the mails, telex, and cables as mediums for communicating international payments between member financial institutions.

Others

There are a number of other experimental paperless message systems. The Western Union Company, for example, has developed an International Mailgram Service (IMS); the Xerox Corporation is experimenting with the Telecommunications Network Service (TNS). In the not too distant future these systems, in conjunction with EFTSs, will make it possible to bank from one's home or office, read electronic newspapers, send electronic mail, and work in an electronic office.

ARGUMENTS FOR AND AGAINST GOING CASHLESS

One of the key benefits, proponents of EFTSs tell us, of going cashless will be convenience; we will be able to bank from the comfort of our homes and offices. However, studies of consumer attitudes toward EFTSs have found that much of the support for these electronic money systems comes from the more affluent groups, who view EFTSs as being valuable time saving devices. Professionals, especially, are favorably disposed toward the cashless society, because of the ease with which it enables them to pay their bills. For the more affluent, EFTSs represent convenience and time savings.

Safety and security are said to be additional benefits society will derive from EFTSs. The incidence of armed robberies and other traditional crimes will decline substantially, since stores, banks, and individuals will carry little or no currency. Forgeries and counterfeiting presently plague the financial sector; these, too, will become things of the past.

We are told that the cashless society will also alleviate the present paper glut in the U.S. Postal Service. EFTSs will make it unnecessary for businesses, government, and individuals to employ the mails for purposes of making deposits, withdrawals, loan repayments, and conducting other financial transactions. EFTSs will also eliminate much of the paper work presently connected with payrolls and social security checks, by making it possible to transfer funds electronically from a business or government account to that of an employee or beneficiary. In the process, the problem of stolen checks will also be resolved; there should also be an easing of the present long bank deposit lines.

Of equal importance, EFTSs will also cut back on the growing costs connected with our present checking system. The volume of checks presently in use has grown dramatically. In 1945, the annual check volume was 5.3 million; by 1970 it had grown to 22.5 billion, and by the mid-1980s it will exceed 100 billion. More than 50 percent of all checks written annually are for amounts of less than 50 dollars; those written for amounts of more than $10,000 represent only one percent. This contributes to the high cost of processing checks; these costs are said to grow daily.

At present, it costs an average of 30 cents to process each check. It is estimated that the total annual bill for handling all the checks in this country now exceeds $11 billion. Proponents of the cashless society note that EFTSs could cut these costs by more than 30 percent. The costs associated with the production, authorization of payment, handling of checks, forgery, fraud, error, and the float would also be largely eliminated under EFTSs.

Proponents also tell us that EFTSs will result in better and increased financial services; they will also augment retail sales, since customers will be able to shop from the convenience of their homes. EFTSs will also serve to give consumers greater access to their funds, prompting them to spend more. The cashless society may also make the smaller financial institutions more competitive by giving them access to national markets.[2]

However, the cashless society is not without its critics; they charge that it will give rise to novel and more complex problems. It will spawn new types of crimes, invasions of privacy, and also open our society to further political/economic manipulation. Some critics even charge that EFTSs will give rise to Orwell's "Big Brother."

Consumer groups have already indicated that they fear EFTSs will open the individual's entire financial history, including his/her most intimate inner secrets, to credit bureaus at the press of a button; it will dramatically augment the dissemination of personal data to third parties. A study by the U.S. Congress concluded that the threat to privacy under EFTSs is a matter of serious concern, one that is founded on a realistic assessment of the present technology.

There is also concern that EFTSs will lessen the individual's control over his/her finances. The ability to exploit the benefits of the float during the check clearing process will no longer be available to the consumer. EFTSs, based upon prearranged transfers of funds, adds limitations to the individual's ability to manipulate personal finances. Consumer advocates are also fearful that the cancelled check, presently used as proof of payment in disputes between consumers and creditors, will no longer be available in the cashless society.

Currently, consumers can direct their banks to stop payment on a check, giving them a leverage in their business dealings. In an environment of instantaneous electronic transfers of funds, this leverage will no longer be available to the consumer. There is also the problem of computer error and

[2] Representatives of the small financial institutions, however, take exception.

malfunction. Human error, once computerized, may prove difficult and expensive to detect or correct.

There is also the serious problem of EFTS-related crimes. We have already seen that computer-related crimes and abuses are on the increase; payment systems where the computer is the workhorse likewise lend themselves to criminal manipulation. A study I headed found that, at present, few computer security programs can withstand a dedicated attack by sophisticated criminals. In addition, many of our police agencies presently lack the training and know-how to investigate and bring to prosecution complex computer-connected frauds; they may fare even worse in a cashless society.

There is also concern by small financial institutions that their larger counterparts, in an effort to create a cashless society, may resort to illegal trade practices. In addition, critics charge that EFTS-related civil disputes may prove both more difficult and costly to litigate than present suits. Existing rules and procedures make it difficult to introduce printouts, magnetic tapes, and disks in evidence in a trial.

However, despite these fears, indications are that we are heading in the direction of a cashless/paperless society. In large part, this financial revolution was made possible by computer technology, but there are also subtle and powerful forces at work. It is these that serve to propel the present EFTSs revolution.

To the powerful financial interests, EFTSs offer vehicles for new markets and opportunities; their smaller counterparts, fearful that unless they jump on the EFTS bandwagon they will be left out, have also demonstrated an interest in the cashless society. Businesspeople and retailers view these systems as a cost saving vehicle, while vendors see EFTSs as potential multibillion dollar annual markets. The secret of EFTSs have been their ability to attract the backing of powerful and diverse economic interests; they have something to offer to each one.

HOW THESE SYSTEMS OPERATE

Currently, bank customers in many of our cities are able to pay their bills by simply dialing their bank's computer. Giving a secret identifying code, the customer can order the computer how much to pay and to whom. Bank customers are also presently able to make deposits, withdraw cash, transfer funds, pay bills, and even obtain an update on their account, through the use of EFTSs.[3] Plans are also afoot to enable them to contact

[3] For a more in-depth review of EFTSs, see A. Bequai, *The Cashless Society: EFTS at the Crossroads* (New York: John Wiley & Sons, 1981).

their bank's computer by portable telephone, and direct it to make payments.

At present, a growing number of individuals pay their utility, insurance, and department store bills without using cash or checks. The vehicles that make this possible are several; among the better known are the automated clearing houses, point-of-sale systems, automated teller machines, preauthorized credits and debits, and the telephone bill paying systems.

Automated Clearing House (ACH)

An ACH is a computerized, interbank transfer system. Through it, an originating bank transmits payment orders electronically or on magnetic tapes. These payments are then routed by the ACH to designated receiving banks. The ACH constitutes one of the more fundamental types of EFTS; it is also one of the oldest. There are presently more than 30 such systems in operation in the United States.

The typical ACH operation commences with a computerized list of payment orders from one or more payers. On the list are recorded the names and account numbers of the payees, those of their banks, and also the amount to be paid each. The list is then transmitted electronically by the payer's bank computer to the ACH computer; the latter sorts out the information, and directs the payment orders to the appropriate receiving bank.

The ACH process has replaced check clearing facilities with electronic entry systems that clear by means of electronic impulses. The key advantage to an ACH is the increased speed by which balances can be adjusted at a common clearing bank, freeing these balances for other uses more quickly than under the manual system employed by many check clearing facilities. What makes the ACH attractive is its simplicity.

Point-of-Sale (POS)

POS systems have been described as the most pure EFTS presently available. The ultimate success of the EFTS revolution may depend, in part, on the widespread acceptance and use of POS systems by the public at large. A POS can be used to process deposits, withdrawals, interaccount transfers, and also to verify account balances and preauthorized credit extensions. In a POS, on-line electronic messages involving the instantaneous verification of accounts and the transfers of funds from customers to merchants replace present traditional paper flow systems. POS terminals serve to eliminate the requirement of paper flow in the initial payments transaction.

A POS can also capture and transmit, electronically, payments information originating at a merchant's location. This is done by transmitting a message from a terminal located at a merchant's counter to a data base in a depository institution's computer. The object is to transfer funds or to provide an information service, such as verifying or guaranteeing a check or authorizing a draw against a preestablished line of credit.

Unlike an ACH transaction, which is preauthorized by the customer and initiated by the company or by the customer through the depository institution, POS transactions are initiated individually at an electronic terminal by the customer through a merchant, or other terminal operator. POS transactions also require immediate and unique authorization by the depository institution where the customer's account resides. Whereas most ACH transactions often entail regional or national distribution, POS transactions often occur in local stores, often involving a customer doing business with a local merchant.

Automated Teller Machine (ATM)

There are presently more than 10,000 ATMs in use in the United States; their numbers are fast growing. ATMs have also found favor with consumers overseas.

Occasionally referred to as Customer-Bank Communication Terminals (CBCTs), ATMs are capable of processing a variety of transactions between a depository institution and its customers. They can accept deposits, provide withdrawals, transfer funds between accounts, and accept instructions to pay third parties. An ATM permits bank customers access to their accounts 24 hours a day, seven days a week.

ATMs can be one of two types: off-line or on-line. Off-line types are not connected to a computer; rather they operate independently. They are equipped with the necessary logic to read and decode a customer's entry card. Bank clerks are assigned the daily task of reviewing services performed by these off-line ATMs. A printed receipt is usually generated for all customer transactions. The customer receives the original document through the ATM cash drawer, and a duplicate is retained by the machine for bank proofing and posting operations.

An off-line ATM can also be equipped with an internal (magnetic core) memory to store lists of delinquent (hot-card) accounts and stolen cards; these lists are updated for each ATM belonging to a particular bank.

The on-line ATM represents a newer and more sophisticated generation. It is directly connected, through the use of telephone communication lines, to a central computer. The on-line ATM provides the customer with the capability of making an account balance inquiry; it can also provide for computer file updating. On-line ATMs can also keep more current hot-card lists than their off-line counterparts.

ATMs, however, are not problem free. They often malfunction, and are open to criminal attack, especially by insiders. The number of banking services they provide is limited. Bank customers often complain that they are impersonal. Some customers, especially those from the lower socio-economic strata of society, are awed by this technology; they do not under-stand it and have difficulty using ATMs.

Fraudulent authorizations pose a serious problem. A criminal who gains access to a customer's card and secret access code (PIN) can easily rip off the system; counterfeit ATM cards can also present a problem. In addi-tion, ATM facilities can be bugged by a concealed electronic listening device; a thief can also be posted across the street, observing a customer use an ATM and noting the PIN typed on the keyboard. Sophisticated criminals can resort to "skimming"; in this scheme, the data from the real card's magnetic strip is transferred to a second (counterfeit) card.

Criminals can also attack the on-line ATMs employing a "spoofer." This is a device that is inserted in the communications lines that connect the ATM to the central computer at the bank. The spoofer is employed to direct the ATM to dump cash until the cash hopper is empty. ATM communication lines are also vulnerable to taps; the thief, through use of a simple tap, can intercept important and confidential financial data. ATMs are also open to physical attack; a criminal may attempt to break into an ATM by striking it with a blunt instrument. However, the amount of money that can be stolen in this manner is limited.

Preauthorized Credits and Debits

The more common of these are direct payroll and social security deposits. An employee who wants to participate in a preauthorized credit program simply signs an authorization form with the employer. Before each pay-day, the employer's computer records on a magnetic tape the employee's bank number, bank account, and amount to be credited to that account. The magnetic tape is then sent, before the date of payment, to the em-ployer's bank; the latter debits the employer's account for the entire de-posit payroll and credits the accounts of any employee who is a customer. Remaining credits on the magnetic tape are then transmitted to an ACH for distribution to the financial institutions where the other employees have accounts. Each participating employee in this program is then sup-plied with a statement as evidence of deposit.

Many government agencies and private concerns presently participate in preauthorized credits programs. The direct deposit program is attractive for a number of reasons: it provides security, convenience, and lowers the payroll handling costs. It also serves to cut down on paperwork by decreasing the number of checks that have to be written.

Federal Reserve Wire (FRW)

The FRW links the 12 Federal Reserve Banks and their 24 branches—with their 300 member banks—into a nationwide network. The FRW, with its nerve center in Culpeper, Virginia, also links the Federal Reserve System with the U.S. Treasury via high-speed communication lines. The FRW handles more than 50,000 wire fund transfers daily, with a value of more than $100 billion. The network also handles transfers of marketable government securities.

Bank Wire (BW)

This is a private communications network, which services 115 subscribers; these are spread out over more than 70 major cities. BW handles 12,000 messages daily, resulting in transfers of more than $25 billion. Its computer nerve centers are based in New York City and Chicago. Some of its subscribers also make use of the Computerized Clearing House for Interbank Payments Systems (CHIPS), for large fund transfers involving foreign financial institutions.

Telephone Bill Paying (TBP)

For a small monthly fee, bank customers can pay their bills by telephone. The customer simply telephones the bank from a home or office (using a dial phone) and gives a secret passcode number to a teller; the customer then tells the teller who and how much to pay.

A bank customer with a touch-tone phone need only punch a seven digit number; this will give access to the bank's computer. Upon gaining entry, the computer will request the account number. After the customer gives this, the computer will then request the secret passcode. The computer will also ask for the payment code—the number assigned the store to be paid. The customer then proceeds to instruct the computer as to the amount to be paid. If the customer makes a mistake, he/she need only press the asterisk button on the phone; the computer will then automatically cancel that entry and request the correct information.

TABLE 1   POTENTIAL FOR FRAUD IN
TELEPHONE BILL PAYING (TBP) SYSTEMS

Lax bank security or a careless bank customer can open a TBP system to criminal attack. The thief (impersonating the customer), armed with the secret account and identification numbers, can easily transfer funds from a customer's account to his/her own. The simplicity of the system makes this possible[a]

Operating a 12-Key Touch-Tone System

Step 1   User calls (the telephone number given). The bank's computer will answer and request his/her account number.

Step 2   User enters eight-digit test number, and then presses the (#) button. The computer then asks the user to enter his/her personal (secret) identification number. The user then presses (numbers) and the (#) button. At this point, the computer tells the user what the current balance is in his/her account, and proceeds to request that the user enter his/her first transaction. (The computer often has a pleasant talking voice.) The user then proceeds to pay his/her bills.

Step 3   The user enters the transaction information:
(a)   The vendor number, and the pressing of the (#) button.
(b)   The amount (of dollars and cents)—the last two numbers are the cents—and then the user presses the (#) button again.
(c)   If payment is to be made the same day, the user presses the (#) button again. If payment is to be made at a later date, the user simply presses the button(s) for the date he/she wants the payment to be made. (For example, if payment is to be made the 5th day, simply press 5 for the date, and then the (#) button.)

Step 4   (a)   If all the information the user has provided is correct, he/she then simply presses the (#) button and proceeds to the next transaction.
(b)   If there is an error, the user then presses the (°) button and re-enters the transaction beginning with the vendor number.

Step 5   When the last transaction is completed, the user presses the (#) button and waits for the confirmation of the total number of payments made and the amount paid.

Step 6   If the user has any problems, he/she can press zero and the (#) button and a bank employee will come on line to assist.

TABLE 1   (Continued)

Operating a 10-Key or Rotary-Dial System

Step 1   The user dials the (number).

Step 2   User then gives his/her account and identification numbers, then the vendor number, payment amount, and date payment is to be made.

Step 3   The bank employee repeats all the information to verify its accuracy, and then proceeds to follow the user's instructions.

---

[a] An impersonator could easily carry out the above steps and transfer funds to his/her account.

Payments such as mortgages, utility bills, insurance premiums, and auto loans easily lend themselves to TBP payments. TBP systems are presently in use at more than 50 depository institutions, in several states. However, TBP systems have met with some consumer reservations; some bank customers are reluctant to switch from the familiar checking system or telephone paying system. Consider, also, the potential problems outlined in Table 1.

The EFTSs revolution appears to be gaining acceptance, especially among the younger and more affluent members of our society. The needed technology is presently available; the economic pressures, at least for the foreseeable future, appear to be on the side of the EFTS proponents. However, the cashless society has its price; it raises numerous problems and challenges. Paramount among these is the use of EFTSs by criminals to steal with impunity.

UNRESOLVED ISSUES

Proponents of EFTSs often point out that society will derive numerous advantages from these systems. Convenience is one of these; through EFTSs, consumers will be able to pay their bills from the comfort and security of their homes. Businesspeople will be able to communicate with their associates from the comfort of their offices. These electronic money systems offer numerous advantages, but they also raise numerous concerns, for which their proponents have no easy answers.

Consumerism

Proponents tell us that EFTSs will help alleviate the present costly paper glut in our financial and postal networks. Under EFTSs, much of the present paperwork and mailing expenses will become a thing of the past. Personal security will also be enhanced; EFTSs offer the advantage of banking from the safety of one's home or office. The elderly need not go out at a late (dangerous) hour to mail their bills; these can easily be paid from the safety of their television rooms.

However, there are also going to be problems for consumers under EFTSs. They will lose control over their personal finances. The ability to manipulate one's finances and to exploit the benefits of the float during the check clearing process will no longer be available. At present, a cancelled check is adequate proof of payment. It is also used in the preparation of tax returns, the resolution of disputes with creditors, and in numerous legal proceedings. In an EFTS environment, this will no longer be true; proof of payment will have to come in the form of a computerized printout, and this can raise numerous problems since some courts may not allow a printout in evidence.

Today's consumer can also direct the bank to stop payment on a check; this gives him/her great leverage in dealing with retailers, creditors, and others. Under EFTSs, the transfer of funds will be instantaneous and the opportunity to stop payment will be minimal. Consumers may also find themselves frustrated by errors and malfunctions in these systems; errors could prove both costly and difficult to remedy.

Privacy

In a cashless society, the individual's entire financial history, including the most intimate personal details of his/her daily life, will be readily available to both government and business at the press of a button. In addition, poor EFTS security may expose the individual to blackmail and other invasions of privacy; these crimes will increase dramatically in the cashless society. Privacy may become a rare commodity under EFTSs.

Costly Litigation

This may arise as a result of EFTS-related errors and malfunctions. The Federal Electronic Funds Transfer Act attempts to assign liability regarding both the card issuer and holder; for example, a card holder may be liable for up to $50 if the losses are connected to his negligence.[4] However, there are a number of gray areas that have yet to be fully addressed. Among these, for example, the question of who is liable in instances involving a fraud where neither card issuer or holder was negligent. Presently, the Uniform Commercial Code (UCC) spells out many of the liabilities connected to the checking system, but under EFTSs, the UCC may well become obsolete.

In addition, EFTSs may make present litigation even more costly; for example, the opposing parties may have to rely on the services of experts more than is currently the case. This would certainly make litigation more costly. Yet it would make little sense for a litigant to spend $5000 on an expert when the entire dispute revolves around $4000. The high cost of EFTS-related litigation may only serve to augment the present problems our legal system faces.

Loss of Competition

There is basis for concern that EFTS may result in lessened competition; for example, will access to the system be limited only to those who can bear the costs? The initial costs of these systems may prove so high that the cashless society could fall under the control of the large financial institutions. Only the large banks would have the capital needed to purchase the expensive technology. This could undermine the ability of the small banks to compete effectively; the financial sector would then be dominated by a handful of giants. There are ample examples of this in other industries, for instance, the auto and the oil industries, just to name two. There is justified basis for concern.

Branching

Federal law restricts branching by national banks, state chartered banks—that are members of the federal reserve system—and nonmember state chartered banks that are insured by the Federal Deposit Insurance Corporation (FDIC). Before any of these institutions can establish a new branch, they must first obtain the approval of the Federal regulators, but power to approve is also limited by state legislation.

Many of the states have imposed limitations on the establishment of branches, especially by out-of-state banks; some, for example, treat point-of-sale systems as branches. State branching laws have been upheld by the Federal courts. Critics, however, charge that these state laws serve to

[4] See P.L. 95-630.

hinder the development of a truly national EFTS. For the small financial institutions, however, the branching laws constitute a needed safeguard against the large banks.

The outcome of the branching debate will certainly have an impact on the direction EFTSs may take; it can also retard the rise of a national EFTS.

A CASHLESS WORLD

The EFTS revolution has also made itself felt in Europe. ATMs are presently found in Great Britain, France, Italy, Belgium, and other European countries. South Korea, Hong Kong, Singapore, and Japan are also well on the road to EFTSs. ATMs have found a surprisingly receptive climate in all of these countries; the bank wires are used daily by their financial institutions to transfer billions of dollars across continents.

ACHs have also made their way to Europe. The ACH movement first gained its momentum in the late 1960s, with the first British ACH becoming operational in 1968. Many European depository institutions now make widespread use of them to process millions of payments. European ACHs are employed to process not only payroll credits and debit transfers, but also cash dispenser exchanges, guaranteed check payments, and check truncation. The Scandinavians, for example, employ them primarily to process payroll credits, while the French use them mostly for direct debit transactions, and the Belgians for check truncation.

Access to European ACHs varies from country to country; in some countries, direct access is limited only to the major clearing banks. In others, it is open to all depository institutions. In Scandinavia, for example, both commercial banks and thrifts have equal access to the ACH, but in Britain, a bank must first sponsor a corporation and accept responsibility for any financial losses it may cause before the corporate entity can send its tapes directly to an ACH. European ACHs also handle the bulk of government assistance payments; many of these are in the form of direct deposits. As a result, the Europeans appear to demonstrate a strong interest in the EFTS revolution.

The highly centralized banking systems found in many European countries also lend themselves to the development of EFTSs. Europe's experience with the postal Giro services has made the public more receptive to EFTSs; as a result, opposition to the cashless society has not been as vocal in Europe as it has been in the United States.

Many of Canada's larger financial institutions have also moved to electronic methods for handling their daily financial transactions. On-line savings account services are in wide use; bank customers can now go to any of a bank's branches and make either deposits or withdrawals. The data is relayed back to the bank's central computer via a branch terminal. A bank's branches are now also able to exchange data with one another in a matter of minutes.

Many of the Canadian banks now record their financial transactions on magnetic tapes; the ACH revolution has taken hold. The Canadian government also encourages many of the large corporations to pay their employees by direct deposit to their accounts.

Canadians, however, live in awe of their giant neighbor. They fear that their EFTSs may fall under the control of the American banks. As a result, the Canadian government requires that EFTS communication processing functions be under the control of domestic corporations. There is also serious concern in Canada that the larger domestic financial institutions may attempt to exclude the smaller institutions from participating in EFTSs. With this concern in mind, the Canadian Finance Ministry has taken the public position that EFTSs should be competitive and open to all domestic financial institutions.

The cashless society poses a special dilemma for nonindustrialized nations. Massive amounts of financial and personal data are exported daily out of these nations for processing and storage in the computers of the West. Increasingly, these nations find themselves dependent on multinational corporations for the processing of their social, economic, and political data. Some of the political leaders in these nations view this as the "rape of their information sovereignty." EFTSs are viewed as only augmenting their dependency on the West.

The nonindustrialized nations also find themselves, at present, in the midst of internal political instability. Coups, assassinations, and wars with their neighbors are often the norm. These nations also face serious economic problems. Large numbers of their populations lead a daily existence of borderline starvation; illiteracy and disease are the norm. Feeding, healing, and clothing their citizenry must by necessity take precedence; few precious resources are left over to develop the requisite resources and pool of trained personnel to man EFTSs.

The cashless society is thus viewed by these countries as a tool of the industrialized West; they see it as a mechanism to control their economies. In response to this perceived threat, they have enacted regulations to limit the development of EFTSs. However, the eventual future of EFTSs will be decided in the industrialized West; it may very well be forced on the Third World.

The EFTS revolution has taken roots not only in the United States, but also in Europe, Canada, and Japan. The industrialized nations presently have both the requisite technology and trained personnel to move into the cashless society. The growing problem of political instability and poverty in the nonindustrial nations, and their fear that Western banking interests may use EFTSs to dominate their economies may stifle the growth of EFTSs in these countries. As for the Soviet Bloc, the outcome of the EFTS revolution may hinge on how their elites perceive the political implications of these technologies. Suffice it to say, however, that, in the West at least, we are heading toward a cashless society; with it will come the problems associated with new types of crimes.

CHAPTER 19

Stealing
Electronic
Money

Thieves armed with a knowledge of computerized bank codes and how to transfer funds electronically nearly stole $2 million by simply transferring these funds over various communication circuits stretching from Florida to Mexico. A civilian pay clerk for the military was charged with embezzling more than $40,000; he allegedly programmed a government computer to print out dozens of checks drawn on accounts from the various military agencies. The checks were made out to several of his associates, who, in turn, cashed them and shared the proceeds with him. Not to be outdone, a group of white collar criminals with ties to organized crime copied key financial and personal data stored in the comptuer of a large retail chain.

These cases serve to illustrate the ease with which computerized financial systems can be bilked by criminals, armed with the necessary technical know-how. Electronic Fund Transfer System (EFTS) related crimes and abuses will increasingly pose a serious problem for both government and the private sector.[1] EFTS criminals are finding that preying on the cashless society can be both easy and rewarding; the computer criminal has already set the example. Lax security, ill-prepared police forces and

---

[1] This includes such EFTSs as wire transfers, automated clearing houses, direct deposits, automated teller machines, and others. EFTSs and their developments are discussed in depth in Chapter 18.

272

prosecutors, and antiquated legal procedures pose little deterrence to this new breed of criminal. EFTS computers, terminals, communication lines, and other components of these cashless systems will increasingly find themselves the objects of attacks by an array of electronic criminals: dishonest employees, extortionists, organized crime, sophisticated white collar criminals, terrorists, the discontented, and others. The dawn of the EFTS criminal is upon us.

TYPES OF THREATS

To date we have no exact data as to the magnitude of EFTS-related crimes. However, based on our experience with computer-related crimes and abuses, we can safely speculate that EFTSs will increasingly become targets of the more sophisticated criminal elements within our society. Cashless systems that will house the wealth of a nation, by their very nature, will invite criminal attack.

From 1940 onward, and well into the present, the underlying philosophy of the computer manufacturers has been one of expediency: improved speed and storage capabilities, and the lowering of costs. The manufacturers and designers have demonstrated, from the beginning, little or no concern for security; the threat of crime has either been dismissed as being insignificant or swept under the rug. This philosophy has carried over, in part, into the EFTS arena. Marketing and public relations concerns continue to permeate the outlook of many manufacturers.

The picture of the amateur EFTS criminal, armed only with knowledge of the system, and motivated by the challenge of beating the establishment, is not always accurate. The amateur criminal often poses a secondary threat to EFTSs; the serious threat comes from the professional class of criminals. It can safely be said that adequate EFTS-connected security measures can be enacted to curtail the activities of the amateur criminal; in addition, the losses the amateur criminal can inflict on EFTSs can be minimized by our existing security (physical, personnel, communication, and other) measures. The serious threat to EFTSs comes from the more sophisticated professional criminal elements of our society; their lengthy experience with white collar and computer crimes can be transferred to the EFTS arena.

One of the more serious threats to EFTSs comes from the professional white collar criminal groups that currently prey with impunity on the diverse sectors of our economy.[2] Studies of securities-related rip-offs,

[2] These are said to account for more than $40 billion in losses annually.

bankruptcy frauds, insurance heists, and an array of illegal trade practices indicate that such groups exist and are more than ready to turn their focus to the cashless society. These criminal elements come from diverse professional backgrounds, and are armed with the requisite arsenal to attack EFTSs. A well organized conspiracy involving such individuals can seriously threaten the viability of EFTSs. Well organized and funded, technically capable, and with access to key EFTS personnel, these white collar criminal rings could easily prey on EFTSs.

Organized crime is also a cause for serious concern. This confederation of well organized professional criminals has increasingly grown in sophistication, and has already made inroads into the computer crime area. EFTSs offer them new and diverse opportunities. Given their tight knit structure, numerous business contacts, and ability to coerce and win over insiders at EFTS facilities, organized crime poses a considerable threat. It brings with it not only its contacts, know-how, and organization, but also both national and international fencing networks. Organized criminal elements can easily dispose of stolen merchandise, goods, equipment, confidential data, and funds through their fencing networks and business fronts. In addition, the mob's loansharking, bookmaking, and narcotics operations provide it with ready-made tools to penetrate and subvert the employees who will operate EFTSs.[3]

Terrorists also pose a potential threat to EFTSs. Professional terrorists are presently active internationally. Unlike the criminal, the terrorist is motivated by ideological fervor. Monetary considerations play a secondary role in the terrorist's activities; what makes the terrorist potentially dangerous is a willingness to sacrifice both himself/herself and others for the cause. EFTSs have already attracted the attention of such groups in France, Italy, and other industrialized nations. Open societies pose a special problem for law enforcement; lax security makes them ideal targets for the politically malcontent.

The terrorist thus poses a twofold challenge to the cashless society: a threat to the security of its economic institutions, and a threat to its political well-being. The terrorist has both the requisite weaponry and the will to severely damage key EFTS facilities, bringing a nation's financial institutions to their knees. Of greater concern to society, however, should be the terrorist's ability to force the governing authorities to impose dragonian measures on their citizenry so as to curtail the terrorist's activities. A technologically advanced society—and one that comes to rely on EFTS for its everyday financial transactions—would find it difficult to

---

[3] Through blackmail, extortion, and other corrupt practices, the mob has already demonstrated its ability to prey on the Wall Street community.

preserve its democratic safeguards if its major financial institutions were seriously threatened. The objective of the terrorist is to cause societal havoc, to disrupt a society's political mechanisms. EFTSs are potentially ideally suited for this task.

Professional spies (both industrial and political) also pose a threat to EFTSs. Corporate and foreign agents may seek to gain access to confidential data stored or transmitted in EFTSs. The interception of valuable confidential economic and political data will attract the professional spy. Unlike the terrorist, the objective of the industrial spy is the theft of data for purposes of a competitive or political advantage. These efforts will be directed at accessing these systems either electronically or through the assistance of corrupt EFTS employees. Data-related crimes, unless EFTSs are safeguarded, will increase dramatically in a cashless environment.

SYSTEM VULNERABILITIES

EFTSs are vulnerable to criminal attack from four key areas: external physical attacks (destruction of all or part of a facility); internal physical attacks (sabotage and vandalism); internal and external manipulation of the system or any of its components; and electronic penetration.

External physical attacks can come from several sources: the amateur criminal (the mentally unstable, disgruntled employees, or former employees); professional white collar criminals; terrorist elements; foreign spies; and organized crime. External physical attacks can have as their objective the destruction of EFTS facilities, their components, or their communications. The end objective may be some economic or political gain or advantage, or even the destruction of a nation's financial base.

As regards internal physical attacks, these can also come from several sources: disgruntled or mentally unbalanced employees (who want to "get even with the boss"); agents of terrorist groups (motivated by ideology or personal feelings for another member of the terrorist group); corporate or foreign spies (driven by monetary considerations or politics); and organized crime or its associates (their tools are often extortion, blackmail, or threats to another or one's family). These attacks can be directed at EFTS facilities or any of their various components; internal attacks can be directed at a system's hardware, software, and/or communications.

Of similar concern is the potential for manipulating these financial systems. Input financial data can be fabricated, altered, deleted, or destroyed. In addition, the software (programs employed to run the computers of these systems) can likewise be manipulated to fit the objectives of the criminal. Output data can also be copied, stolen, or destroyed.

Also of serious concern is the threat of electronic penetration of these systems.[4] Especially vulnerable to criminal attack are the communication links of EFTSs; data being transmitted back and forth between computers and terminals is open to interception. The threat at this stage comes from sophisticated criminals armed with electronic interceptive tools; their use, however, requires a degree of sophistication and technical know-how that is not readily available to the amateur criminal. However, organized crime, terrorist groups, industrial spies, and professional white collar criminals have both access to such electronic interceptive tools and the needed technical know-how to operate them successfully.

One of the more widely employed forms of electronic interceptions is wiretapping. Taps can easily be connected directly to the communication lines of EFTSs; this enables the criminal to intercept and record, modify, or delete the data. Also readily available are electromagnetic devices; these are designed to intercept the radiation generated by a computer, its telephone/teleprinter lines, and microwave communications.

A criminal can also connect an unauthorized terminal to a valid private line, and thus enter the system whenever a legal user is inactive but still holds the communications channel. Another common electronic interceptive technique involves the tying of an unauthorized terminal into a system that does not authenticate terminal entry; the criminal thus gains access to the system at will. A criminal can also probe a system for any unprotected entry points caused by error, malfunction, or lax security; the criminal can then selectively intercept and alter messages. The modified message is then released to the valid user.

The electronic revolution will provide criminals with added and more innovative tools with which they can penetrate EFTSs. Access to these technologies is a simple matter in an open society; adequate countermeasures will thus be needed to safeguard the integrity and viability of the cashless society. Whether the financial institutions and other EFTS constituencies will be willing to do this remains to be seen; at present, many of their efforts have been half-hearted.

CRIMES BY INSIDERS

The diversity and complexity of human skills needed to operate EFTSs also makes them vulnerable to attack, manipulation, and subversion by the insider. Crime, in general, is a "people problem"; EFTSs will face the same problems. Dishonest employees and consultants can pose a serious

---

[4] This is discussed in greater detail in other chapters of the book.

security problem for the cashless society. Safeguarding these financial systems will entail being able to identify their potential adversaries.

Of special concern for those delegated the responsibility of safeguarding EFTSs should be the potential threat posed by the following system personnel:

Data entry and update clerks. They can change the direct access file data or the magnetic tape data by means of terminal entries or unit record entries. They can also cause physical damage to the on-line terminals.

Communication operators. They have access to the concentrators, multiplexers, modems, line switching units, and similar equipment necessary for these systems to operate. They can modify, destroy, or disclose the data; they can also overload or misdirect the data.

Media librarians. They are responsible for storing, preserving, and retrieving the data stored on magnetic tapes, disks, floppy disks, cylinders, or similar media. They can destroy, disclose, or substitute programs and data files.

Systems programmers. They write, debug, and install usually resident machine instructions relating to the execution of compilers, utilities, operating system software, communication monitors, data base management software, and other common software not directed at a specific application. They can destroy, modify, or disclose the data, peripheral equipment, and the computer.

Communication network managers. They are responsible for the configuration of the communication network through a terminal, placing lines and terminals into/out of service, establishing alternate paths, and starting/stopping polling. They can modify, destroy, or make unauthorized use of the system's communications equipment.

Operations managers. They are responsible for the operation of computers, peripheral equipment, job controls, console operators, communication operators, off-line data custodians, and for repairing the system hardware. They can direct their subordinates to engage in erroneous or intentional acts that will cause damage to the system.

Data base managers. They are responsible for the data base files. They can modify, disclose, or destroy the data base.

Application programmers. They write, debug, and install usually nonresident machine instructions relating to the execution of logic to control the processing of a particular application. They can copy application programs, or modify, disclose, or destroy data files and programs.

Terminal engineers.   They can identify hardware failures, isolate faulty components, and repair or replace hardware to restore the system to operational status. They can modify, destroy, or disclose programs and data files.

Facilities engineers.   These check, adjust, repair, modify, and replace equipment supporting computer and terminal facilities (for example, air conditioning, power, lights, heat, and water). They can cause the air conditioning, backup power, and lights to fail.

Programming managers.   They supervise the system development functions and application programmers. They can modify, destroy, disclose, or use computer programs and test data.

Identification control clerks.   They are authorized to designate account numbers, issue PINs (for EFTS cards), and monitor the manufacture, encoding/embossing, and mailing of EFTS cards. They also monitor microfilm paper audit trails, and log jobs into/out of the EDP center. They can thus modify, destroy, or disclose personal identification data.

EDP auditors.   They check the adequacy of accounting, financial, and operational controls. Since they are responsible for all the system's controls, they can commit numerous unauthorized acts.

Terminal operators.   These can be merchants, retail clerks, bank tellers, or consumers. They key into a terminal to initiate an EFT transaction; they can modify, destroy, or disclose the contents of the system and data files. They can also make unauthorized use of the system.

Equipment operators.   They enter jobs, data, and utility execution cards through the system card readers. They can destroy or remove equipment, modify job scheduling, and disclose or destroy input/output data, media, supplies, and negotiable instruments.

Job set-up clerks.   They cause jobs and data to be entered into the job schedule. They can modify, disclose, or destroy data files, computer programs, and data media.

The above should not be taken as an indication that all (or most) personnel are dishonest; on the contrary, insider-connected crimes are committed often only by a handful of dishonest employees. However, system managers should be aware of the potential for fraud, theft, and abuse by men and women placed in positions of trust and responsibility. Being aware of these potential insider threats, and acting within the guidelines of the law, will only serve to help minimize the threat of EFTS-related crimes.

ATM- AND POS-RELATED CRIMES

At present, various types of automated teller machines (ATMs) and points-of-sale systems (POSs) are common features in many cities and suburbs in this country, Western Europe, and Japan. These computerized financial systems constitute rudimentary forms of EFTSs; they are a prelude to the coming cashless society. They have, however, proven vulnerable to criminal attack; our experience with ATM- and POS-related crimes should thus serve to better prepare us for more complex and sophisticated future EFTS crimes. These ATM/POS capers have, generally, taken one or more of the following forms:

Fraudulent authorizations
Insider crimes
Physical penetrations
Vandalisms
Data link interceptions

ATM crimes usually take several forms; the more common involves a thief who gains access to a customer's plastic card and PIN (identification number). Armed with these, entering the system becomes a simple matter. Counterfeit ATM cards have also proven a problem. The magnetically encoded data on the card can be transferred to a counterfeit one; this can be done in one of two ways:

Skimming. This involves placing a piece of recording tape over the stripe of the genuine ATM card; heat is then applied to this with a common household iron. The recording tape is then placed over the stripe on the blank (counterfeit) card, and the heat is applied a second time.

Buffer recording. This technique will produce a higher quality counterfeit; however, it can prove more complex and costly. It requires an electromagnetic reader and a buffer storage. The card is read and its encoded data is stored in the buffer memory; it is later written out on the blank (counterfeit) card.

Data link interceptions can also prove to be a problem for on-line ATMs; in this case, the criminal intercepts the transmissions between the ATM and the central computer and then proceeds to instruct the ATM to dispense cash. The thief may also employ a tap to intercept the data; the data can then be used at a later time to transfer funds to phony accounts that the thief controls. Since these interceptions can prove difficult to detect, communications security is recommended.

ATMs are also open to criminal attack from dishonest bank employees, and vendor installation and service engineers. Physical attempts to break into an ATM and vandalism should also be considered; these, however, represent a minimum risk since the amount of money the thief can steal is limited. In addition, security alarm systems connected to the ATM under attack would be activated and bring the police to the scene.

POS crimes can take various forms; the more common (and less sophisticated) of these involves the thief who gains access to a customer's plastic card and PIN (identification number). Armed with these, the theif simply bills purchases to the real owner. It has been suggested that if the real owner's photograph were used in conjunction with the POS card, this could serve to minimize the misuse of another's card. However, experts note that, since many retail clerks are often part-time employees (especially during the summer months of the year, when students join the labor force), they are not security conscious; in an effort to provide speedy service, they may pay scant attention to any photograph.

A POS is also vulnerable to attack by a criminal who accesses the computer files and alters financial transactions or transfers funds to phony accounts. A dishonest computer programmer could also pose a threat to a POS, planting a "trapdoor" in the software; this would enable the thief to later bypass the system's safeguards and access it directly. As is the case with on-line ATMs, detecting POS penetrations can prove difficult; adequate security measures, however, should prove of some value.

A POS is also open to vandalism and sabotage. A disgruntled employee can physically attack the system's terminals, electronic cash registers, or its computers. At present, the best that can be hoped for safeguarding a POS is adequate security measures and a willingness by management to vigorously prosecute all offenders. As with other cashless crimes, there are no simple solutions to the problem.

CASHLESS WHITE COLLAR CAPERS

The cashless society could easily lend itself to crimes and abuses by white collar criminals. Financial systems that replace paper-based economic transactions with electronic blips could easily facilitate the commission of traditional white collar capers and make their detection and prosecution more difficult; our police have been trained to investigate paper-based transactions. In addition, EFTSs make it possible to transfer millions of dollars at the press of a button across state lines and continents; these electronic transfers will make it easier for criminals to "launder" their ill-gotten gains; it will also make it more difficult for the authorities to trace and seize these funds.

White collar crime is not a new phenomenon; however, cashless financial systems, which employ thousands of computers, millions of terminals, and billions of feet of wire, will make it easier for white collar criminals to steal the money and property of others.[5] Among some of the white collar capers that EFTSs will facilitate are:

Abuses of trust.   The misuse of one's position to acquire money, property, or some privilege.

Bribery.   This will become easier to pull off and more difficult to detect, especially where it involves multinational corporations and foreign political figures.

Banking frauds.   Violations by bank insiders will become both more prevalent and difficult to detect. These could take the form of embezzlement, false entries in bank (computerized) records, transferrence of funds to phony accounts, and many others.

Collateral frauds.   By opening a phony EFTS account, a criminal could use it as a security for a private loan.

Consumer rip-offs.   These can take the form of bait and switch schemes, false advertising, merchandising frauds, business opportunity schemes, and many others. At present, a defrauded consumer has a cancelled check as proof of payment; this can be used in a trial to recoup losses. Under EFTS, this will not be the case; without a cancelled check as proof of a payment, recouping the consumer's losses may prove more difficult.

Credit rating frauds.   These involve the use and extension of credit. For a fee, a criminal could alter, falsify, modify, or destroy an individual's credit report (rating).

Frauds against government.   These can take the form of phony payments to nonexistent suppliers or beneficiaries.

Ghost payrolls.   Phony employees could easily be added to an EFTS payroll. Both business and government can fall victim to such rip-offs.

Insider dealings.   The storage of voluminous confidential and valuable business-related data in EFTSs can lead to serious abuses by insiders.

---

[5] EFTSs will also make it easier for low-level managers and employees to pull off many of the white collar capers that are currently the monopoly of top management

These could take the form of using the data for personal dealings in securities of publicly held corporations, real estate, and other valuable investments.

Investment rip-offs. By simply creating phony assets, suppliers, and profits, criminals could convince consumers to invest in their bogus company.

Pension frauds. The theft or diversion of a pension fund's assets by its trustees or others will prove easier.

Restraint of trade. Conspiracies, combinations, and other actions to monopolize an industry or interfere with the marketplace will become more common.

Revenue violations. Efforts to deprive a governmental authority of revenue to which it is entitled may become easier.

Welfare rip-offs. Abuses involving government assistance will grow. Dishonest insiders can place friends, relatives, or ghost beneficiaries on the computerized welfare rolls.

Others. At present, experts have identified more than 1000 forms of white collar crime. EFTSs should, for the most part, facilitate their commission and make their detection and prosecution more difficult.

EFTSs make it possible to steal large sums of money at the press of a button. They make it possible to rip off a company or government agency at the press of a button; the ill-gotten funds can be transferred electronically to secret bank accounts in foreign havens. Sophisticated EFTS-related crimes constitute the next evolutionary stage of computer criminology.

RECOMMENDED SAFEGUARDS

EFTS-related crimes are not only on the increase, but the losses connected with them are equally on the rise. For example, in one such caper involving a California bank, an insider was able to siphon off more than $20 million in a phony wire fraud scheme; the theft went undetected for several years. In another case, a clerk for a money market fund with assets in excess of $1 billion ripped off her employer for more than $1 million; the funds were transferred electronically to a Swiss bank account.

EFTS-related crimes, as is the case with most white collar capers, often involve insiders; they may be acting alone or may be part of a conspiracy. Often, these insider capers thrive in a corrupt organization. However, these insider-related EFTS crimes can be curtailed through personnel control measures; these are often inexpensive and simple to implement. They do, however, require an organizational commitment to see them through.

The personnel safeguards most often recommended for EFTSs are as follows[6]:

Organizational ethics. System personnel should be encouraged to behave ethically. Codes of ethics should be established and prominently displayed and disseminated.

Responsibility. Assign to specific individuals responsibility for EFTS safeguards, controls, and security; ensure that these responsibilities are then carried out.

Management role. It is the responsibility of management to set the goals, standards, and policies of the organization; the staff should be sensitive to management's attitudes, especially in the area of integrity and ethics. Management should also demonstrate a willingness to devote adequate resources to security, and it should delegate sufficient authority and responsibility to its auditors and security officers.

Documentation. All security policies and procedures should be in writing, periodically reviewed and updated.

Sensitivity. Management should be sensitive to the personal needs and problems of its staff.

Audits. These should be an integral part of the operation; auditors should be assigned to review the system's controls.

EFTS security, although far from foolproof, can play an important role in safeguarding the cashless society. However, it must be periodically reviewed and updated; it must also have the full support of top management. Cosmetic security will not suffice; EFTSs can be protected from criminal theft, fraud, and abuse.

PROSECUTING THE CRIMINAL

Only a handful of states have, to date, enacted legislation to address the problem of EFTS crimes. At the Federal level, Congress has passed the Electronic Fund Transfers Act (EFTA). It attempts to address some of the legal problems connected to EFTSs, including that of EFTS-related rip-offs.

[6] Some of these safeguards are discussed in greater depth in other chapters of the book.

Among other things, the EFTA makes it a Federal crime for anyone to:

Knowingly use, or attempt or conspire to use, any counterfeit, fictitious, altered, forged, lost, or fraudulently obtained EFTS debit instrument to obtain money, goods, services, or anything of value.

Knowingly transport, or attempt or conspire to transport, any counterfeit, fictitious, altered, forged, lost, stolen, or fraudulently obtained EFTS debit instrument (knowing the same to be counterfeit, fictitious, altered, forged, lost, stolen, or fraudulently obtained).

The EFTA specifically addresses crimes that make use of EFTS debit instruments to gain entry into the system; however, it remains to be seen whether the courts will expand the EFTA to cover EFTS frauds that are not connected to debit instruments.[7]

In addition to the EFTA, there are several other Federal criminal statutes that can be employed to address some EFTS-related crimes. The wire fraud and mail fraud statutes have proven of some value, but they come into play only when a criminal uses the wires or mail in interstate/foreign commerce to commit the crime.[8] The Federal forgery laws may also prove of some limited value; however, at the Federal level, new statutes that are specifically directed at EFTS-related crimes may soon be necessary.[9]

At the state level, the authorities have to rely on traditional criminal statutes to combat EFTS-related crimes. The arson statutes can be employed if an EFTS facility is set on fire; the burglary, embezzlement, and larceny statutes may also be used where there is an illegal taking of property. The state conspiracy, forgery, and false pretense statutes may also have some limited application, but here, too, legislation that specifically addresses the problem may be needed.

The authorities, both at the Federal and state levels, will also encounter procedural and evidentiary problems when dealing with complex EFTS crimes. These bear much semblance to the problems connected with prosecuting computer-related capers.[10] Although simple EFTS-related

---

[7] The EFTA would cover any fraudulent card, code, or other means of access to a consumer's account. See Public Law 95-630 for added details.

[8] See Title 18 of the United States Code, Sections 1341 to 1343, for more specifics.

[9] The U.S. Secret Service received more than 2000 computer/EFTS criminal referrals from the private and public sector in 1982 alone. Lack of adequate resources and laws have stifled its efforts in these areas.

[10] For an in-depth discussion of problems connected with computer-related litigation, see August Bequai, *Computer Crime* (Lexington, Mass.: Heath, 1977).

crimes such as arson and vandalism should pose no more of a problem for prosecutors than any other traditional criminal case, complex EFTS frauds raise serious investigatory/prosecutorial problems.

The cashless society raises—as do computers—serious legal issues for our criminal justice system. These have to be addressed in the near future; a failure to do so may open our financial institutions to an electronic crime wave. There are no simple solutions—only difficult choices.

Conclusion

A former programmer for a Federal agency is said to have duplicated more than 90 valuable computer programs, before leaving it for private employment. A computer operator at a Maryland hospital used his employer's computer to embezzle more than $40,000 in a "ghost employee" scheme. An airline carrying the Soviet Ambassador to the United States is said to have flown for about six miles at the wrong altitude, in the crowded and dangerous skies of New York; government investigators concluded that someone had tampered with the air traffic control computers.

Crime by computer is here to stay; wishing that it would "go away" will neither diminish nor eliminate the problem. The proliferation of computers in every sector of our society has made it possible for anyone with some EDP training and access to the technology to wreak havoc on our private and public institutions. As our schools integrate computers in their daily curriculums, the potential for abuse and misuse by young men and women, devoid of ethics, will grow dramatically.

The lone computer criminal—whether a dishonest insider or outsider—will, for many years to come, prey on society. Armed with the requisite know-how, and often occupying a position of trust, he/she will continue to steal with impunity. Computer security measures and swift prosecution may eventually contain this threat; however, both business and government have demonstrated a reluctance to adequately address the problem. As for those who shape law enforcement policies and strategies, they continue to concentrate their efforts in the area of traditional crime. If the present trends continue, the lone computer criminal seems to have a bright future.

Of equal concern is the rise of the supercriminal. Armed with these new technologies, organized crime and professional white collar criminals can wreak havoc on our economy. No industry will be free from attack; they will steal with impunity. Unless law enforcement makes an effort to rectify this problem, we may very well be living in the age of the super-criminal.

However, it is not only the dishonest employee and professional criminal who pose a threat; their ranks have been enlarged by ideological zealots. These have already attacked computers in Europe and Asia. They have amply demonstrated that it is a simple matter for a handful of trained fanatics to sabotage computer facilities that run the trains, airplanes, nuclear facilities, and financial institutions of modern societies. Electronic terrorism is not science fiction; it should be taken seriously. There is sufficient evidence to convince even the most skeptical among us that the potential for terrorist attacks against EDP facilities is both real and growing. Modern Western societies are fragile structures; the computer may prove to be their "Achilles heel."

Privacy may soon become obsolete; the electronic revolution has made it possible to intrude on the individual's private realm at the press of a button. Even a 12-year-old, armed with the requisite technology, can gain access to most data bases in the Western world. Thieves, dishonest businesspeople, corrupt bureaucrats, and others threaten our privacy daily. Privacy-connected crimes are on the increase; information has a price, and there are an increasing number of willing buyers.

While the superpowers race to increase and improve their armaments, a subtle revolution is taking place in the art of warfare. Just as the invention of gunpowder made it possible for the peasants of medieval Europe to break the monopoly the knightly class held over warfare, so too has computer technology begun to erode the military monopoly of the superpowers. Small nations, armed with the requisite technology, could bring a highly developed industrialized society to a halt by simply sabotaging its key computer facilities and data bases. Destroy a nation's data base, and you destroy its ability to function. A renegade nation-state could pose a serious threat to its larger and more developed neighbors.

The computer revolution has also created the basis for a new elite. The medieval gentry had its power base in land; the mercantile class exploited commerce, while the moneyed and propertied classes of the twentieth century employed manufacturing. The electronic elite, because of its monopoly over the flow of information, will be able to manipulate the social, political, and economic environment. Such elites have already demonstrated an ability to affect the outcome of the political process; in the long run, they may pose a greater threat to society than the computer criminal who simply steals for private gain.

The present legal system, both in America and Europe, has demonstrated an inability and unwillingness to come to terms with computer-related litigation. Outdated laws and procedures continue to govern; litigation drags on without end. The new technology, unless our jurists address the problem, may make the cost of computer-connected litigation prohibitive.

Computers, however, are not only vehicles for crime and destruction. Like other technologies before them, they have helped elevate humanity; our lives have been, in many instances, greatly enriched. They are employed to guide airplanes, ships, trains, and even space vehicles; we use them daily in hospitals, banks, manufacturing, and every other industry imaginable.

The police employ this new technology to locate missing persons, analyze evidence, and track down dangerous criminals. Our financial institutions would collapse without computers, and the modern state could not govern today's mobile society without their assistance.

It is a technology fraught with the potential for good and evil; how it is employed is a reflection of the ethical fiber of a society. Computer crime need not be a problem; it can be contained. The electronic criminals can be stopped in their tracks; the needed tools are currently available. What has been lacking has been our willingness to employ them to meet the challenge head on.

Computer-related crimes can be prevented; we must take steps to do so, for we have few other choices. The alternative may be the fragmentation of our societal fiber, a return to the Dark Ages.

Glossary

Audit Trail. A sequential record of system activities that is sufficient to enable the reconstruction, review, and examination of the sequence of states and activities surrounding or leading to each event in the path of a transaction from its inception to output of final results.

Communications Engineer/Operator. One who operates communications equipment including concentrators, multiplexers, modems, and line switching units. Ordinarily, this person reconfigures the communications network when failures or overload situations occur.

Computer. An electronic device that performs logical, arithmetic, or memory functions by the manipulations of electronic or magnetic impulses and includes all input, output, processing, storage, software, or communications facilities that are connected or related to such a device in a system or network.

Computer Network. The interconnection of communications lines (including microwave or other means of electronic communication) with a computer through remote terminals, or a complex consisting of two or more interconnected computers.

Computer Operator. A person who operates a computer, including duties of monitoring system activities, coordination of tasks, and the operation of equipment.

For a more detailed glossary, see U.S. Department of Justice Manual, *Computer Crime: Criminal Justice Resource Manual* (Washington, D.C.: U.S. Government Printing Office, 1979).

Computer Program. A series of instructions or statements, in a form acceptable to a computer, that permits the functioning of a computer in a manner designed to provide appropriate products from such computer system.

Computer-Related Crime. Any illegal act for which knowledge of computer technology is essential for successful prosecution.

Computer Security Specialist. A person who evaluates, plans, and implements operational, procedural, personnel, and technical safeguards and controls that are related to the use of computer systems.

Computer Systems. A machine, or collection of machines, used for governmental, educational, or commercial purposes, one or more of which contain computer programs and data, that performs functions including, but not limited to, logic, arithmetic, data storage and retrieval, communication, and control.

Data. Any representation of fact or idea in a form that is capable of being communicated or manipulated by some process.

Data Base. An organized collection of data processed and stored in a computer system.

Data Communications. The transmission, reception, and validation of data.

EDP (Electronic Data Processing) Auditor. A person who performs operational, computer, computer program, and data file reviews to determine integrity, adequacy, performance, security, and compliance with organization and generally accepted policies, procedures and standards. This person also may participate in design specification of applications to ensure adequacy of controls, performs data processing services for auditors.

Facilities Engineer. A person who inspects, adjusts, repairs, modifies, or replaces equipment supporting computer and terminal facilities, for example, air conditioning, light, heat, power, and water.

Hardware. The computer and all related or attached machinery, such as mechanical, magnetic, electrical, and electronic devices, used in data processing.

Machine Language. A computer programming language that is used directly by a computer, without having to pass through a translation program, such as a compiler.

Master File. A file of data that is used as an authority in a given job and that is relatively permanent, even though its contents may change from run to run.

Media Librarian. A person who files, retrieves, and accounts for off-line storage of data on disk, tape, cards, or other removable data storage media.

The person provides media for the production control and job set-up areas and functions, and cycles backup files through remote storage facilities.

On-Line. The state of devices or computer users in direct communication with the central processing unit of a computer. Also a computer system in an interactive or time-sharing mode or other processes.

Operations Manager. The manager of a computer facility responsible for the operation of the computer system. He/she may also be responsible for the maintenance, specifications, acquisition, modification, and replacement of computer systems or computer programs.

Programming Manager. A person who manages computer programmers to design, develop, and maintain computer programs.

Software. Computer program, procedures, and associated documentation concerning the operation of a computer system.

System Engineer. A person who designs, configures, tests, diagnoses, assembles and disassembles, and repairs or replaces computer system devices and components.

Systems Programmer. A person who designs, develops, installs, modifies, documents, and maintains operating system and utility programs.

Terminal Engineer. A person who tests, diagnoses, assembles and disassembles, repairs and replaces terminals or their components.

Bibliography

Akin, Richard H. *The Private Investigator's Basic Manual.* Springfield, Illinois: Charles C. Thomas, 1976.

Allen, Brandt. "Embezzler's Guide to the Computer," *Harvard Business Review,* **53,** 79–89 (July 1975).

Allen, Brandt R. "Computer Fraud," *Financial Executive,* **39,** 38–43 (May 1971).

American Institute of Certified Public Accountants (Statement on Auditing Standards No. 3). *The Effects of EDP on the Auditor's Study and Evaluation of Internal Control.* New York: AICPA, 1974.

Anderson, Ronald A., and Kumpf, Walter A. *Business Law.* Cincinnati, Ohio: South-Western Publishing Company, 1972.

Awad, Elias M., and Data Processing Management Association. *Automatic Data Processing—Principles and Procedures.* Englewood Cliffs, New Jersey: Prentice-Hall, Inc., 1973.

Barmash, Isadore, Ed. *Great Business Disasters: Swindlers, Bunglers, and Frauds in American Industry.* Chicago: Playboy Press, 1972.

Baruch, Hurd. *Wall Street Security Risk.* Washington, D.C.: Acropolis Books, 1971.

Becker, Robert S. *The Data Processing Security Game.* New York: Pergamon Press, 1977.

Benson, George C. S., and Engerman, Thomas S. *Amoral America.* Stanford, California: Hoover Institution Press, 1975.

Bequai, August. *Computer Crime.* Lexington, Massachusetts: D. C. Heath, 1977.

Bequai, August. *White Collar Crime: A Twentieth Century Crisis.* Lexington, Massachusetts: D. C. Heath, 1978.

Bequai, August. *Organized Crime: The Fifth Estate.* Lexington, Massachusetts: D. C. Heath, 1979.

Bequai, August. *The Cashless Society: EFTS at the Crossroads.* New York: John Wiley & Sons, Inc., 1981.

Bequai, August. "Crooks and Computers," *Trial Magazine,* **12,** 48–53 (August 1976).

Bequai, August. "Litigation under the EFTS," *Federal Bar News,* **23,** 174–177 (June 1976).

Bequai, August. "Wanted: The White Collar Ring," *Student Lawyer*, 5, 44–48 (May 1977).

Bequai, August. "The Binary Burglars," *Student Lawyer*, 5, 18–24 (February 1977).

Bequai, August. "White Collar Plea Bargaining," *Trial Magazine*, 13, 38–43 (July 1977).

Bequai, August. "Legal Problems in Prosecuting Computer Crimes," *Security Management*, 21, 26–27 (July 1977).

Bequai, August. "White Collar Muggers Have Reason to Feel Safe," *Barrister*, 4, 26–29 (Summer 1977).

Bequai, August. "The Forty Billion Dollar Caper," *Police Chief*, **XLIV**, 66–68 (September 1977).

Bequai, August. "Computer Fraud: An Analysis for Law Enforcement," *Police Chief*, **XLIII**, 54–57 (September 1976).

Bequai, August. "The Cashless Society: An Analysis of the Threat of Crime and the Invasion of Privacy," *University of Utah Journal of Contemporary Law*, 3, 45–60 (Winter 1976).

Bequai, August. "The Electronic Criminal," *Barrister*, 4, 8–12 (Winter 1977).

Bequai, August. "Prosecutorial Decision-Making," *Police Law Quarterly*, 4, 34–42 (October 1974).

Bigelow, Robert, and Nycum, Susan. *Your Computer and the Law*. Englewood Cliffs, New Jersey: Prentice-Hall, Inc., 1975.

Binns, James. "The Internal Auditor's Role in Questioning Fraud Suspects, Part I," *The Magazine of Bank Administration* (October 1977).

Blake, Ian F., and Walker, Bruce J. *Computer Security Structures*. Stroudsburg, Pennsylvania: Dowden, Hutchinson & Ross, Inc., 1977.

Canadian Institute of Chartered Accountants. *Computer Audit Guidelines and Computer Control Guidelines*. Toronto, Canada, 1970.

Carroll, John M. *Computer Security*. Los Angeles: Security World Publishing Company, Inc., 1977.

Comptroller General of the United States, Report to the Congress. *Computer Related Crimes in Federal Programs*. U.S. General Accounting Office, 1976.

Coughran, Edward H. "Prosecuting Computer Abuse," *Criminal Justice Journal*, 1, 1978.

Finch, James H. "Espionage and Theft Using Computers," *Assets Protection*, 2 (1), 1976.

Finkel, Jules. *Computer Aided Experimentation: Interfacing to Mini-F Computers*. New York: John Wiley & Sons, Inc., 1975.

Glick, Rush G., and Newsom, Robert S. *Fraud Investigation*. Springfield, Illinois: Charles C. Thomas, 1974.

Hagen, Roger E. *The Intelligence Process and White-Collar Crime*. Report prepared for Battelle Law and Justice Study Center, Seattle, Washington, 1978.

Hoffman, Lance J. *Modern Methods for Computer Security and Privacy Symposium*. Phoenix: Honeywell, Inc., 1978.

Hoyt, Douglas. *Computer Security Handbook*. New York: Macmillan Information, 1973.

IBM. *Data Security and Data Processing*. Volume 5, Study Results. IBM (No. G320–1375).

Inbau, Fred E., Moessens, Andre A., and Vitullo, Louis R. *Scientific Police Investigation.* Philadelphia: Chilton Book Company, 1972.

Jancura, Elise G., and Berger, Arnold H. *Computers, Auditing & Control.* Philadelphia: Auerbach, 1973.

Jaspan, Norman, and Black, Hillel. *The Thief in the White Collar.* Philadelphia: J. B. Lippincott, 1960.

Krauss, Leonard I. *SAFE: Security Audit and Field Evaluation for Computer Facilities and Information Systems.* New York: AMACOM, American Management Associations, 1973.

Leininger, Sheryl, Ed. *Internal Theft: Investigation and Control, An Anthology.* Los Angeles: Security World Publishing Company, Inc., 1975.

Martin, James. *Security, Accuracy, and Privacy in Computer Systems.* Englewood Cliffs, New Jersey: Prentice-Hall, Inc., 1973.

Mauer, David W. *The American Confidence Man.* Springfield, Illinois: Charles C. Thomas, 1974.

Miller, Charles A. *Economic Crime: A Prosecutors Handbook.* Chicago: National District Attorneys Association, 1974.

Meyer, John N. *Accounting for Non-Accountants.* New York: Hawthorne Books, 1974.

Parker, Donn B. *Crime by Computer.* New York: Charles Scribner & Sons, 1976.

Parker, Donn B. *Computer Abuse Assessment.* A Stanford Research Institute Report prepared for the National Science Foundation, Washington, D.C., 1975.

Parker, Donn B., Nycum, Susan, and Oura, Stephen S. *Computer Abuse.* Springfield, Virginia: National Technical Information Service, 1973.

Ralston, Anthony, and Meek, Chester L., Ed. *Encyclopedia of Computer Science.* New York: Petrocelli, 1976.

Russell, Harold F. *Foozles and Frauds.* Altamonte Springs, Florida: The Institute of Internal Auditors, Inc., 1977.

Ruthberg, Zella G., Ed. *Audit and Evaluation of Computer Security,* U.S. Department of Commerce, National Bureau of Standards (NBS No. 500–19), 1977.

Schabeck, Tim A. "Computer Crime Investigation, Part 3," *Assets Protection,* 2, (4), Winter 1977.

Schabeck, Tim A. *Computer Crime Investigations Manual.* Madison, Wisconsin: Assets Protection, 1979.

Sutherland, Edwin H. *White Collar Crime.* New York: Dryden Press, 1949.

Van Tassel, Dennis. *Computer Security Management.* Englewood Cliffs, New Jersey: Prentice-Hall, Inc., 1972.

Walker, Bruce J., and Blake, Ian F. *Computer Security and Protection Structures.* Stroudsburg, Pennsylvania: Dowden, Hutchinson & Ross, Inc., 1977.

Whiteside, Thomas. *Computer Capers: Tales of Electronic Thievery, Embezzlement, and Fraud.* New York: Thomas Y. Crowell Company, 1978.

Index